Metadata and Digital Library Systems

Metadata and Digital Library Systems

Neelesh Kashyap

RANDOM

RANDOM PUBLICATIONS

NEW DELHI (INDIA)

Metadata and Digital Library Systems

ISBN 978-93-5111-560-1

Published in 2015 in India by

RANDOM PUBLICATIONS

4376-A/4B, Gali Murari Lal, Ansari Road
New Delhi-110 002
Phone : +9111-43580356, 011-23289044, 011-43142548
e-mail: sales@randompublications.com,
info@randompublications.com, randomexports@gmail.com

Reprinted 2025

Type Setting by : Friends Media, Delhi-110089
Digitally Printed at : Replika Press Pvt. Ltd.

Preface

The kinds of metadata associated with an information resource can address different aspects. Descriptive metadata identifies the resource and provides data about its content. Administrative metadata is used to help manage the resource; version numbering is an example. Technical metadata provides system related information about the resource such as the file type or format or resolution level of an image. Use metadata can keep track of usage and users. Metadata may be added manually, created through the use of an automated process like an indexing algorithm, or computer generated "on the fly". Most Integrated Library Systems are still bibliographic / reference based—they were not designed for the storage and retrieval of full text and multimedia. However, because of the increased demand for systems to support digital libraries, some ILS vendors have created add-on modules; others are providing integration "hooks" for third party products or tools that can be used to add access to full text documents or images.

Data and Meta-data can enter into Invenio powered repositories through different ways. They can be manually deposited by an author, through custom and fully configurable web interfaces, backed by an equally configurable work-flow architecture, that lets the submission administrator set up any kind of procedure triggered by a deposition. Meta-data and data can as well be harvested regularly from OAI-PMH compatible repositories. Data can also be input into the system from any non-standard format by writing ad-hoc conversion scripts either in XSLT or in the proprietary BibConvert's language. Users also have the possibility to upload records by sending e-mails that will be parsed automatically. The system can be configured to accept submission by robots thanks to the availability of a simple web API.

The book will suit to the needs of students, teachers, scholars and general readers.

I would like to thank my team for standing beside me throughout my career and writing this book. My special thanks go to "Random Publications" who have published the book.

– Neelesh Kashyap

Contents

1

Metadata and Library System

METADATA

Metadata is typically defined as "data about data." Many libraries are looking to Non---MARC/AACR2 schemes for cataloging certain types of materials, including but not limited to Web-accessible electronic resources and items in locally digitized collections. Metadata schemas are rapidly being developed as a solution not only for libraries but also for many other organizations that collect or develop information resources and want to make them more accessible. The use of metadata to "catalog" information resources can:

- Improve accessibility and retrievability;
- Provide more effective relevance ranking of search results;
- Act as a surrogate for a resource such as a large file that could be time-consuming to download or view, raw data that requires an explanation to understand, or even a resource not available in electronic form; and
- Aid in legal issues of intellectual property rights identification, tracking, and management.

The kinds of metadata associated with an information resource can address different aspects. Descriptive metadata identifies the resource and provides data about its content. Administrative metadata is used to help manage the resource; version numbering is an example. Technical metadata provides system related information about the resource such as the file type or format or resolution level of an image. Use metadata can keep track of usage and users. Metadata may be added manually, created through the use of an automated process like an indexing algorithm, or computer generated "on the fly". Most Integrated Library Systems are still bibliographic / reference based—they were not designed for the storage and retrieval of full text and multimedia. However, because of the increased demand for systems to support digital libraries, some ILS vendors have created add-on modules; others are providing integration "hooks" for third party products or tools that can be used to add access to full text documents or images.

These modules and tools increasingly include support for the creation, maintenance, search, and display of Non--MARC metadata schemes. Numerous metadata standardization projects exist. Many are detailed schemas that build on a more general one; some are discipline or data type specific; most can be mapped to other metadata schemas to create interoperability. ISO, ANSI, and the World Wide Web Consortium (W3C) all have committees working on metadata-related standards and registries of metadata schemas. Three metadata standards of particular interest to libraries are the Dublin Core, the VRA Core, and the Encoded Archival Description (EAD). Following discussion of these schemas, a protocol for harvesting metadata information that libraries should be aware of is described.

METADATA SCHEMAS

DUBLIN CORE

The Dublin Core Metadata Initiative began at a 1995 workshop (in Dublin, Ohio—thus the name) to improve discovery for networked information resources. Since then, the Dublin Core has developed into an official ANSI/NISO standard and today is probably the most well-known and referenced metadata standard. Dublin Core's strength lies in its simplicity. Fifteen elements are defined for describing any type of resource: Title, Creator, Subject, Description, Publisher, Contributor, Date, Type, Format, Identifier, Source, Language, Relation, Coverage, and Rights. Each element is optional and may be repeated as needed within the set.

Most elements also have a limited set of recommended qualifiers which can be optionally utilized to further refine an element's content or to indicate the encoding scheme used in recording the element's value. Information systems can conform to the standard without supporting qualifiers—such implementation of the standard is known as Dublin Core Simple. Dublin Core is ideally represented in XML (eXtensible Markup Language) syntax. However, Dublin Core Simple can also be represented in HTML (using "DC" elements in the "meta" tags) or even in a generic format (using Element="value"). Communities are encouraged to build on the Dublin Core to develop their own more specialized metadata element sets and many have done so. In theory, if a metadata scheme is based on the Dublin Core, cross-domain searches of the core descriptive information could be done more effectively while still providing specialized access points within a domain. Dublin Core has been given official standing with the World Wide Web Consortium (W3C) and Z39.50 standards initiatives.

Dublin Core Simple is specified for the schema for the Z39.50 Bath Profile cross-domain searching conformance. It has also been mapped to the MARC format to simplify development of automated methods for interchanging Dublin Core and MARC data. The Dublin Core Metadata Initiative (DCMI) is the

Maintenance Agency for the standard. DCMI has several working groups including one for libraries which is developing a Library Application Profile to clarify the use of the Dublin Core Metadata Element Set in libraries and library-related applications.

VRA CORE

The Visual Resources Association (VRA) has developed a metadata set of 28 elements, called the VRA Core, designed to describe works of art, architecture, artifacts, and comparable cultural objects. A visual resources collection frequently needs two or more records for a given item: one record to describe the physical object (the "Work"), and one record to describe each surrogate of the object which is created for viewing on or offline (the "Image"). The VRA Core includes a Record Type element used to clearly distinguish whether a record applies to a Work or an Image. All category elements are optional and repeatable.

The specification provides for the use of qualifiers to clarify a category's content and allows the addition of local use categories. Controlled vocabularies are recommended for many of the categories. A guide to good practices for cataloging visual works using VRA Core is in development. It is assumed that most Work records will be linked to one or more related Image records but the specification does not define how record linking is to be done—that is left as a local database implementation decision. VRA categories have been mapped to Dublin Core and MARC format as well as to several other related visual art cataloging schemas.

EAD (ENCODED ARCHIVAL DESCRIPTION)

The Encoded Archival Description is an encoding scheme for archival and manuscript collection finding aids, which provides access to other information by describing, often in detail, an archive's holdings. The specification currently accommodates registers and inventories of any length. Currently, MARC records for archives are usually at more of a summary level than an individual finding aid. The EAD standard supports the interrelationship between the data content of catalog records and finding aids by providing a MARC equivalency attribute, matching MARC field numbers, for related finding aid elements. The scheme can be represented as either an SGML (ISO 8879, Standard Generalized Markup Language) or an XML DTD (document type definition).

There are three parts to the specification: the SGML compliant DTD, a tag library with definitions of the standard elements and attributes, and an application guideline with extensive examples. The defined elements address both information about the finding aid itself and information about the archival materials covered by the finding aid. Attributes can be used to designate, for example, that a particular controlled vocabulary was used for a particular element's content. Use of controlled vocabularies or authority lists is not required. The Library of Congress, Network Development and MARC Standards Office is the Maintenance Agency for EAD, in partnership with the Society of American Archivists.

Sample RFP language for metadata schemas

The following are examples of language that could be included in an RFP to address metadata schemas:

- The system must support the use of Dublin Core (ANSI/NISO Z39.85) metadata for digital information resources. Describe any built-in functionality or add-on modules that provide support of metadata for cataloging and/or search and retrieval including customizable templates for data entry and edit, user-readable display of metadata, and validation of data against authority lists.
- Identify any metadata schemas, other than Dublin Core that are supported and describe how they are implemented. Describe any conversion tools or utilities that will translate from one metadata schema to another.
- Describe how search and retrieval of Non--MARC metadata records and MARC bibliographic records are integrated.
- Discuss if the system's Z39.50 server allows both MARC data and Non--MARC metadata to be searched. Describe if and how Z39.50 broadcast searches can be combined with metadata searches.
- Describe any tools within the system or available as separate modules that can be utilized to create, encode, and modify metadata records. Describe whether the metadata record can be embedded within the digital object, must be separate, or if either is supported. Describe to what level these tools can be customized. Define the skill sets that are needed to use these encoding tools.
- Describe how metadata records can be linked to one another within the information system's database. Identify whether one-to-one, one-to-many, or many-to-many linkages are available.
- Describe any data import / export functionality between MARC record cataloging and metadata encoding that would reduce duplicate cataloging effort and ensure consistency.

Assessing compliance

Currently, integration of library bibliographic systems and metadata encoding / searching is in the embryonic stage. Often, libraries use systems from multiple vendors to address both traditional and digital library system implementations. This results in the traditional library catalog and the digital library being totally separate with perhaps a low level of integration by providing a link within the MARC record that will take the user to the corresponding full-text or image.

This situation is changing, but varies significantly from one system to another in what is supported, how it is implemented, and how transparently the two types of data are accessible. Two main areas of concern in assessing metadata support are in the input / creation of metadata and in search and retrieval.

On the input side, the library evaluation team will want to determine what kind of input tools are available to support metadata creation, which metadata schemas have built-in templates, and how user-friendly and customizable the tools and templates are. Ideally the metadata input templates should be similar in look and feel to the templates used for MARC record cataloging. To reduce duplication of effort in cataloging, the tools should allow data fields from a MARC record to be easily transported to a metadata record and vice versa. Many of the metadata schemas have tools available to validate whether a particular record complies with the standard; these should be used to test sample metadata records created through the system's input tools and through any conversion tools from MARC to metadata or one metadata schema to another.

On the search and retrieval side, the system would ideally allow a single user interface to simultaneously search the library's MARC records and metadata records and present a single list to the user with associated records linked. A Z39.50 broadcast search combined with a metadata search of collections and resources outside of the library would also be desirable. If third party tools for search and retrieval are being considered, then the configuration requirements of both the library system and the third party tool need to be carefully assessed to ensure interoperability.

PROTOCOL FOR METADATA HARVESTING

The Open Archives Initiative (OAI) Protocol for Metadata Harvesting (PMH) was initially developed to support federated searching of metadata for distributed electronic archives of scholarly papers. The concept was deemed to have wider applicability and has since grown to encompass a standard harvesting protocol for multiple forms of metadata in any type of information repository. PMH defines a mechanism for a designated "data provider" to expose its metadata to one or more "service providers." Designated service providers could use the protocol to harvest metadata and to offer value-added services, such as a metadata search engine. This architecture differs markedly from the Z39.50 model of distributed search and retrieval.

While lacking in some of the advanced functionality of Z39.50, PMH has a simpler implementation and shifts the operational responsibility and processing away from the data providers to the service provider. It is considered particularly useful for collections of locally digitized or born-digital materials, which can now be included in the databases of large search engines. Currently, the protocol requires all data repositories to be able to export their metadata for harvesting in an XML schema. All repositories must also support export in the Dublin

Core Simple metadata set to ensure a common baseline. However, the protocol does support the concept of multiple types of metadata sets and data providers may offer their metadata in additional schemas as well. The protocol also requires repositories to datestamp all records at time of creation or modification to allow service providers to do selected harvesting within a specified date range. OAI maintains a registry of PMH compliant data providers, but registration is optional so it is expected that more providers are using the protocol than have registered. The protocol and its related documentation do not currently provide guidelines related to issues of intellectual property protection and acceptable use of exposed metadata. Libraries that become PMH data providers need to consider what their policies for these issues will be and how they will address enforcement of those policies by service providers who harvest their data.

Sample RFP language

The following are examples of language that could be included in an RFP to address OAI Metadata Harvesting compliance:

- Describe how the system supports the OAI Protocol for Metadata Harvesting (PMH) for a data provider, including any optional features that have been implemented. Discuss in particular how selected metadata records can be restricted from harvesting and how datestamping is handled.
- Identify any metadata schemas other than Dublin Core which are supported for exposure to the OAI Protocol for Metadata Harvesting (PMH).

Assessing compliance

Many of the data providers' compliance issues for the OAI PMH specification relate to how the metadata gets created and encoded, which was in the Metadata Schemas section. Some additional questions which the library evaluation team will want to explore include how the metadata gets XML-encoded (if not natively in that format), how the system assigns the required unique identifiers, how datestamping is done to allow for accurate incremental harvesting, and how access controls are applied to restrict selected metadata records from being harvested. Metadata and protocol harvesting support may not be provided as an out-of-the-box implementation, but instead be supported through the availability of toolkits. In such cases, the flexibility, ease of use, and learning curve for the toolkit will be a key factor.

INFORMATION RETRIEVAL

Z39.50Z39.50 defines a standard protocol for two computer systems to communicate for the purpose of information retrieval. Based on client/server architecture, the protocol standardizes the messages that clients and servers use, regardless of the underlying software, systems, or platforms. A client system that implements the Z39.50 protocol allows communication with diverse servers, and a server system that implements the protocol is searchable by clients developed by different vendors. The protocol is independent of the underlying transport mechanism, however most current implementations are done using TCP/IP over the Internet. Originally Z39.50 was designed to help with searching library bibliographic catalogs utilizing different library system software.

Today Z39.50 is used to access a wide range of databases in many disciplines across a variety of organization types. A library implementing Z-client technology can provide their users access to any Z-server compliant database without the user having to know that system's native search interface. A library implementing Z-server technology can open up their catalog to other libraries' or organizations' users without individual customized set-ups. Z39.50 has a "broadcast search" capability that allows a user to simultaneously search multiple databases from different providers. Libraries can adopt a single standardized Z39.50 interface for their patrons to concurrently access the library's catalog, purchased CD-ROMs, subscriptions to online databases, and Internet resources.

And data from a variety of sources can be extracted, using the protocol, to a common format for offline use or import into a local database. The Z39.50 standard identifies a number of "facilities," *e.g.,* Initialization, Search, Retrieval, etc. Each facility contains one or more "services" which are the specified protocols to perform a particular task within the facility, *e.g.,* Sort. Queries are qualified by various "attributes" which are grouped into types. A "Use" type of attribute indicates the query access points, such as title or author. A "Relation" type of attribute qualifies the relationship of two query values to one another, *e.g.,* less than, greater than, or equal to. Other attributes that control queries include truncation or omitting of characters in search terms and the structure of the query itself. Attribute types and values are clustered into related sets.

An example of an "attribute set" is "bib-1", which specifies the attributes that could be used in a typical bibliographic query. The specification for "extended services" in version 3 allows libraries to go beyond catalog searching and utilize Z39.50 protocols for many other library processes such as finding and importing cataloging records, creating "virtual" union catalogs, making ILL requests, saving and running Selective Dissemination of Information (SDI) profiles, and updating databases. Additionally, the Z39.50 standard is becoming accepted as a solution to the challenge of retrieving multimedia information including text, images, and digitized documents. The Library of Congress is the designated Z39.50 Maintenance Agency. A voluntary group, the Z39.50 Implementors Group (ZIG), meets regularly to discuss implementation issues and recommend improvements to the protocol.

Sample RFP language

The following are examples of language that could be included in an RFP to address Z39.50 compliance:

- The system must include a Z39.50 client and server that are compliant with ANSI/NISO Z39.50 version 3. Describe how the system has implemented Z-client and Z-server, and indicate how compliance has been tested and verified. Discuss how new Z-connections are set-up for both client and server, how customizable the set-up configuration is, and the skill set required to create and maintain set-ups.
- Identify and describe any Z39.50 optional facilities, services, or extended services that have been implemented.
- The system's Z-server must be accessible over a TCP/IP connection by at least two different remote Z-clients that are not the vendor's own products. Vendors will be required to demonstrate this capability or provide test documentation.
- The system must provide a Z39.50 version 3 client interface integrated with the system's patron Web client or has the same "look and feel." Vendors must be able to demonstrate that searches via their Z39.50 client and the native search interface return the same records.
- The system must include bibliographic data, holdings, circulation status, and user-understandable diagnostic messages in Z39.50 result displays. Identify the holdings schema that is utilized.
- It is desirable that the system include a Z39.50 cataloging client which supports import / capture of MARC bibliographic and authority records from any Z39.50 compliant server. Describe the system's Z39.50 support of the MARC records structure and identify any other record syntaxes that are supported.
- The system must have the ability to enable broadcast searches of Z39.50 servers. Describe how multiple Z39.50 connections and simultaneous searches are handled and how retrieval sets are merged, sorted, and displayed.
- Describe how the system will support seamless Z39.50 search and display interface with Non--MARC internal or external databases (CD-ROM or online) that support the Z39.50 protocol. Identify any particular systems or databases which have been pre-configured for Z39.50 access from the library system.

Assessing compliance

Libraries should first determine if they need both the Z-client and Z-server functionality. If only database searching of other Z39.50-compliant systems is envisioned, then the Z-client functionality may be all that is required.

Z39.50 implementations can vary depending on which version of the standard is supported. Section 4.4 of the Z39.50 standard defines conformance, requiring at minimum that version 2 be supported. Generally, libraries will want a system that complies with version 3, which adds more powerful Boolean and proximity searching; greater security, authentication, and resource controls; and a number of "extended services" that provide mechanisms for Z39.50-enabling systems. Many of the added features in version 3, especially the extended services, are optional. A system could be in conformance with version 3, but not provide many features that the library might want. It is important that the library evaluation team understands the various options in the standard and identifies those facilities and services which are needed or desirable for their application.

Examples of some enhanced version 3 features libraries might want are Scan, which allows index browsing; Explain, which allows users to obtain information about the target system; and Persistent Query and Periodic Query, which allow the saving and re-running of searches. The following section discusses Z39.50 Profiles, which can be helpful in identifying which Z39.50 features to require in the RFP. When evaluating the system's Z39.50 broadcast search capability, the evaluation team should determine any limits (or ability to set them) on the number of targets or result set sizes, how result sets are sorted and merged, and if preliminary results from one target can be displayed while others are still being searched. Even if a library implements version 3 compliant protocols, there may still be interoperability issues with other target systems that have implemented earlier versions or chosen different optional features. The University of North Texas is conducting a Z39.50 Interoperability Testbed Study whose goal is "to develop rigorous methodologies, test procedures, and measures to assess interoperability between systems using the Z39.50 standard protocol for information retrieval."

The results of this project should help both libraries and vendors in understanding and improving interoperability. A Z39.50 Register of Implementors is available on the Maintenance Agency's Web site. To further aid in both the selection of optional features and the interoperability issues, profiles have been developed that further define conformance requirements in specific application areas. The next section discusses three profiles that should be of particular interest to libraries.

Z39.50 PROFILES

As discussed in the previous section, ensuring that separate Z39.50 implementations interoperate can be challenging due to the different options that can be chosen. To address these challenges, many organizations and user groups have developed "profiles" which detail a subset of Z39.50 features and functions that an implementation conforming to that particular profile will support. When all the databases being searched support the same profile, search results should be more consistent and accurate. Some 25 profiles have been registered with the Z39.50 Maintenance Agency, crossing numerous organization types, geographic areas, and subject disciplines, including geospatial data, museum information, and thesaurus navigation. There are three profiles of particular interest to most U.S. libraries: the Bath Profile, the U.S. National Profile, and the GILS Profile. Other library related profiles exist or are in development that may be of interest in other geographic regions or particular subject disciplines. Consult the Library of Congress Z39.50 Maintenance Agency site for a list of these profiles.

BATH PROFILE

The Bath Profile was developed to improve interoperability of Z39.50 accessible library catalogs. It was designed to be international in scope with the expectation that it would be incorporated into more detailed national, regional, or provincial profiles. Release 1.1 of the Profile has been endorsed as an ISO Internationally Recognized Profile (IRP). Release 2 is expected to be issued in late 2002. Three functional areas are addressed in the current release:

- Basic bibliographic search and retrieval with primary focus on library catalogs,
- Bibliographic holdings search and retrieval, and
- Cross-domain search and retrieval.

For each area, three levels of conformance are defined, with each higher level inheriting the requirements of the lower level(s). Conformance Level 0 has limited requirements as it was intended to encompass as many existing Z39.50 products as possible. Conformance Level 1 adds requirements to improve searching and interoperability; libraries specifying new or enhanced Z39.50 systems should require adherence to at least this level.

Conformance Level 2 defines a number of enhanced functions that may not yet be widely available in existing implementations. Level 2 requirements are not detailed in the current release of the specification but are included in the forthcoming Release 2. The profile also defines a core set of typical library user searches and how to express those searches using Z39.50 "vocabulary." The National Library of Canada is the Maintenance Agency for the Bath Profile.

U.S. NATIONAL PROFILE

The soon-to-be issued U.S. National Z39.50 Profile for Library Applications is a compatible superset of the Bath Profile. It includes additional specifications and requirements than the Bath Profile to address national requirements for U.S. and Canadian libraries. The first version of the U.S. National Profile focuses on two areas 1) Bibliographic search and retrieval from library catalogs, and 2) Bibliographic holdings retrieval. It follows the same modular structure as the Bath Profile, using functional areas and conformance levels, but has some different requirements and criteria for each level.

The U.S. Profile also specifies exact Z39.50 attribute combinations for expressing a set of typical library catalog searches. The Holdings functional area currently focuses on presenting holdings information related to bibliographic records retrieved from a search. Searching of holdings will be addressed in a later release of the profile.

GILS (GLOBAL INFORMATION LOCATOR SERVICE)

The Global Information Locator Service (GILS) is a Z39.50 profile developed to provide a uniform search and retrieval method for accessing U.S. federal government information. The U.S. Government's information runs the gamut of disciplines from the arts to sciences, social sciences, and legislative information; the complexity of both the government's information and its management bureaucracy makes it difficult to prescribe any standard formats for its vast array of resources.

GILS seeks instead to specify a common set of access points and a search and retrieval gateway to the information regardless of where it is located as long as the server is GILS-compliant. The GILS Profile specifies a "GILS Core" utilizing Z39.50 requirements and, in addition, provides specifications relating to other aspects of GILS conformant servers that are outside the scope of Z39.50. Servers compliant with the ISO 23950 Geospatial Profile (GEO) or the Catalog Interoperability Profile (CIP) are also compliant with the GILS standard. Although developed for federal information, GILS is widely used for state information and many state libraries have implemented GILS. Government libraries, libraries doing cooperative ventures with government agencies, or libraries in government contractor organizations will want to seriously consider including GILS conformance in their RFP specification. Any libraries that want to make government information more accessible to their patrons will want to have GILS interoperability at least at the Z-client level.

Sample RFP language

The following are examples of language that could be included in an RFP to address Z39.50 profile compliance:

- The Z39.50 client and server functionality provided with the system must comply with Conformance Level 1 of the Bath Profile for all Functional Areas defined. Describe any deviations from this conformance and indicate how compliance has been tested and verified.
- The Z39.50 client and server functionality provided with the system must comply with Conformance Level 1 of the U.S. National Profile for all Functional Areas defined. Describe any deviations from this conformance and indicate how compliance has been tested and verified.
- Identify and describe any Z39.50 client or server functionality that

conforms to Level 2 of the Bath or U.S. National Profiles. Where Level 2 functionality does not currently exist, describe any plans for adding this conformance.

- The Z39.50 client and server functionality provided with the system must support the GILS profile specification. Describe any deviations from this conformance and indicate how compliance has been tested and verified.

Assessing compliance

Z39.50 profile-specific compliance issues relate to whether specific features from the standard have been implemented as specified in the profile. Ideally, the system will be pre-configured to support the desired profile, however, since these profiles are relatively new and still evolving, their support may not be widely implemented yet. The profiles will also have changing and/or added requirements as new releases are issued. Vendors should be asked which release they have implemented and if not the current one, what the timeframe is for supporting the latest release. If the profile is not supported "out-of-the-box," the library evaluation team will first need to determine if the profile can be supported at all. If the native system, as well as the default Z39.50 implementation, doesn't include a service or facility that is identified in the desired profile, no amount of configuration will make the system profile-compliant. If the features are available, then the library will want to know if the vendor will do the configuration as part of the local installation (and at what cost) or if and how the library can do the configuration itself.

The configuration tools or process to match a desired profile should be fully understood, including the required skill set needed by someone doing such a configuration. Another issue to consider is that local database indexing choices can impact a library's ability to conform to any of the Z39.50 profiles regardless of the information system's conformance level. For example, a library may have chosen not to index a particular field that is identified in the profile, or may have indexed a field in a way that would not support features like truncation or proximity searching. Full compliance with any of the Z39.50 profiles may require a library to change their indexing policy and reindex their database. Guidelines have been developed as part of the Z39.50 Interoperability Testbed Study to assist libraries in making indexing choices to best support Z39.50 profiles.

Command searching

- ISO 8777, Commands for interactive text searching

ISO 8777 names and defines 30 search and retrieve commands, eight symbols or punctuation used to qualify the commands, and the expected system response to each command. The goal is to provide a common language for conducting searches in a command mode. With the widespread use of browser-based graphical user interfaces, command searching is not utilized as much in library systems, particularly in the patron access modules. However, it may still be useful to have commands as an alternate search method for those who are familiar with and like Boolean searching. Command searching can be very useful for library technical staff to find and retrieve records for administrative, maintenance, data clean-up, and reporting purposes. A number of Integrated Library Systems offer "CCL" searches as an "Expert Search" or "Command Search" option because of the power of such a search and the speed of entering the search criteria.

Sample RFP language

The following are examples of language that could be included in an RFP to address command searching compliance:

- The system must support command level searching utilizing the standard commands as defined in ISO 8777, Commands for interactive text searching. Describe any deviations from this standard.
- Describe any additional search command functions or languages, different from those defined in ISO 8777, that are available with the system.
- Describe any database records and system functions or modules that cannot be accessed with a command level search.

Assessing compliance

Section 4.2 of the standard defines an information retrieval system as being in conformance "when it recognizes and responds to every command specified by this International Standard." The commands and qualifiers listed in the standard are fairly basic, thus missing any of them would definitely limit the retrieval capabilities with a command method. It is likely that a library would want more retrieval commands and functions than the standard defines. If that is the case, the RFP should state any additional requirements. A system may utilize a proprietary search language, however the vendor should be able to map the commands and functionality in their proprietary system to those in the standard. Where the commands perform the same function, it is desirable that the proprietary system would use the standard's command name.

WEB ACCESS

WEB ACCESSIBILITY INITIATIVE

The Web Accessibility Initiative (WAI) is an activity of the World Wide Web Consortium (W3C) to make Web content accessible to people with disabilities. The guidelines do not discourage the use of multimedia in Web content, but rather they explain how to make such content more widely accessible. Many libraries have an interest in making their information more accessible to disabled people and some have already incorporated the accessibility guidelines into the inhouse development of their Web pages. This same accessibility should be required of the Web interface to the library system.

There are three different guidelines, each directed to a different participant in the provision of Web content. Each specification details the guidelines, associated checkpoints, priority (*i.e.*, criticality) levels for each checkpoint, and conformance level requirements. The Web Content Accessibility Guidelines are directed to Web content developers. The Authoring Tool Accessibility Guidelines are directed to developers of Web page creation and editing tools or Web site management tools. The User Agent Accessibility Guidelines are directed to developers of Web browsers or other user interfaces to Web content. Separate supporting documents for each guideline provide information on implementing the checkpoints and testing and validation of the content or Web software products.

Sample RFP language

The following are examples of language that could be included in an RFP to address Web accessibility compliance:

- All Web-based interfaces in the system must comply with the Web Accessibility Initiative Web Accessibility Guidelines (WAG) or supply alternative versions of Web pages that comply with the guidelines. Describe how your system addresses Web accessibility support and identify the level of conformance with each of the WAG guidelines. Indicate how compliance has been tested and verified.
- Describe any Web page development and editing tools, available with the system or as add-ons, and discuss how the tools support creation of Web pages that comply with Web Accessibility Initiative Web Accessibility Guidelines (WAG).

Assessing compliance

There are a number of tools available to verify that a Web page meets WAI guidelines; these are listed on WAI's Web site. Even if the system's default Web pages have been tested by the vendor using one of these tools, there is usually some level of customization to the Web pages and interfaces during implementation. Therefore, the library evaluation team will need to retest the final design of their Web pages. Since Web page interfaces used with the library system will typically be modified and customized inhouse on some periodic (possibly even frequent) basis, the library should include a requirement of running a WAI compliance test as part of their ongoing Web page development and modification process.

OPEN URL

The OpenURL standard was designed to allow a library user who has retrieved an information resource citation to obtain access to the most "appropriate" copy of the full resource. The standard defines a mechanism for attaching an OpenURL link to a reference, usually a bibliographic citation. When the OpenURL is clicked, the user is presented with an option to request the full-text. When the user selects the option, it is fulfilled with the given the user's and organization's preferences related to cost, contractual and license agreements in place with suppliers, access rights, etc. Consider the scenario of three users in three different libraries accessing the same vendor's database product and wanting to retrieve the full-text of a particular article found in a search. If the database product were OpenURL encoded and the three libraries had implemented OpenURL services, then UserA could have the article retrieved from an inhouse collection of electronic journals, UserB could have the article retrieved from a publisher's Web-based journal database which the library had licensed, and UserC could have the article automatically requested from a document delivery supplier under the library's volume purchase agreement. All of the decisions, routing, and licensing necessary to make this happen would be transparent to the users. An OpenURL differs from a standard Web URL (Uniform Resource Locator) in two ways:

- It delivers metadata as well as identifiers that can be used to initiate action requests beyond linking to a referred site.
- It is context sensitive, in that the request is processed differently based on the context of the user initiating the request.

When the OpenURL is clicked, the associated metadata stored with the URL is sent to an OpenURL-compliant link server where the "rules" about target link preferences for the particular user base are stored. The link server presents the user with the available extended services for that user, such as electronic full-text, and fulfills the requested service on demand using the method determined by the stored rules. While electronic delivery of full-text articles was the initial impetus of OpenURL, the standard can be applied to the provision of other services such as ordering of full-text from document delivery suppliers, searches of selected library's holdings for ownership of a referenced title, citation searches of a referenced article, links to book reviews, author searches for additional works, links to author biographies and personal websites, Web searches for related information on the same topic, etc. A NISO version of OpenURL is currently in draft and expected to be issued for trial use in early 2003. However, the first version of the specification has existed for several years and has been implemented by a number of library and information suppliers. The forthcoming NISO version is expected to generalize and add to the defined syntax to better address extended services beyond scholarly journal articles.

Sample RFP language

The following are examples of language that could be included in an RFP to address Open URL standards compliance:

- Describe any built-in or add-on capability to support a locally managed OpenURL-compliant link server. Discuss how this server interoperates with the various library system modules.
- Describe any capabilities of the system to integrate with a third party supplier of an OpenURL-compliant link server system or service. Discuss how this third party system would interoperate with the various library system modules.
- The system must support input and editing of OpenURL links as part of its cataloging / editing modules for both bibliographic MARC records and metadata records. Describe how the system supports OpenURL link input and discuss options for handling OpenURL identifiers.

Assessing compliance

The standard focuses on the syntax for the OpenURL but does not address or specify software design for link server management or technologies to manage the user identification, which is where many of the difficult implementation issues reside. These technologies would generally be supplied through some type of add-on modules or through a third party product or service. Thorough testing of all the technologies and interfaces with the library system will be needed, as this is not currently a plug-and-play type of implementation.

Similar to the situation with many library's digital resource collection, current implementations of the OpenURL and link server technology are often separate from the integrated library system. If the OpenURL related functionality is integrated with the library system, the main compliance issues will be with the creation and management of OpenURL links, how the system handles the links in their Web interface, and how the system and its Web interface would interoperate with a link server.

Many library systems allow the storing of a URL in a MARC 856 field and present it as a live hyperlink in the Web interface. This type of implementation should be tested to ensure that it can support the input and storage of an OpenURL (which is both longer and more complex than a standard URL) and pass the entire OpenURL intact to the Web interface. Other questions for the evaluation team to ask the library system vendor are: How does the library system recognize an OpenURL vs. a standard URL and how are they handled and displayed differently?

When an OpenURL link is clicked in the library system's Web interface, does the system recognize it as an OpenURL and pass it correctly to the designated link server? How is the user's identity and preferences handled so that they are included or referenced correctly when the OpenURL is sent to the link server? If the library system is using a common Z39.50 interface to access additional resources beyond the library's catalog, such as an abstracting and indexing service database, how are OpenURL links embedded in those resources handled? Can the common search interface correctly display and act on an OpenURL link of a retrieved citation from another Z39.50 compliant product?

XML

The eXtensible Markup Language (XML), one of the latest incarnations of "markup" languages, is quickly becoming the universal format for structured documents and data on the Web. While HTML, also a markup language, addresses the presentation and look of information, XML defines the structure of the information and describes the role of its structured components. XML is a subset of SGML, the international Standard Generalized Markup Language defined in ISO 8879, which was developed for technical documentation before the Web existed. XML kept the best, most functional features of SGML and dropped many of the optional, complex aspects to make a markup language suitable for the Web environment. Some key components of XML that make it such a powerful tool are:

- Open system approach – XML is Non--proprietary and utilizes ASCII, making XML data machine-independent and accessible across computing platforms.
- Separation of Content and Display – XML coding focuses on the structure of the document with the intent that it can then be re-used and customized for different purposes. Separate stylesheets can be created using eXtensible Style Language (XSL) (or other tools) to define particular display or print formats. This separation grows in importance with the widespread use of different sizes and types devices to read Web content, from PCs to PDAs to cell phones and whatever new device gets invented tomorrow.
- Extensibility – XML is called extensible because it allows the creation of customized markup tags and applications. The customized tags and rules to be used are defined in a Document Type Definition (DTD)—a name inherited from SGML—which is the collection of tags defined for a particular application. This allows groups of people or organizations to create their own customized XML applications for exchanging information in their domain, however they choose to define that domain.
- Internationalization – XML utilizes Unicode, a single comprehensive character set that encompasses virtually all of the world's written languages.
- Database interoperability – XML uses the concept of a document composed of a series of entities, which can contain one or more elements. This component nature of XML accommodates interfacing with a database, since XML tags can be mapped to database fields, and makes it very suitable for storing the XML in a database, as

whole documents or in components for greater repurposing capability.

- Extended linking – XML's linking capabilities go beyond the simple HTML one-way hyperlinking from point A to point B. X-links can be to multiple targets, activate automatically, embed or replace information, or be defined "out of line" in a separate document. Not many tools have implemented extended linking features yet, but the possibilities are there.
- Metadata support – The metadata describing a document can be explicitly tagged with XML, making the data much more useable and searchable than HTML's meta-tags allow.

XML offers many opportunities for library applications:

- MARC – The Library of Congress Network Development and MARC Standards Office is developing a framework for working with MARC data in an XML environment, including DTD schemas, stylesheets, and software tools. This would allow MARC data to be fully converted to XML format or to be selectively output to XML for publication or use in another application or schema. There is even some controversial discussion about whether XML should completely replace MARC.
- Integrated library system interfaces – By using XML as the common input/output format, the traditional library system could be more easily integrated with Web technology and other proprietary systems. Newly developed tools or systems would not require separate special interfaces to be written. A totally XML-based integrated library system is likely in future years.
- A&I Databases – Output from abstracting and indexing databases could be offered in XML format which allows the record to be more easily re-used in applications such as interlibrary loan.
- Domain specific metadata searching – Organizations with common interests can define an XML-compliant schema for "cataloging" their data or tagging multimedia documents, then create virtual databases of the combined data or export the data for harvesting by a search engine.
- Digital publishing – XML is tailor-made for digital publishing and can provide a common format for e-books and other electronic documents The Open eBook Forum has developed a standard for encoding e-books in XML that would allow them to be read in a variety of reading devices.

XML is in its early development phases and its use in library applications is just beginning. Supporting tools and new applications are rapidly growing and it is clear that XML will have a significant role in electronic information management and delivery. A number of the standards discussed in this guide are already being implemented using XML and more XML implementation approaches are planned or expected in the future. RFP language is not included here as the RFP requirements need to be specific to the particular application which is using XML, *e.g.,* EAD, or Dublin Core, or MARC-XML.

DATA ELEMENTS FOR BINDING LIBRARY MATERIALS

Z39.76 identifies and defines common data elements used to process and track library materials for binding when information about the material is exchanged between a library management software system and a binding preparation software system. Use of the specified data elements in an automated library system can reduce duplicate data entry when preparing binding orders, improve accuracy and consistency of binding labels, and allow for more automation of binding processes. The standard incorporates other identifying codes and standard numbering systems such as ISBN, ISSN, and SICI.

Holdings information fields are based on the MARC 21 Format for Holdings Data. The standard does not define any of the communications protocols required for the information exchange, but the expectation is that EDI is utilized for the transfer of data.

Sample RFP language

The following are examples of language that could be included in an RFP to address Z39.76 binding data elements compliance:

- The system must support ANSI/NISO Z39.76 Data Elements for Binding Library Materials. Define which binding element fields are included by default in the system and discuss how optional elements are handled.
- Describe how binding element information is input and how it is linked to the bibliographic and holdings record information to ensure consistency.
- Describe the process for generating binding information from the system to send electronically to a vendor. Describe the methods and formats for exporting binding information to a file.
- Identify which communications protocols can be used to transmit binding information.

Assessing compliance

A small subset of the data elements defined in the standard is considered mandatory; these elements should be supported in the selected system. Many of the optional fields are defined as such only because they would not be utilized with every binding order thus it is likely that many of the optional fields would be desirable to have. Additionally, some libraries may be using a binding preparation software package that might require some of the standard's optional data fields. The evaluation team should review all the optional elements and identify the additional fields that would be "mandatory" to their library's binding process. Determine how the desired optional data elements are supported and how easily additional data elements can be added at a later time. Ask if there are any limitations on the number of binding related fields which the system can support. Determine that the system supports both serial and Non--serial materials in the binding processes and that the binding module can access needed data from the serials and acquisition modules. Have the vendor create a test file of binding data from the system as it would look when transmitted and verify that the information is compiled and reported correctly. If the library's binding vendor accepts electronic transmissions, a test transmission to that vendor and the vendor's verification of how the data was received would be useful.

Clarify with the vendor which communication protocols are supported for binding information. If the system supports EDI transmission for acquisition and claiming activities, can it also be used for the binding transmission? If the binding data is exported to a file, determine what file formats are available and if these are compatible with what the library and the binding vendor use.

NISO CIRCULATION INTERCHANGE PROTOCOL (NCIP)

The NISO Circulation Interchange Protocol (NCIP) defines and specifies the objects, services, messages, and data elements needed to facilitate interoperability between dissimilar circulation systems. Three applications are addressed: direct consortial borrowing, circulation/interlibrary loan interaction, and self-service circulation. Functions that permit a circulation system to manage controlled access to electronic materials, such as e-books and music files, are also included in the protocol. Currently, many libraries have to record an interlibrary loan in both their circulation system—to track the patron's check-out or the item's nonavailability status—and in the shared ILL system—to track the loan or outstanding loan request.

Use of the NCIP will allow disparate circulation systems and ILL systems to communicate, exchange information about users and items, and update status automatically—eliminating duplicate data entry, lessening manual interventions, and ensuring consistency in loan information and updates. Library consortiums where individual libraries are using different library systems can utilize NCIP to turn consortial loans into circulation transactions.

Self-service circulation transactions can be improved and expanded beyond the patron's home library. The NCIP standard separates the specification of services and data objects from implementation details to allow the protocol to be deployed using different encoding and transport methods, as well as permit the use of future technologies without rewriting the entire standard. Implementation specifics are handled through Implementation Profiles, which specify methods for message exchange using particular technologies, and Application Profiles, which describe the particular service requirements needed to support typical circulation applications. Templates and rules for developing these profiles are provided in the standard. A basic Implementation Profile, utilizing current Web and XML technology, is included as part 2 of the standard. Eight Application Profiles associated with Implementation Profile 1 have been defined and are available on the NISO NCIP Web site along with the schemas referenced in the Implementation Profile.

Sample RFP language

The following are examples of language that could be included in an RFP to address NCIP compliance:

- The system must support the NISO Circulation Interchange Protocol, ANSI/NISO Z39.83. Describe any successful demonstrations of NCIP implementation between: 1) the system's circulation module and other ILL systems, and 2) the system's ILL module and other circulation systems.
- The system must support NCIP Implementation Profile 1, ANSI/NISO Z39.83, Pt. 2. Describe how the system implements this profile.
- Identify the specific NCIP Application Profiles which the system supports.

Assessing compliance

NCIP Implementation Profiles and Application Profiles include conformance requirements, specifically, which of the services, messages, and data structures are required as well as the rules defining Behaviour for conformance. Implementation Profile 1, provided with the standard, defines two levels of conformance: strictly conformant and conformant, each of which is further explained in the profile. This particular Implementation Profile requires the use of XML for message encoding, DTD to encapsulate the structure, Unicode UTF-8 for character encoding, and one of three transport protocols—HTTP, HTTPS, or TCP/IP. Current implementations of NCIP should demonstrate compliance with these protocols and schemas. Libraries should determine which of the eight application profiles are relevant to their environment. The event tables in the application profile can be used as a kind of checklist to determine if the system being evaluated supports the services needed in the desired application environment. NCIP was approved in mid-2002 and a newly formed implementors group plans began meeting in October 2002. It is expected that this group will develop further guidelines on conformance interoperability.

BARCODES

A barcode is an optically readable array of black and white "bars" of varying widths where a fixed pattern of bars and spaces represents a particular machine-readable character. An optical scanning device "reads" the barcode and sends the information to a decoder which converts the scan to its correct machine-readable characters. The ratio of the bar widths, the print density and quality of the label, the accuracy of the scanning device, and the capability of the decoder all play a part in whether the right information is ultimately fed into the computer system. Libraries typically use barcodes to uniquely identify a physical library collection item and link the physical item to a bibliographic and holding record. Barcodes are also used on library patron identification and link to the patron's database record. During a circulation transaction, the barcodes of the library item and the patron are scanned resulting in a faster and more accurate circulation transaction. An accurate and effective barcode scan is dependent on the interaction of the barcode label, the barcode reader, the decoder, and the library system software interface. Readers and especially the labels are often purchased from different vendors than the library system supplier, which makes standards conformance of all the vendors critical. There are over 200 barcode symbol "languages" in existence worldwide. Each "language" specifies rules for how data is encoded into the "bars," label printing requirements, decoding rules, and error checking. Only a fraction of the bar code specifications are in wide use. The two bar code standards most in use by libraries are Code 39 and Codabar.

CODE 39

Code 39 is a general barcode standard utilized in many industries. It is sometimes called the "3 of 9 code" as it uses 9 bars, 3 of which are wider than the others, to define a character. An alphanumeric system is used which can have up to 43 characters with 1 start/stop code pattern. Code 39 is considered one of the easiest codes to use because of its self-checking capability.

CODABAR

Sample RFP language

The following are examples of language that could be included in an RFP to address barcode compliance:

- The system must support the use of both Codabar and Code 39 barcodes for bibliographic items and patron IDs, with the ability to interpret a minimum of 14 digits.
- The system must accept input from third party suppliers' barcodes and readers, or another library system barcodes, that comply with Codabar or Code 39 standards. Describe any limitations on support of these standards or standard-compliant third party products.
- Barcode numbers on items or patron IDs should be able to be scanned or manually entered into the system.
- The system must be able to create output that can be used by a vendor to create Code 39 or Codabar standard barcodes.
- Barcode numbers should be entered into MARC field 949 or an appropriate 8XX field of the record.

Assessing compliance

Bar code technology and readers supporting both Code 39 and Codabar are fairly commonplace. Their commodity nature has caused libraries to shop around to find the best prices. As a result, it is not unusual for different vendors to supply the barcodes, the readers, and the system software. Thus it is important that tests be performed using the proposed products from all vendors involved to ensure accurate interoperability. In particular, test check digit computation, readability, and reliability should be verified.

BIBLIOGRAPHIC FORMATS

MARC 21 FORMATS

The *Machine Readable Cataloging format* (MARC) was originally developed by the Library of Congress to automate the production of catalog cards. Over time, MARC has become widely used internationally and expanded to support advances in technology and library practices. The USMARC formats have evolved into the MARC 21 specifications, becoming the defacto standard for bibliographic formats in library computer applications. The MARC 21 formats specify three content designators:

- Tags – A 3 digit number that uniquely identifies all the possible "fields" of the cataloging record, such as title, author, series, etc.
- Subfield codes – A lower case letter or digit, preceded by a delimiter, used to further differentiate the data within a field.
- Indicators – Two one-character positions for single digit numbers whose use or meaning varies depending on which field tag the indicator follows.

The specifications address the format encoding necessary for representation and exchange of bibliographic data between systems. Display formats and database storage technologies are not included in the specification and are determined by the design of the particular information system product. There are five MARC 21 format or content specifications, each addressing a specific type of data:

- The MARC 21 Format for Bibliographic Data
- The MARC 21 Format for Holdings Data
- The MARC 21 Format for Authority Data
- The MARC 21 Format for Classification Data
- The MARC 21 Format for Community Information

At this time the only system using MARC 21 classification data is the centralized database of Library of Congress Classification records maintained at the Library of Congress. Other libraries would not reference the classification data standard in their RFPs. The Library of Congress is the official Maintenance Agency for the MARC 21 specification.

MARC 21 FORMAT FOR BIBLIOGRAPHIC DATA

Bibliographic data is the core component of an automated library system. It forms the basis of all online catalogs and shared cataloging processes. All the functional modules of an integrated library system utilize or interact with the bibliographic data in some way. In earlier versions of MARC, each type of material had a separate format defined. In the 1990s, however, the concept of "format integration" was implemented—now all material types are addressed with one format and all MARC 21 fields may be used with any material type.

Sample RFP language

The following are examples of language that could be included in an RFP to address MARC 21 bibliographic format compliance:

- The system must encode all bibliographic records in MARC 21 Format for Bibliographic Data without limitation on record length. Describe how the system supports this format. Discuss any limitations on the use of 9XX or X9X locally defined tags and fields.
- The system must be capable of importing and exporting bibliographic records in MARC 21 Format for Bibliographic Data without vendor intervention and with full preservation of all content designators. Discuss how import and export is handled. Address whether 9XX locally defined fields are included in import and export.
- The system must provide for display of all MARC content designators on the cataloging workstation and suppress display of codes on all patron access workstations. Describe how record display is handled for each of the following clients: librarian/cataloger workstation, OPAC, Z39.50 client, and Web browser.

Assessing compliance

A library will want a system that supports the full MARC 21 bibliographic format, allowing use of the complete spectrum of content designators, even when it is not intended to use all of them. It is desirable that the system has some validation mechanisms for content designators and selected controlled values. Additionally, the system should accurately import and export records with all content designator tags intact. The system should preserve the order of MARC fields as created or imported, so as not to lose context of related data. The many data elements contained in MARC can result in a powerful search system; the evaluation team should assess how effectively the system uses the wealth of data in the record. The system should support all functionality expressed through indicator values. For example, if an indicator is defined as meaning a display constant should be supplied or a certain number of characters are Non--filing, then the system should provide that functionality. Format changes to MARC 21 are issued annually and the vendor should discuss how the system is kept current with these changes. If the system uses a vendor-supplied tag table, ask about the update frequency of these tables by the vendor and the lag time from when tag changes are issued by the Library of Congress and incorporated into the vendor's tables. Since record display is not specified in MARC 21, demonstrations of display on different types of workstations for different types of users—cataloging workstations, OPAC terminals, Z39.50 clients, and Web browsers—should be performed to determine how each display might differ

MARC 21 FORMAT FOR AUTHORITY DATA

Authority data acts like an online thesaurus, allowing for control of authorized names and subjects used in designated fields of bibliographic records. These records may also generate cross references from unused to preferred terms and interrelationships between authority entries. The MARC 21 Format for Authority Data identifies seven kinds of authority records—established heading, reference, subdivision, established heading and subdivision, reference and subdivision, node label—and defines how each type is to be encoded.

Sample RFP language

The following are examples of language that could be included in an RFP to address MARC 21 authority data format compliance:

- The system must support MARC 21 Format for Authority Data and allow all relevant bibliographic fields to be authority controlled. Describe how the system implements this format and identify which fields can be authority controlled. Describe the default authority control policies and the ability to customize these policies.
- The system must generate SEE and SEE ALSO references from authority records and display them in the OPAC. Discuss how the system creates, manages, and displays cross-references.
- The system must be capable of importing and exporting authority records in MARC 21 Format for Authority Data without vendor intervention.
- The system must be capable of editing authority records individually and globally and allow easy access to authority records editing from within the bibliographic module.

Assessing compliance

The system should be evaluated for the ability of authority records to interact with bibliographic records in generating references and validating entries. Compliance issues generally relate to the implementation of cross references—specifically how and when the system displays simple and complex cross references from the tracings information. Additionally, authority records have import and export requirements that differ from those of bibliographic records and thus should be tested separately. Libraries that import authority control lists from more than one source should determine if and how these lists are merged and how overwriting is prevented.

MARC 21 FORMAT FOR COMMUNITY INFORMATION

Many libraries, especially public ones, identified a need for storing and making accessible to patrons local information about their organization and community that cannot be described by the traditional bibliographic record. The MARC 21 Format for Community Information was the answer to that need. It identifies five types of community information records—individual, organization, Programme or service, event, and other—and defines how each type is to be encoded.

Sample RFP language

The following are examples of language that could be included in an RFP to address MARC 21 community information format compliance:

- The system must support MARC 21 Format for Community Information. Describe how the system implements this format.
- The system must be capable of importing and exporting Community Information in MARC 21 format without vendor intervention.
- The system must be able to limit searches to the community file only. Describe how this is accomplished.
- It is desirable for the system to provide linkages to an authority file. Describe how authority records for Community Information are handled.

Assessing compliance

There are minimal requirements for community information format compared to the other formats. Support for all the identified data elements, import and export capability, and the validation routines should be verified. If authority control is desired for community information, determine if a separate authority file is available.

MARC 21 FORMAT FOR HOLDINGS DATA

The holdings data describes the particular items and copies in the library's collection that are associated with a bibliographic record. Proper holdings format and coding is critical to the operation of circulation related functions, serials check-in, and integrated acquisitions. The MARC 21 Format for Holdings Data specifies data fields and tags for three types of holdings—single-part items, multi-part items, and serial items—as well as rules for embedding holdings in or linking holdings to the bibliographic record. The current version of the standard has incorporated the required holdings elements specified in ANSI/NISO Z39.71 and includes a chart mapping MARC data elements to those in

Z39.71. An encoding level tag has been added to identify the specificity of the holdings statement at 5 defined levels.

Sample RFP language

The following are examples of language that could be included in an RFP to address MARC 21 holdings format compliance:

- The system must support MARC 21 Format for Holdings Data at both summary and detailed levels, and as either embedded or linked records. Describe how the system supports this format. Discuss the ability of the system to automatically generate summary holdings. Discuss how the system is kept current with modifications to the holdings format.
- The system must be capable of importing and exporting holding records in MARC 21 Format for Holdings Data without vendor intervention and with full preservation of all tags.
- The system must provide for display of all MARC 21 holdings tags on the librarian workstation and suppress display of codes on all patron access workstations. Describe how record display is handled for each of the following clients: librarian/cataloger workstation, OPAC, Z39.50 client, and Web browser.
- The system's serials check-in system should automatically update the MARC 21 holdings record including all content related to the 85X/86X paired fields. Describe how the system serials check-in module integrates with the MARC holdings records.

Assessing compliance

Full compliance to the MARC 21 Format for Holdings Data is not as widespread in current library systems as is compliance with the bibliographic format. Libraries frequently differ in their interpretation of what constitutes a "copy"; the evaluation team should determine whether the system will support their local definitions and handling. Identify any limitations on the number of holdings records that can be linked to a bibliographic record. Serials holdings can be especially complex due to the "pattern" variety of issues, irregular issues, and special extra issues. The integration between the serials check-in functions and the holding records should be discussed. Ideally, the pattern information in the 853 field should match the pattern used for serials check-in and the 863 field should update automatically as an issue is checked in. Import capability is important when migrating from one system to another. Export capability in either detailed or summary format should be reviewed if there is any expectation of contributing to a union catalog or listing. Tests of holdings data should include embedded and linked holdings records, summary and detail holdings, and how the different types of holdings are displayed. Import and export of a sample of the libraries holding data should be tested to ensure that field codes are intact.

HOLDINGS STATEMENTS FOR BIBLIOGRAPHIC ITEMS

Z39.71, supporting the concept of format integration, supersedes and merges two previous holdings standards, Z39.44 for serials and Z39.57 for Non--serials. The NISO standard was based on the international standard, ISO 10324 Information and documentation – Holdings statements—Summary level, but goes further in defining holdings at a detail level. Use of the specified display formats provides consistency in the communication and exchange of holdings information among libraries and between disparate information systems. Z39.71 works in conjunction with the MARC 21 Format for Holdings Data; MARC defines the structure and encoding for implementing holdings data while Z39.71 addresses the content and display of those holdings. The standard defines four levels of specificity of holdings, mandatory and optional data elements for each level, punctuation / format to be used for the data content, and display options.

Sample RFP language

The following are examples of language that could be included in an RFP to address Z39.71 holdings statement compliance:

- The system must support holdings statements of both serial and Non--serial multi-part items as defined in ANSI/NISO Z39.71 Holdings Statements for Bibliographic Items, including summary and detailed holdings, mixed level holdings, itemized and compressed formats, and enumeration and chronology displays. Describe the system's support for all mandatory data elements at all four levels and discuss how optional elements can be utilized.
- The system must support holdings display as defined in ANSI/NISO Z39.71 Holdings Statements for Bibliographic Items, with respect to formats, punctuation, and order of data. Describe how holdings statement display is handled for each of the following clients: librarian/ cataloger workstation, OPAC, Z39.50 client, and Web browser.
- The system must support export of holdings data, with full retention of content formats as defined in ANSI/NISO Z39.71 Holdings Statements for Bibliographic Items, to allow participation in union lists or library data exchanges.
- Describe how the system links holdings data and bibliographic data.

Assessing compliance

Full support of holdings data at any of the four levels defined in the standard is the main compliance issue. The system should accept the newly defined option of having an open-ended holding in an OPAC display. Available display options should be verified and tested on all types of clients that the library intends to use. Linkages between holdings data and bibliographic data should use an item identifier. While not specified in the standard, limitations, if any, on number of holdings linked to a given bibliographic item or holdings record length should be determined. Z39.71 accommodates the use of holdings data created under the earlier standards. Libraries that plan to migrate data using older formats and use the new standard requirements for future holdings should understand how the system will handle and display both the old and the new formats.

RECORD STRUCTURE, CHARACTER SETS, AND EXCHANGE MEDIA

In addition to the MARC 21 format specifications, discussed in Section I, there are also specifications that relate to the more technical structure, coding, and labeling of data that is needed for the exchange of information between computer systems. The MARC 21 Specifications for Record Structure, Character Sets, and Exchange Media define the standards for ensuring that all the bibliographic formatted information is retained, understood, and translated correctly.

MARC 21 – RECORD STRUCTURE

The record structure is the key for the computer's understanding all of the MARC bibliographic formatted data and is an integral reference in all the format specifications. The MARC 21 record structure specification is an implementation of ANSI/NISO Z39.2, Information Interchange Format, and ISO 2709, Format for Information Exchange. It defines how bibliographic and related records should be structured so that any compliant computer software can translate the codes and data into understandable, editable, and searchable information.

The specification details three parts of the record:

- The leader tells the computer how to process the subsequent record by defining the length and type of the record and kinds of coding being used.
- The directory provides an index to the record by identifying the field tags that are used in the record and their length and start position.
- Variable fields are all the control and data fields that make up the actual record.

Sample RFP language

The following are examples of language that could be included in an RFP to address MARC 21 record structure compliance:

- The system must comply with the record structure specified in MARC 21 Specifications for Record Structure, Character Sets, and Exchange Media. Discuss how the system has been tested to validate this compliance and provide copies of relevant test documentation.
- The system must be capable of importing and exporting all types of MARC 21 formatted records without vendor intervention and with

full preservation of all tags. The system must be able to import and export individual records as well as the entire database in MARC 21 format.

- Describe the system's capability of importing and exporting bibliographic utilities' versions of MARC records, *e.g.,* OCLC-MARC and RLIN-MARC.

Assessing compliance

The system should accurately import and export records of all MARC 21 format types with all structure and content designator tags intact. The system should provide all the tools and utilities needed to do imports and exports without additional programming or services from the vendor. Some bibliographic utilities, such as OCLC and RLIN, have subtle differences in their implementation of the Z39.2 standard, usually in the leader format and how records are blocked on tape. The library evaluation team should determine if import and export of MARC records from the bibliographic utility they use has been implemented and tested. Since record indexing and storage are not specified in MARC 21and could vary greatly from one system to another, the evaluation team should ask for a full explanation of the underlying database structure and indexing routines.

MARC 21 – CHARACTER SETS

All computerized characters have to be encoded at the binary level. While early automation systems used the EBCDIC character set, since the 1970's ASCII has been the most commonly used code across all types of computer applications. But ASCII, which has only 256 possible combinations, falls short when a single application, such as the typical library catalog, utilizes multiple languages, transliterations, and diacritics. The MARC 21 specification defines two character set formats:

- MARC-8, an 8-bit coding system which utilizes the ASCII set from ANSI X3.4 and its international counterpart ISO/IEC 646, the ANSEL extended Latin character set, the East Asian Character Code, as well as a number of other sets specific to particular languages and symbols.
- UCS/Unicode UTF-8, a variable 8/16-bit coding system based on the Unicode and UCS standards. Unicode defines a single character set that encompasses most written languages. The MARC standard does not currently define the full Unicode character set. The supported MARC-8 character codes have been mapped to Unicode with the intent of enabling transition from 8 bit to 16 bit systems and round trip movement of data without loss of information.

The character sets supported in an automated library system will determine how bibliographic text is input, stored, and displayed. To accurately import records in electronic format, the library system must either natively support the records' character set or have a reliable conversion Programme. While all types of libraries may encounter character set issues, libraries with diverse multilingual collections will need to be most concerned with how a potential system implements character sets.

Sample RFP language

The following are examples of language that could be included in an RFP to address MARC 21 character set standards compliance:

- The system must support the importing, inputting, editing, displaying, printing, storing, and exporting of all characters defined in the character sets of MARC 21 Specifications for Record Structure, Character Sets, and Exchange Media. Identify any character sets specified in MARC 21 that are not fully supported by the system for importing, inputting, editing, displaying, printing, storing, and exporting. Explicitly describe the areas of Non--support.
- The system must support the MARC 21 character sets utilizing standard hardware peripherals for input, display, and printing. Describe any specific requirements for peripheral hardware to ensure this support.
- Describe how Non--Roman alphabets, Latin script characters, and specialized symbols are handled with a standard Web browser client.

Assessing compliance

Each character set that the library plans to use should be tested separately in the proposed system. After testing input on a cataloging workstation, the display and printing of the characters should be tested on the different types of peripherals the library expects to use. Display should also be checked using a Web browser. Sample records utilizing the different character sets should be imported and checked for editing, display, and printing. Record exporting options should also be tested and round trip export / imports should be tried.

MARC 21-EXCHANGE MEDIA

The MARC 21 Exchange Media specifies media format and labeling for mechanisms that may be utilized to exchange MARC 21 encoded records between computer systems. The requirements for labeling, volume, organization, and sequence of data are defined for three types of exchanges: electronic file transfer, microcomputer diskettes, and magnetic tape. Magnetic tape interchanges are based on three related ANSI standards: ANSI X3.27, ANSI X3.39, and ANSI X3.54.

Sample RFP language

The following are examples of language that could be included in an RFP to address MARC 21 exchange media compliance:

- The system must support the MARC 21 Specifications for Exchange Media with the capability to import and export, without vendor intervention, by FTP electronic transfer, disk, and tape.
- Describe all tools and utilities that come with the system, or are available as separate modules, which are utilized to import or export MARC formatted records.
- Describe all tools and utilities that come with the system, or are available as separate modules, which are utilized to import MARC records from bibliographic utilities.

Assessing compliance

Adherence to media format and labeling specifications is essential for successful exchange of MARC 21 records. Vendors should be asked for documented test results or demonstrations for the type of transfers the library requires. Electronic file transfers utilizing Internet *File Transfer Protocol* (FTP) can be easily tested using the library's own data or sample data files. Magnetic tape transfer specifications were changed in 1977 to support record spanning across media. Libraries should verify that the vendor supports the new tape specifications.

SERIAL ITEM AND CONTRIBUTION IDENTIFIER (SICI)

The SICI standard defines a coding structure to assign unique identifiers to serials. The code builds on the *International Standard Serial Number* (ISSN) for the serial item portion of the identifier. The SICI code is derived algorithmically from bibliographic information about the serial and/or article and may be generated by the creator/publisher of the items and contributions, by a third party vendor such as a document delivery supplier or abstracting and indexing service, or by the library which acquires and holds the materials.

Use of the SICI code in a computer system allows the items and contributions to be uniquely identified in many library automated transactions including ordering, claiming, bibliographic database linking, ILL and document delivery, check-in, reserve room, and rights management and royalty collection. The code was designed to be compact enough to be easily converted to a barcode. SICI has also been assigned a use value in the Z39.50 bib-1 attribute set.

This assignment allows the SICI to be used as a qualifier in a Z39.50 information retrieval search. SICI also could be used as the identifier in conjunction with an ILL Protocol request, EDI order, or a GEDI electronic document transmission.

Sample RFP language

The following are examples of language that could be included in an RFP to address SICI compliance:

- The system must support the use of the Serial Item and Contribution Identifier as specified in ANSI/NISO Z39.56. Describe how your system implements SICI for both serials and contributions. Discuss how the SICI is stored, indexed, and searchable.
- Discuss how your system does SICI code matching and validation.

Assessing compliance

It is more likely, currently, to find support of SICI at the Serials Item level than the Contribution level in a library system. However, the use of the Contribution Identifier through the entire ILL or document delivery cycle is becoming more crucial. Even libraries that do no currently identify items at the contribution level should look for a system that allows the code's use. Since the standard allows that some data elements can be omitted when creating a SICI, the algorithms a system uses to match or validate SICI codes can be complex. Demonstrations and tests of this functionality should be requested from the vendor.

The 1996 version of the standard changed the rules for Title Code, clarified the distinction between serial items and contribution identifiers, added a method for indicating the medium of the material, and better delineated the segments of the identifier. Libraries should confirm that the system supports the changes in this version.

RESOURCE SHARING AND INTERLIBRARY LOAN

ILL PROTOCOL

- ISO 10160, Information and documentation—Open Systems Interconnection—Interlibrary Loan Application Service Definition
- ISO 10161-1, Information and documentation—Open Systems Interconnection— Interlibrary Loan Application Protocol Specification—Part 1: Protocol specification
- ISO 10161-2, Information and documentation—Open Systems Interconnection— Interlibrary Loan Application Protocol Specification—Part 2: Protocol implementation conformance statement proforma

The ISO ILL Protocol standardizes the exchange of interlibrary loan information between computer systems. Currently, most automated ILL systems or consortia require the borrowing and loaning libraries to access a common database and system. Loans are generally available only from those libraries participating in the common system. Loans outside of the common system usually have to fall back on paper ILL requests that are mailed or Faxed. The ISO ILL Protocol takes a distributed view to handling automated ILL transactions. Borrowing and lending libraries, whose systems are compliant with the standard, would enter information into their own systems which would then send messages in the standard protocol format directly to each other or through an intermediary. In addition to allowing the library to use the ILL system of its choice or the ILL module in its own integrated library system, use of the ISO protocol approach widens the resource sharing base—potentially to anywhere in the world where the protocol is being used—an increasingly important capability in today's global society. The ILL Protocol breaks transactions down into separate activities or tasks, each of which is defined as a "service." These services have defined specific data elements and "messages" that get transmitted during the ILL transaction in a specified sequence. Three standards make up the full protocol:

- ISO 10160 defines the ILL roles, models the different role combination interactions, and defines the various ILL services, messages, status states, and sequencing rules.
- ISO 10161-1 is the "meat" of the protocol, specifying the "ILL Protocol Machine's" behavior requirements and the procedural rules to support the services defined in ISO 10160.
- ISO 10161-2 details the requirements for completing a conformance statement.

Three roles—requester, responder, and intermediary—are defined along with their respective events, actions, and procedural rules. Services supported by the protocol include ILL requests, renewals, recalls, tracking, and overdue notification. Provision is made for the identification of the delivery mechanism and the item medium / format; however the standard does not prescribe the actual delivery mechanisms or telecommunication transport protocols. The National Library of Canada is the official Maintenance Agency for the ISO ILL Protocol standards.

Sample RFP language

The following are examples of language that could be included in an RFP to address ISO ILL Protocol compliance:

- The system must support the ISO ILL Protocol standards, ISO 10160 and 10161-1. Describe how the system enables input and output of ISO ILL Protocol requests. Discuss any implementation decisions related to optional protocol requirements.
- The system must conform to the Interlibrary Loan Protocol Implementors Group (IPIG) Profile. Vendors should submit a copy of their completed IPIG Profile Conformance Statement Requirements List.
- Identify which communications protocols can be used by the system to transmit ISO 10160 and 10161-1 compliant ILL protocols.
- Describe how the system's ISO-compliant ILL Protocol Machine application interacts with the other modules of the library system, particularly circulation and finance applications.

Assessing compliance

Section 10 of ISO 10161-1 describes the standard's conformance requirements. A system can be compliant with the protocols for one or any combination of the three roles and only the simple transaction functions are mandatory. In order to effectively evaluate a system's compliance, the library needs to be clear about which role(s) it intends to perform and which optional services and parameters are needed for its particular ILL operations. The Interlibrary Loan Protocol Implementors Group (IPIG) was established by the North American Interlibrary Loan and Document Delivery Project to facilitate implementation of the protocol.

To address the complexity of understanding and implementing conformance with the protocol, IPIG created the ILL Protocol Implementors Group (IPIG) Profile for the ISO ILL Protocol reflecting a common set of decisions, options, and values for implementation. The IPIG Profile imposes some additional constraints on implementation, beyond those specified in the base application standards. A claim of conformance to this IPIG Profile is a claim that all requirements in the relevant base standards are satisfied and that all the requirements of the Profile are satisfied. Similar in purpose to the ISO 10161-2 PICS proforma, for the vendor to complete to indicate levels of compliance with the specified roles, services, and parameters.

The library evaluation team should go through of the IPIG Profile and identify which optional parameters are important to their specific library situation. The library's requirements can then be compared to the completed forms submitted by the vendors. For those features which are designated as having conditional support, the evaluation team should determine whether the identified conditions would be relevant in their implementation. A separate publication, IPIG Guidelines for ILL Application Developers, provides advice for understanding and achieving conformance with the ILL standard and IPIG profile.

Although created for developers of ILL computer systems, the guidelines can also be useful to the library evaluation team in understanding the standard, developing their own requirements, and interpreting the vendor's conformance statement and implementation approach. The ILL Protocol Maintenance Agency Web site includes resources on how to conduct system tests including a list of participating testbed sites. The ILL Protocol Implementor Group Web site includes updated information on the status of system testing by IPIG members.

GENERIC ELECTRONIC DOCUMENT INTERCHANGE (GEDI)

- ISO 17933, Generic Electronic Document Interchange (GEDI)

The Generic Electronic Document Interchange (GEDI) standard defines the formats and protocols for exchanging electronic documents. It was created to avoid the development of disparate Non--standard automated systems as electronic document delivery continues to grow in availability. A standard set of formats and transport mechanisms will encourage the use of electronic document delivery, allow the use of automated systems to increase speed and lower delivery costs, and utilize the same networking technology for ordering and delivering documents.The GEDI format consists of two parts: the header or cover information and the electronic document itself. To facilitate use of GEDI with the ISO ILL Protocol, the header tags have been mapped to equivalent data elements defined in ISO 10161-1, Interlibrary Loan Application Protocol Specification. Document formats currently supported are TIFF, PDF, and JPEG, however the standard is designed to accommodate registration of additional formats as they become widely accepted. While the standard is designed to allow utilization of any transfer protocol agreed upon by the involved parties, it defines profiles for FTP and MIME e-mail transmission. Three roles of participating organizations are defined—Supplier, Consumer, and Relay—the latter being an intermediary store-and-forward facility.

Sample RFP language

The following are examples of language that could be included in an RFP to address GEDI compliance:

- The system must support the transfer of electronic documents in compliance with ISO 17933, Generic Electronic Document Interchange (GEDI). Describe how the system provides these capabilities. Identify which document formats and transfer protocols are supported.
- Describe how the system integrates ISO ILL Protocol (ISO 10160 and 10161) functionality with GEDI functionality.

Assessing compliance

The GEDI standard specifies the conformance requirements based on the role being performed—Supplier, Customer, or Relay. An information system at the highest level of compliance would have to both send and receive in all the listed formats and transfer protocols, receive and interpret all header data elements, and even accept and ignore Non--standard header elements. Libraries should identify which role(s) they intend to perform and identify which formats and transfer protocols are needed to perform those roles in their environment. Except for mapping of the header data elements, the standard does not specify the integration functionality with the ISO ILL Protocol or a library system's ILL transaction module. Discussions with the vendor will be necessary to determine if this integration exists and how it was implemented.

ELECTRONIC DATA INTERCHANGE (EDI)

- ANSI X12, Electronic Data Interchange (series of standards)

- ISO 9735, Electronic data interchange for administration, commerce and transport (EDIFACT)—Application level syntax rules

EDI, the electronic exchange of information to conduct business transactions is commonplace today in many industries, especially for purchasing and invoicing. Both the customer and supplier can benefit by the use of EDI through reduced data entry time, improved accuracy of data (no rekeying errors), and faster speed of response and transaction fulfillment. Many publishers and book / serial agents are set up to utilize EDI with libraries for orders, invoices, claims, claim responses, and shipping notices. EDI implementation requires the use of a highly structured format. Two major standards: ANSI X12 and EDIFACT are the specifications utilized most widely, X12 in the U.S. and EDIFACT internationally, especially in Europe. Each standard defines the EDI messaging structure, syntax, codes, transaction sets, directory of elements, and rules of Behaviour. Both of these standards are quite complex; in fact, each is actually a series of standards. Additionally, neither X12 nor EDIFACT are static standards; new versions and interim releases are scheduled periodically to address technology and industry changes.

Different releases are not always fully compatible with one another. To ensure interoperability, the two communicating systems must be supporting the same version and release level for transaction sets, segments, and data elements. Like many standards, there are numerous elements designated as optional, further complicating implementation. To address the complexity and options of the standard, many industry groups have developed guidelines "translating" the standards to specific recommendations for their industry's applications and specifying particular transaction sets or subsets. Several organizations in the publishing and library community have created such guidelines.

BASIC, a standards group formed through the merger of BISAC and SISAC has developed formats for EDI for the publishing community based on ANSI X12. ICEDIS has published formats for subscription orders based on X12. Basically, the BASIC and ICEDIS guidelines identify selected X12 transaction sets and map them to book and serial related activities. The X12 transaction sets that are typically used in library applications include:

- 810 Invoice
- 850 Order
- 855 Order acknowledgement
- 997 Functional acknowledgement
- 869 Order status inquiry/ Claim
- 870 Order status response / Claim response

Both BASIC and ICEDIS are migrating their guidelines to EANCOM, a widely used subset of EDIFACT developed by EAN International. EDItEUR has already taken the X12 guidelines for serials developed by SISAC and created EDIFACT versions.

Sample RFP language

The following are examples of language that could be included in an RFP to address EDI compliance:

- The system must support *Electronic Data Interchange* (EDI), in conformance with ANSI X12 standards, for ordering, claiming, canceling, invoicing, and reporting for both monographic and serial materials. Describe how the system implements EDI. Discuss how the system verifies EDI data elements and provides error alerts.
- Describe your plans and timeframe for EDIFACT support for EDI transactions.
- The system must support all of the X12 transaction sets as specified in the BASIC (BISAC/SISAC) Guidelines. Describe any deviations from the guidelines.
- Describe how data sent and received in EDI transactions is integrated with the different modules of the library system, particularly bibliographic, serials, acquisitions, and finance.
- Describe to what extent and how EDI related transactions can be completely automated, *e.g.,*, claims sent without operator initiation.
- Identify which telecommunications protocols can be used for EDI transmission.

Assessing compliance

The critical compliance issues for EDI relate to both the handling of the needed transaction sets and the methods in which the library system creates and receives this transaction information. Many systems have a software module that "translates" the relevant information in the library system to and from an EDI formatted message. The library evaluation team will want to understand which data fields are extracted for sending transmissions and in which fields received data is loaded. In particular, support of the subscription renewal invoice from a serials agent can be more problematic than dealing with individual book orders or new subscriptions. The timing of the EDI transmission data extracts / loads and the amount of operator intervention needed can also be issues. There are both pros and cons to real-time vs. batch functioning as well as totally automated vs. operator-initiated actions. The library team needs to consider how these choices fit in with their processes and which options are available within the system. Earlier implementations of EDI transmission generally required the use of a *Value-added Network* (VAN) communications supplier, which can add to the costs of using EDI. Some implementations now support transmission over the Internet. The various transmission options should be discussed along with their costs and available security controls. Most library system vendors and major book / serial agents have experience in EDI interchanges between their respective systems.

The library evaluation team should discuss with the library system vendor which book / serial agents they have worked with directly and ask for documented tests of interoperability. Likewise, the current book and serial agent used by the library should be consulted for input on their experiences with different library systems and any issues the library will need to address with a particular system, if chosen.

MODERN DIGITAL LIBRARY SYSTEM

Invenio is an integrated digital library system originally developed at CERN to run the CERN Document Server, currently one of the largest institutional repositories worldwide. It was started over 15 years ago and has been matured through many release cycles. Invenio is a GPL2 Open Source project based on Apache/WSGI + Python + MySQL architecture. Its modular design enables it to serve a wide variety of usages, from a multimedia digital object repository, to a web journal, to a fully functional digital library.

The development strategy used to implement Invenio ensures it is flexible in any layer. Being based on open standards such as MARCXML and OAI-PMH 2.0 its interoperability with other digital libraries is guaranteed. Being originally designed to cope with the CERN requirements for digital object management, Invenio is suitable for middle-to-large scale digital repositories. Records can be of any nature. This presentation will introduce the different features of Invenio, their usage in the CERN context and how other institutions and projects are also driving some of its development.

USAGE

Besides being used to run the CERN Document Server, Invenio has also been chosen by several other big institutions or projects. Among them it is about to be used to serve the SPIRES High Energy Physics information through the recently launched INSPIRE service, that will become the repository of reference for high energy physics. It is used by the EPFL. ADS has expressed interest to move to an Invenio-based platform, while starting a collaboration at the data level between astrophysics and high energy physics worlds. For example in Spain Invenio is already used by the *Dipòsit Digital de Documents* (DDD) and by the "Repositorio Digital de la Universidad de Zaragoza". Recently the European Commission has chosen Invenio to become part of two important projects D4ScienceII, and OpenAIRE, with the latter having the goal to set up a portal where all the EC funded research project documents will be available.

FEATURES

Let us demonstrate the key Invenio features by following the lifetime of a record in the system, from ingestion to dissemination. As an integrated digital library, Invenio is built to allow the management of digital objects and the meta-data associated with them. Meta-data are stored in the MARCXML format, which has the flexibility to store any kind of information and which can be easily converted, thanks to XML style-sheets to any other meta-data format.

INGESTING RECORDS

Data and Meta-data can enter into Invenio powered repositories through different ways. They can be manually deposited by an author, through custom and fully configurable web interfaces, backed by an equally configurable work-flow architecture, that lets the submission administrator set up any kind of procedure triggered by a deposition.

Meta-data and data can as well be harvested regularly from OAI-PMH compatible repositories. Data can also be input into the system from any Non--standard format by writing ad-hoc conversion scripts either in XSLT or in the proprietary BibConvert's language. Users also have the possibility to upload records by sending e-mails that will be parsed automatically. The system can be configured to accept submission by robots thanks to the availability of a simple web API.

DIGITAL OBJECT MANIPULATION

Fully fledged tools to integrate and manipulate digital objects are available. In particular Invenio can manage multiple formats for the same document, multiple revisions, automatic conversions between formats, automatic stamping of PDF documents with watermarks, creating icons, automatic text extraction to allow for full-text searching, automatic meta-data extraction and many more. Data consistency is also ensured by MD5 checksum being continuously verified.

INDEXING AND RANKING

All the new records ingested into the system and their modifications are indexed by a very fast indexing engine that has been developed in-house. All the indexing stages are configurable; which metadata fields to index, how to extract tokens, which language is expected in order to apply stemming and removing stop words, and so on.

A plug-in based ranking engine takes care of creating special indexes to be used at search time for sorting results based on word similarity, citations, download statistics, and to present citation networks.

CURATING RECORDS

Curators have powerful web-based tools to manipulate records, whilst maintaining change histories, auto-completion of fields based on fully configurable knowledge bases, multi-record modification, assisted duplicate record finding and an efficient AJAX-based record merging tool, and so on. Curators can also exploit flexible tools to perform meta-data compliance checks against configurable rules. Automatic tools are also available to extract citations and references from scientific papers and to extract keywords based on a given ontology, to enrich the available meta-data. Distributed curation activities can be instantiated through integration of Invenio with RT, one of the most famous open source ticketing systems.

DISPLAYING RECORDS

Bibliographic records can be displayed in any format, thanks to an easy and fully-configurable formatting layer, which allows creation of record-based rules to choose which representation of a record to use, while each representation can be fine tuned to fit any particular need. Thus any kind of content can be hosted and properly displayed, such as multimedia documents, books, address book contacts, and so on.

Records can be organized in a flexible hierarchical structure using real and virtual collections. Each collection can in turn be customised to choose the look and feel and the kind of features enabled. The whole web appearance of Invenio can be fully customised thanks to an integrated templating system, thus facilitating integration of Invenio into an existing institutional portal. Since Invenio is being developed in an international environment it supports internationalization and comes translated already in 25 different languages.

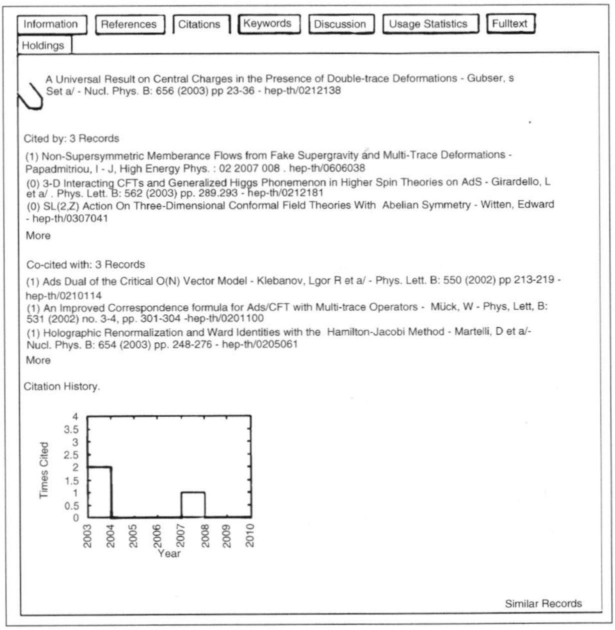

SEARCHING AND BROWSING RECORDS

A powerful search engine resides at the core of Invenio Fig Supporting a Google-like syntax, it can be used to dig into the repositories in a very easy way, while allowing the more experienced users to take advantage of many advanced features such as regular expressions, range queries, selection of meta-data, and many more. Results can be clustered by collections and ranked with respect to word similarity, number of citations, downloads based rankings, and any other pluggable algorithm.

Any search query can automatically turned into an RSS feed to add to a personal news aggregator. Thanks to integrated support for MODS and UnAPI standards, search results can be stored in Zotero, a powerful Firefox plug-in useful to organize a personal digital library. The system offers users powerful citation and author analyses.

COLLABORATIVE TOOLS

Invenio integrates several collaborative and typical web 2.0 tools such as baskets, to store and share records or external resources with other users, personal e-mail notification alerts, record commenting and reviewing, internal web-based messaging tools, approval/reviewing work-flows.

EXPORTING RECORDS

Data and meta-data can be exported in several ways, the most important being through OAI-PHM protocol and by means of a pluggable exporting module.

AUTHENTICATION AND AUTHORIZATION

While offering for free local accounts management, Invenio can be integrated with institutional user databases to delegate the authentication phase and to exploit externally available user details. Using the *role based access control* (RBAC) model of Invenio one can define a list of roles, attach users to particular roles, and grant rights to perform actions such as view-restricted-collections based on user group membership, user IP address, and more.

CIRCULATION

Invenio supports the operation of a physical library by integrating a circulation module, as well as by supporting inter library loans. Users can submit loan requests, and follow the request status, the librarians have a web interface to accept/reject loan requests, to send overdue letters, to set up sub-libraries, etc.

CREATING JOURNALS

As an example of an application that has been built on top of the core Invenio, the web journal module lets repository administrators create online web journals with regular issues built from articles stored in the repository itself. A specific appearance can be set up in order to have a layout providing journal-like reading experience. This is currently used today for producing the official CERN Bulletin, which is issued every two weeks.

2

Managing Administrative Metadata

INTRODUCTION

A growing need exists for metadata management of administrative issues related to electronic resources. Some of these issues include license restrictions, authentication means, technical contacts, and statistics availability. *Integrated library systems* (ILS) do not easily accommodate such metadata, and paper files maintained by serials librarians have proven inadequate both in accessibility and organization. Making e-resource metadata quickly available to interlibrary loan and reference staffs is facilitated by an online gateway of the ERTS model.

IN THE BEGINNING

Discussions about the state of Tri-College e-resources were held in 2001. The focus of these discussions, which were sponsored by a Mellon Foundation grant, was ensuring consistent access to e-journals throughout the consortium. This original charge was broadened later that year and resulted in development of the ERTS system. The authors comprise the founding members of the ERTS Team. We held a number of brainstorming sessions to identify the results each library hoped to achieve with ERTS. Particularly due to our consortium status, numerous discussions were necessary so as not to overlook any one library's specific needs. Some of the goals for ERTS included:

- Immediate access to license information for all e-resources purchased by the Tri-College Consortium libraries
- Various statistical reports not easily available, if at all, through our integrated library system
- Notification services that alert staff when e-resources are about to expire

We began identifying data elements based on these needs.

The suggested fields, and the information we expected to place within them, fit into four categories:

- *Licensors:* Entities from whom we license e-resources
- *Items:* Individual e-resource titles
- *Purchases:* Acquisitions data concerning e-resources
- *Vendors:* Entities from whom we purchase e-resources

After consulting established element sets, particularly those maintained by the University of Washington and Johns Hopkins University, it was comforting to see that our direction was quite similar.

SCOPE

ERTS exists in large part because of limitations inherent within integrated library systems. That said, the ERTS Team was wary of duplicating information already held in our local catalog. Thus we sought to restrict ERTS's scope to those data either unavailable, or not easily retrievable, through our ILS. Since the predominant mission of ERTS is to track license information, few freely available electronic resources are entered. Only in cases where a certain aspect of a freely available e-resource requires tracking, such as how the consortium has decided to catalog it, is it entered in ERTS. In cases of volatile aggregators, only a collectionlevel record is maintained.

Resources we have decided to exclude from ERTS generally fall into these categories:

- Extending less than a year's guarantee of access
- Delivering incomplete holdings
- Not providing ready title-level access

LICENCE INFORMATION

As in many institutions, electronic resources are heavily used in our libraries. As a result, serials and acquisitions personnel field numerous questions from public services staff regarding license restrictions. The paper files we maintained before ERTS were not an adequate medium for promulgating license-related information. Ellen Finnie Duranceau's efforts with license tracking at MIT were influential at pointing the way towards a networked file for staff use. Apart from the license terms related to legal responsibilities, ERTS stores elements that directly address what library services we can provide and what our patrons can do with a given resource.

Some of these data include:

- *ILL Allowability:* We have buttons for yes, no, n/a, and unknown. There is also a free text box to allow for further details. Our ILL staffs need to know this information, and occasionally reference librarians are asked about such restrictions.
- *Number of Simultaneous Users:* Because certain resources carry this restriction, this element helps public services staff troubleshoot the cause of a user not being allowed access. Documenting simultaneous

user limits in ERTS provides a check that may help public services staff before assuming a more involved access problem is the culprit.

- *Print Restrictions:* Some resources limit the number of pages printed per session, and others even prohibit printing. This element prevents the expenditure of valuable time trying to diagnose an apparent printing problem.
- *Reserve Restrictions:* Staff responsible for electronic reserves need to know if such mounting is restricted in any way. An example of such a restriction is having a strict time frame for the duration of the e-reserve link. As with print restrictions, the licensor may obligate us to inform users of such restrictions or other license terms.
- *SDI Availability:* This element indicates the availability of a service allowing patrons to register for e-mail notification when new content becomes available. Often, such content is in the form of journal issues or tables of contents.
- *Archival Guarantee:* As we exchange print subscriptions for electronic equivalents, access to this information has become a great concern, especially since it is often hard to tease out of veiled licensing language.
- *Negotiation Contact:* This element stores the name of the licensor's negotiation representative. This information is useful when we wish to alter the language in our license.
- *General Comments:* This catch-all field is used to capture license data not covered in the fields, such as a note concerning licence revision dates.

CATALOGUING INFORMATION

Cataloguing electronic resources in the Tri-College setting poses complications beyond the natural challenges inherent with this ever-changing media. When the Tri-Colleges first purchased electronic resources, a commitment was made to provide individual bibliographic records in our local catalog for each title. During this time, many journal publishers provided online access to their content, often free with the print subscriptions. As aggregators and large publisher collections became available, the challenge to provide title and subject access grew into an even more formidable task.

In order to continue providing individual title access in this environment, the Tri-Colleges employed several methods of cataloguing, including a locally derived batch method, along with the more standard copy cataloguing via cooperative resources like OCLC.

Further adding to this quandary, the consortium libraries share a catalog. Although the libraries purchase many online resources collectively, there are numerous eresources unique to a single library. Maintaining consistent cataloguing standards across three separate technical services units is a challenge. ERTS supports sharing of these standards by centralizing cataloguing information for the Tri-Colleges. Initially, the cataloguing elements in ERTS were linked to the licensor database.

This architecture posed three problems, however:

- The licensor name is generally not used by cataloguing and reference staff to identify an electronic resource.
- Catalogue librarians describe information about individual and collection titles that is not always consistent across multiple resources offered by the same licensor. For instance, a licensor may place title lists and holdings information for one of its collections on the Web, but not for another. This may affect the way the resources are cataloged. Appending these cataloguing data to title records, rather than licensor records, gives us the flexibility necessary to record differences among collections.
- Several freely available collections for which the Tri- Colleges maintain cataloguing procedures do not warrant a licensor record.

The cataloguing database consists of approximately sixteen fields that are divided into four sections on the cataloguing information page:

- Title;
- Tripod Searching Information;
- Technical Cataloguing Information; and
- Publisher-Related Information.

Title

Cataloguing uses this section, consisting of one element "Title", to identify the individual journal, collection-level, or aggregator title. The Tri-Colleges use the MARC 130 tag for local collocation and retrieval purposes within Tripod. The title field in ERTS replicates the locally derived 130 field. The intention is to facilitate ease of searching for public services staff. If they require more information about an electronic resource, they can then search the title in ERTS.

Tripod Title Searching Information (for Public Services)

This section, designed for use by public services staff, consists of two elements that identify the search keys necessary for retrieval of all titles in a collection or aggregation. The first field contains a URL that invokes an OPAC search in Tripod. The second element contains the Tripod search key and search term. Such a field might look like this: author=Project Muse.

Technical Cataloguing Information

This section centralizes local decisions for Tri-College cataloguing staff. It consists of three elements. The first field notes, whether individual titles within a collection, aggregation, or database, are analysed. The second field indicates what method is used to catalog analysed titles and where the file used for the locally batch-created records resides. The third field records any MARC fields that are unique to each collection, aggregate, or database. For instance, a cataloger might decide to use a series entry to help collocate related electronic resources. When this is the case, the 4XX field would be recorded in this field. Also, if a 7XX field is recorded for a person or corporate body, it would be accordingly noted in this area.

Publisher-related Information

This section incorporates URL and note fields. The URL field directs catalogers to a title list, usually located on the licensor's Web site, that is used in our batch load procedures. A brief note about the update pattern and frequency of these titles lists is also located here. The final element in this section is a note about whom to contact at the vendor for service updates. Overall, the cataloguing database is a modest component of ERTS. Yet it provides the Tri-College's cataloguing community an invaluable tool. ERTS circumvents the need to record cataloguing decisions on paper files or "in our heads," making for a stronger, more fluid approach to cataloguing electronic materials throughout the consortium.

PURCHASE INFORMATION

Although much purchase information is available in our local catalog, we felt it would be useful to be able to view a title's cost over a five-year period, as well as to easily distinguish any one-time fees. Additionally, we wanted to have the ability to gene0rate reports that would tell us how much we were spending on different categories of electronic titles.

Each purchase event is captured in ERTS by entering the following data:

- *Library:* This is the purchasing library or in some cases may be the consortium as a whole.
- *Licensor:* Selected from a drop-down list of licensors; this is usually the publisher/creator of the title.
- *Vendor:* Also selected from a drop-down list; this is from whom we purchase the title. For cases in which one of the libraries acts as purchasing agent for the other two, that library would be recorded as the vendor.
- *Purchase Type:* We have a need to distinguish among titles that are paid as electronic only, titles that carry an added cost over the cost of the print subscription, and titles that offer free online access as a consequence of a print subscription.
- *One-time Charges:* We wanted to record this information separately so that it could be distinguished from annual costs. Price, paid date, expiration date, and ILS order number are also entered.

Generally, much discussion surrounds the initial decision to purchase a particular resource. The decision to renew a resource, however, is often made with less thought and in a very short time frame. It is most often the case that the need to make the renewal decision is prompted by a renewal form or invoice from a vendor and is sometimes received after the previous subscription has expired.

We often do not take the time to ask ourselves important questions such as: How often was this resource used? Has the licensor provided good service in the case of technical problems? Can we justify the cost? Instead, we often rely on the gut feeling of our bibliographers. While their sense of the usefulness of the resource may be valid, we want to be able to provide more data and more time for them to make the renewal decision. Therefore, we have added an e-mail-alerting component to ERTS which uses the expiration date in the purchase record and notifies selected staff sixty days prior to the expiration of a title. This is a strategy we learned from the HERMES system implemented at Johns Hopkins University. We believe this gives us sufficient time to analyse usage statistics, cost, and service issues so that we can make informed renewal decisions.

A 'renew' button in the purchase record moves the previous year's purchase data to a new column, retaining the ILS order number and purchase type. ERTS uses the price entered for the new year to calculate the price change from the previous to the current year. A variety of reports can be generated from the purchase data in ERTS. For example, we can create reports totaling electronic acquisitions by purchase type for the fiscal year or for any selected time period, giving us the title, the most recent paid date, and amount of each electronic resource, sorted by type of resource, then by title. A report on the number of records by purchase type and an annual expenditure comparison report can also be generated. Other report types can be created as needed.

TECHNICAL SPECIFICATIONS

ERTS runs on FileMaker Pro, currently version 5.5 desktop software at Haverford's Magill Library. ERTS was developed on a Mac, but currently runs on Windows. Staff use Macintosh and Windows computers to access the database, which performs well on both platforms. Readonly access to ERTS is restricted to the three college campuses by IP address; editing privileges are restricted by passwords.The staff functions of inputting, editing, and reporting are available in all three campus libraries through FileMaker's sharing system. Search functions for public services staff are available through a Web interface using the FileMaker CDML tags. Through the Web, users on the three campuses can search by licensor name or title and view the license restrictions that apply. Staff can also enter comments about an e-resource's system performance or access difficulties, which can then be made available to them at renewal time. *ERTS consists of six interrelated files or "tables"*:

- Licensors—One record is entered for each licensor and used by all three libraries.

- Items—One record is entered for each title and used by all three libraries.
- Purchases— Each library maintains a separate purchase record.
- Vendors—One record is entered for each vendor and used by all three libraries.
- Service comments
- Administration

METADATA ISSUES

While initially we had standardized on Qualified Dublin Core, moving forward with WordPress required us to make two substantial modifications, one to the metadata itself and the other to the WordPress functionality. First, although the libraries had followed the recommended QDC date format wherever possible (but had created Non--standard dates when days/months/ years were not known specifically), WordPress required a well-formed date value. Because of this, we had to zero-fill any un-specified values. This allowed WordPress to make decisions and appropriately place Non--specific dated posts.

The second major issue we faced occurred due to the size of some areas of the taxonomy. The standard functionality of WordPress categories includes a retrieval of all the related child categories when a user is interacting with the category browse interface. While this is preferable in some cases, database response times for our project were leading to time-out issues whenever category values exceeded several hundred.

In order to solve this issue, the category retrieval functions had to be re-written to make this process more efficient and to pull child values only when they were needed.

WordPress allows local implementations to make modifications like this using a local functions file that is related to specific interface themes. While this will require us to re-examine these functions with each WordPress upgrade, it also allows us to continue expanding the use of the taxonomy to create new relationships between the images in our collection.

In general, we used the following four approaches to modify WordPress in the Digital Forsyth project:

- First, the implementers downloaded pre-developed plug-ins. These plug-ins allowed us to quickly extend or modify the functionality of WordPress without significant effort.
- Second, we modified existing functions to fit our local needs. While using pre-defined functions makes these modifications much simpler to do, they can also affect the system when upgrades are made to WordPress.
- Third, in some cases we chose to modify the core functionality of WordPress.

- This was required in special cases where the WordPress default behaviour was not in sync with our expectations for Digital Forsyth. A simple example of this is the fact that blogging software by default returns posts in reverse chronological order. However, for our project we wanted posts to be returned in increasing chronological order; therefore, in such cases we modified basic WordPress functions accordingly.
- Fourth, we created new local functions. While this approach was not used extensively, in the case of category retrieval new functions were required to make data retrieval more efficient. This final approach is probably the most susceptible to issues related to system upgrades.

As the Digital Forsyth project moves into its third year, we are looking Towards merging the library cataloger experience with public feedback and tagging experience. This may allow us to stop using a back-end digital library for record creation and simply use it for archiving, which will significantly simplify the processes of data creation, loading, user-tagging, and updating currently in place.

Creating a user Interface using Themes

We were able to use the theme platform in WordPress to easily create a custom look and feel for our digital library. Two of the major modifications required were modifying the theme to display hierarchical tags more prominently and including our custom metadata fields at the correct place in the blog posting. Other modifications included style and layout customization. Some high level uses and benefits of themes are:

- Enabling multiple user/organization centric views of the data
- Enabling rapid prototyping of interfaces during initial development
- Using splash pages to provide deep links to searching and browsing interfaces.

In general, Word Press themes provide a simple platform for creating user interfaces, and involve approximately 8-10 files. Themes can be based on templates and specific pages where required. In some cases, we found ourselves deciding whether to use external plug-ins for themes or to develop them locally. An example of this is the development of 'photoblogging' style functions without using the photoblogging plug-in that comes with Word Press.

While we found the use of local functions was appropriate at the time we made our decision on this matter, being willing to re-investigate/re-develop this area as upgrades occur is an important component of using social software. Because so many possible features exist and are developed in the blogging user community, deciding which features to include and use can be challenging. Here again, the presence of such a large community of developers and users means that we are able to embed and deploy new services quickly, without a large amount of local development. We found that using the WordPress software allowed development to start at a much deeper level. For example, rather than writing a batch loader or indexer, we were able to make small modifications to the WordPress software using existing modules. A prime example of modification is the revision to the tag-cloud plug-in. While traditional tag-clouds emphasize the most popular terms, with regard to our project we found that emphasizing the un-common facet categories in the tag cloud using a Term Frequency/Inverse Document Frequency (TF/IDF) approach yielded a more relevant and usable interface.

We accomplished this by creating a function that counted the number of times a facet was used in the corpus of blog posts and comparing those counts against the facets in the individual post. Based on the assigned weights using class definitions in the HTML, the interface uses CSS (Cascading Style Sheets) to modify the style of the resulting tags.

Data Migration

In order to load data from the digital library system to WordPress, we modified the existing RSS loader to support Qualified Dublin Core tags. The RSS loader was used because it already had a framework to support XML and employed a generic approach to the import functions. By adding control structures and modifying the mapping approach of data, we were able to map QDC fields to the appropriate custom fields and categories in WordPress. We also modified the loader in a few ways, such as excluding certain records and category matches in order to ensure that existing records are not overwritten and that duplicate categories are not created. In order to handle record updating, a separate update script was written.

As we begin to collect user-contributed data, data export and archiving is becoming a more significant problem. We are looking at different approaches for exporting and preserving this data, including extending the Qualified Dublin Core data in the back-end digital library system to support new blog-centric fields and storing data in archival packages.

Two fundamental questions arose while we worked on data loading and exporting. First, while we were committed to using external standards to represent and store data, it became obvious that it might be just as useful to define a local standard and then rely on mapping applications to make data available to external systems. Using a locally defined standard could have allowed us to approach some fields (such as record state, cataloger) more specifically while preserving the standard descriptive fields.

A related need to add qualifiers to different types of links could have been achieved via either a local standard or simply a different approach. As the project moves into its third year, we are considering different metadata standards or approaches that might allow more specificity at the administrative levels. Second, we found that the blogging software had sufficient functionality to support all of the data creation, management, and social-contribution needs of the project. It became obvious that using a digital library system for archiving rather than data creation might be a more efficient approach.

While we adapted the WordPress import/export functionality to suit the needs of our digital library, the issue of scalability might make it necessary in the future to take different approaches with large metadata batches. While current loading practices for our project are acceptable, loading larger batches through direct database interaction could lead to more flexible system interoperability.

The Content of the Blog Post Record

For our project, we use the blog record to represent an individual photograph. The QDC record title is mapped to the blog posting title. Post content contains the QDC identifier field mapped to the image HTML element, and the QDC description field is mapped to a Paragraph.

The Post excerpt contains an image element referencing a thumbnail representation of the photograph. The rest of the blog posting uses custom fields to store the rest of the QDC elements. By making extensive use of WordPress's custom fields to store QDC metadata, the interface and search functionality is enhanced.

OBSERVATIONS AND DISCUSSION

Many of the main benefits of using WordPress or other social software as a digital library interface have already been mentioned. Using a pre-developed system can enable rapid and flexible system development, enables the project to be more focused on user-driven functions, and benefits from the development focus of a larger community.

ISSUES

Data Management

One of the primary issues with the use of social software applications as a digital library interface is data management. While digital libraries have multiple goals (including creation, management, and preservation of digital objects and their metadata), the goals of social software are often focused on ease of content creation, user-friendly interfaces, and data presentation.

Making sure that digital objects are accurately represented and displayed means: utilizing primary identifiers from the core digital library system; taking steps to ensure that metadata is accurately represented in the social software application to ensure no degradation of accuracy or specificity; and accurately managing metadata and digital object versions to ensure that the most accurate data is preserved.

While WordPress required us to manipulate some functions to ensure that these goals were met in our project, its flexibility as a content creation and display system has resulted in a significant reduction in the amount of work required to create and manage our user interface. Future developments in the use of WordPress as a content creation and management system are expected to save time and allow Digital Forsyth to employ systems that can focus on metadata management and preservation.

Technical Skills

A common criticism of social software is the skill level required to implement and manage these applications. Using social software in a custom environment such as the one described in this article exacerbates this situation, as specific skills are required to make the software work in specific ways. In general, programming skills, XML skills, metadata skills and digital object skills are essential for a project like ours. In addition, some specific skills are required to work with WordPress and common digital library applications, including skills using:

- PHP
- SQL
- CSS/HTML
- Web server software
- JavaScript

Two issues that took time for us to work through were:

- Lack of familiarity with the WordPress programming framework
- Lack of documentation of software

In addition, while theme creation is relatively straightforward, customizing a theme beyond simple colour and layout decisions required more extensive work. WordPress is rather complicated software, so finding the appropriate function can be difficult at times. Working with these functions can get confusing, regardless of the extent of documentation provided.

SUSTAINABILITY

Project sustainability should be a key concern when selecting software for a digital library project. Commercial systems can have a host of sustainability issues, including vendor support, ease of system use and customization, and system flexibility. Social software and open source software applications have other sustainability issues to consider as well.These include the inability to guarantee service stability and permanence. While commercial systems typically have market permanence or vendor-supplied migration options, open source and social software is often only as permanent as the user community surrounding it. This means that an organization must be willing to find new solutions when required, and it also means that these organizations will have to carry the burden of system migration on their own. Further, while there are many hosted low cost and free options for digital libraries (including hosted blogs/wikis, hosted image sites such as Flickr), the system being considered should be compared against the needed stability and uptime of the system. In short, it does not make sense to base key parts of a digital library on a free, hosted service if the digital library cannot sustain itself outside of that service.

In choosing the approach we took for Digital Forsyth, we found that the implementation of the user interface was accomplished quickly and with community-centric features that serve as the centerpiece of the project site. Despite the issues that we experienced with metadata management, system assumptions/limitations, and interoperability, overall the use of WordPress lowered our development and maintenance costs.

We are hopeful that the system will benefit from increased sustainability and portability as future releases of WordPress are installed, and as special functions are developed and deployed. In selecting an existing open source application to serve as an interface to your particular digital library, some key questions to ask are:

- Will the system scale to the level that your data requires?
- Are the data models used in the system compliant with your digital library metadata structure?
- Is migrating data between the applications sustainable?
- What needs can be filled with these social software/open source applications? Is the software appropriate just for user interfaces or can it serve other functions of the digital library system?
- How will system sustainability be ensured with the selected options?
- Will developing the customized parts of the software be more manageable than other solutions?
- What core functional requirements exist, and is this application the best approach?

By choosing the solution we did, we hope to be able to incorporate a number of approaches to public interfaces while keeping our digital library applications centralized and focused on key functions of storage and preservation.

DOCUMENTS IN A LARGE DIGITAL LIBRARY

Creating relationships between similar documents is an activity that has a long distinguished history in Information Retrieval. In his textbook on the subject Korfhage (1997) writes "Probably the single key concept behind information storage and retrieval is document similarity". A practical motivation for the search for similarity is to improve information retrieval. When users have found one document they can be directed to similar documents that may be worth their attention. A more theoretical motivation is the discovery of patterns of thought within a body of knowledge that is dispersed across a collection of documents. There are, of course, many ways in which similarity between documents can be assessed. One way is to use the Judgement of an expert.

This is typically done by classifying documents according to a subject classification. This is a tried and trusted method. However, it requires human expertise and labour. These do not come cheap these days.

Therefore many collections have no classification data. Within the collection of documents that we study in this paper, three in four documents do not have a subject classification. Other classic measures of relationship between academic papers are the strengths of co-citation and bibliographic coupling. Such an analysis presumes that a citation index for the papers is available. Producing one manually is even more expensive than subject classification.

It is possible to use recently available software for autonomous citation indexing. Barrueco Cruz and Krichel report on on recent effort s using the same digital library that we study here. In this paper, we introduce a completely new concept of similarity that is user-centered.

We start with the idea that two documents are similar if they respond to the same information need. Thus roughly speaking we can think of two document as similar, if many users will withdraw the papers together while they are working on the system. Provided that we have a digital library with a long log of usage, we can find which papers have frequently been used together. This is what we will refer to as "co-usage" in the following. We are not aware of a study that has developed and tested this concept within a digital library context. We are, of course, aware that commercial systems use a related concept. Amazon.com, for example, suggests to a customer who is considering to purchase an item x that other people who bought x also bought item y. But since users are anonymous in our digital library, within the scope of our collection, the evidence on common usage is more difficult to gather.

MEASURING CO-USAGE

Our dataset comes from logs of the usage of the RePEc digital library. We have built this library over many years. RePEc is the largest free distributed academic digital library in the world. It is a pioneering effort in three respects.

First, RePEc pioneered the business model of the Open Archives Initiative distinction between data providers and service providers. RePEc has grown over 200 archives that are used in 10 different user services.

Second, RePEc is more than a collection of data about documents. RePEc offers a comprehensive picture of academic output by describing collection of documents, persons that are involved as authors of documents or editors of collections, and the institutions to which they belong in a relational database scheme.

Third, RePEc is essentially volunteer driven and has no owner. It is a public good much like the Internet. The data that we examine comes from the WoPEc user service. This service, founded in 1993 is available on the web at three locations since 1994. These are Hitotsubashi University in Tokyo, Japan, Manchester Computing in the UK, and Washington University in St. Louis in the USA. The web site has static pages for each paper. In addition, there are a number of pages that link different papers together.

There are pages that list papers that have been issued within same series, and there are pages that group papers with the same subject classification. The log data also contains indication about what searches users have been making. However, as far as we are concerned, only the access to the description of the individual papers is relevant.

To begin with, recall that WoPEc is a Non--commercial service. WoPEc does not enter into a contractual arrangement with a customer, with or without an exchange of money. Contractual arrangements with customers are expensive to arrange because they involve complicated negotiations, privacy issues etc. On the other hand contractual arrangement—even without exchange of money—generate customer data. The customer data itself has considerable value, see Shapiro and Varian for an illuminating discussion.

In the period that we examine, cookies have not been used. Therefore we need to wade through the log to find traces of usage by the same persons. All that the log offers is a trace to the Internet address (*i.e.,* IP number) of the client machine, a file or action performed, and a time when this happened. Over recent years, the Internet is more and more accessed through personal computers rather than through multi-user systems.

However, we can not be completely sure that an IP number corresponds to the machine of an individual user, because there are caching sites. Therefore we must be watchful of IP addresses that appear particularly frequently. Let us for the moment make the assumption that the usage data from one single machine comes from one single user. We are then in the happy situation that we have identified the user.However, to be able to claim that papers that are appearing together are joined together because they correspond to the same user need, we still have to assume that the information need of the user remains the same throughout the period of observation. This is problematic. Typically users will regard WoPEc as a reference source, and therefore naturally turn to it with different information needs. Therefore it is likely that the log contains material that corresponds to different information needs, even if they are expressed by the same user.

Therefore, we have chosen to think of users using the system within sessions. We typically think of a session as an academic, using a web browser on a desktop machine, going to the WoPEc site, make a few searches and look at a few results. Or we can think of it as a student, walking into a computer lab, uses a search engine, finds a page on the WoPEc service and navigates it for further data. Technically, we define a session as a subset of the total log that comes from the same IP address within a certain time frame. In fact we assume that there must not be more than one hour between two consecutive log entries for them to qualify to be within the same session. In addition, we do not consider repeat access to the same paper as two different accesses to that paper. Such access is likely to occur mainly for technical reasons, such as that the user did not have time to read the article at the first discovery.

Under these restrictions it appears to be convenient to model sessions as sets of papers. We can now proceed to a formal definition of co-usage. Let D be the set documents in the library and S be the set of sessions. Each session s contains a subset of the set of documents, *i.e.,* s Ì D. Introduce | · | as as notation for the number of elements in a set. Let there be two documents di and dj. Let u(di, dj) be the set of all sessions that contain both di and dj. For convenience of notation, write u(di) = u(di, di). Then we propose to call the co-usage coefficient c(di, dj) as follows

$$c\left(d_1, d_j\right) = \frac{\left|u\left(d_i, d_j\right)\right|}{\left|u\left(d_i\right)\right|\left|u\left(d_j\right)\right|}.$$

The motivation for introducing the product in the denominator is to ensure that we do not have situations where one paper appears frequently with another by the sheer size of its own usage. It also leads c(di, dj) to gain the attractive properties that 0 <= c(di, dj) <= 1 and that c(di, di) = 1. It is clear that the measure that we propose here is an intuitive one. It is not a scientifically developed metric of the likelihood that, whatever size the session is, we will see the two papers appearing together in the session.

It is possible to evaluate that probability. However that calculation is not attempted here. It is left for future work. Even if we can theoretically ascertain how to calculate the probability, we can not in practice calculate it for all possible document couples, because of the amount of calculations that would have to be made within a large digital library as ours.

Results

We ran a programme to search for co-usage on a log for three years 1999–2001. There are 102551867 lines in the log. We discarded 24836221 requests for images, 401614 requests for CSS files, and 9315 contained another error. 3164598 requests contained a 404 error and were omitted. Most of them went to robots.txt. 3966837 distinct hosts accessed the system.

We exclude all accesses from hosts that accessed robots.txt. In addition, there are cache and proxy sites that we would like to remove as well. This is a more difficult terrain. The rule that we chose was to look at each day's log, and detect all hosts that issued more than 100 requests. In total, we detected 23068 such hosts, and discarded 17484961 lines because they were made by these hosts. This left us with 23413849 to analyzed. We detected 5251337 sessions.

We limited ourselves to sessions that had more than 3 accesses and less than 100, and that included at least one search. There were 69179 sessions that remained for analysis. We can not make the results available here, for obvious reasons of space.

Therefore we have placed them at http://openlib.org/home/krichel/kumegawa/report.htm. We print the top couples that have the highest co-usage, up to a rounded coefficient of 50%. The following results appear when we look through the data.

First, papers in the same series seem to be much more prone to co-usage than papers from different series. It is often papers by the same authors, over different periods of time, available in the same working paper series or journal that appeared to be co-used a lot. This observation suggests that the original split of the data in different series does not only provide an organizational layer to the data, but also a semantic one. Second, from reading through the related couples, it appears that a key concept that appears in the title immediately explains the co-usage. Thus, it should be possible to gain insights into key concepts that are of user interest by looking at the title data of papers that are co-used, and find the common words. This would be an interesting subject for further research.

This paper has introduced co-usage as a means to make document to document relationships. The concept of co-usage has been found to lead to excellent empirical results. Our results suggests that the concept of co-usage is a valid and interesting one.

Any remaining problems that we are experiencing to make it work in practice are consequences of poor measurement of usage, rather than flaws in the underlying theoretical reasoning. Just in the case of co-citation and bibliographic coupling, there will be a debate on how useful co-usage analysis really is. We have opened that debate with this paper.

There are two further consequences from this paper. In the short run, we intend to incorporate co-usage similarity into future developments of WoPEc, to build links from the description of one paper to the description of another as suggested by co-usage analysis.

NON--STANDARD USAGE MEASUREMENT

A requirement for international standards is clear but development of such standards is a lengthy process. While this process is ongoing, each individual digital library initiative requires feedback to inform development and, thus, must unilaterally adopt an approach to performance measurement. Electronic library projects in the UK, Europe and the USA have used a variety of different definitions and methods of usage measurement and analysis. Thus, neither analyses nor data from different projects can be compared.

Most Internet usage analysis tools are applicable to digital library activities and WWW server log file analysis Programmes still predominate. In 1997 the eLib supporting study referred to above found that most work in the electronic library field relied on transaction logging for management information. If users are authenticated (*i.e.,* have usernames and passwords), it is possible using these tools, to monitor individual use by logging the username alongside the URL. Hits can also be time stamped. In this way, an individual's progress can be tracked from page to page. It is possible also, using cookies, for a service supplier to track an individual's movements on the Internet beyond that supplier's site. However, this is likely to be considered a breach of privacy and librarians 58 make it an issue in negotiation with content suppliers.

To comply with the library ethos, performance indicators should not rely on information about individuals' reading habits. Many academic subscription services authenticate whole sites by registering and restricting access a list of IP addresses. Not only does this overcome privacy issues related to individual users as names and time stamps cannot be recorded on accesses, but it also removes the need for costly password management. An alternative means of reducing the cost of authentication in the UK is use of the ATHENS service which provides an individual with a username and password which may be used to access a variety of services.

Unfortunately, use of ATHENS greatly reduces the management information that can be gathered by individual service suppliers. This is deliberate to protect the privacy of individual users. For example, it is not possible for a supplier to monitor use of her service within a specific discipline if neither individuals nor even whole classes are identifiable by user ID.

Limitations of Current usage Measurement Tools

It is important when designing performance measurement activities that they be justified in terms of the benefits derived. Because it is automatic, transaction logging is a cheap way of gathering data in an electronic environment. Unfortunately, the type of data that can be collected is often restricted by the delivery format. In 1996, when Michigan University intended to test economic models during the TULIP Project, it was unable to do so because 'the Web does not support the kind of data collection required to test economic models'.

Project MUSE is still unable to distinguish between downloading/printing and browsing as the Web is a stateless environment. SuperJournal know that although users claim to prefer HTML documents for onscreen viewing, given a choice of formats, a large majority 59 chooses PDF over HTML. As most users print documents if they intend to read more than a few lines, it can be assumed that they select PDF as a superior format for printing. Unfortunately, SuperJournal cannot verify this assumption by monitoring use as it is not possible to differentiate downloading from printing. Thus, although data gathering is cheap, as yet, it is also limited. Furthermore, analysis of such data tends to be time consuming and thus expensive and interpretation is not always straightforward.

For example, it may be assumed that more hits indicate a better service, as a high number suggests that users return and that they recommend a site to others but, of course, this may not always be the case. A subject-based gateway which generates search results that closely match a users needs will record very few hits before that user leaves the site satisfied with the result. If the search results supplied are poor and include a number of extraneous links or if the user is required to conduct several searches before she retrieves useful links, the gateway will record many more hits before the user leaves.

However, if a subject-based gateway offers not only access to a database of catalogue records but also holds a local archive, it should record a larger number of hits as users are likely both to search the database and to retrieve local resources. Furthermore, attempts to make more efficient use of internet bandwidth by caching and mirroring can subvert attempts to monitor use. Access to resources from site A from a cache or mirror held at site B will not be included in usage measurement unless site B informs site A about the cache and agrees to supply site A with use data. This type of shortfall makes WWW statistics unreliable or, worse, misleading.

Inferring user Behaviour from Transaction Logs

Use of transaction logs for performance measurement requires digital library practitioners to infer meaning from specific types of user act in a digital environment. For example, A. Dawson of the BUBL service (http://www.bubl.ac.uk) suggests that to view a list of journal issues with dates and contents is the equivalent of browsing a library shelf. He also asserts that searching is a deliberate activity which is not easily mistaken and that to access full-text is a likely indication that the user is reading the article. The latter assertion is qualified by the acknowledgement that the reader may access text to scan for relevance rather than, necessarily, to read the article. However, Dawson argues that this ambiguity need not influence the accuracy of any performance measure as it applies to all journals.

This type of inference helps digital library practitioners to make sense of quantitative data. However, knowledge of user behaviour in the digital environment is limited and it can be dangerous to base inference entirely on assumptions and prior experience.

For example, Dawson's assumption that the frequency with which a reader accessing full text is in fact scanning for relevance will apply equally to all journals is contradicted by the findings of the SuperJournal project. SuperJournal found evidence that the way in which scientists and social scientists use journal elements differs. For example, scientists are more likely than social scientists to identify a relevant article from its title and to print it on that basis. Social scientists more often read the abstract to establish relevance because article titles in the social sciences can be more ambiguous. There may be similar differences in the way that scientists and social scientists approach full text.

It is clearly difficult to derive qualitative research findings from quantitative information. Qualitative methods such as interviews and 61 observation should be used to inform assumptions about the meaning of quantitative information and for triangulation.

Training and Awareness

Some of the eLib projects in the Training and Awareness programme area have now migrated to a service model and offer training courses in the use of new technologies for teaching and learning. HEIs are likely to continue to pay for this type of training from staff development budgets. Training of users in the use of IT is unlikely to fall within the remit of libraries although libraries will probably continue to offer training in information skills and the use of specific resources. It is beyond the scope of this project to explore the economics of this activity and compare the costs and benefits of training academics and students in the use of electronic and print resources. Clearly, the transition from a traditional to a digital or hybrid library involves dramatic changes in the infrastructure that supports the production and use of information resources. At present people prefer not to read on screen so they print articles from electronic journals.

As resources for teaching, learning and research are increasingly delivered in electronic form there is likely to be a mass shift from photocopying to printing; the latter is more expensive than the former but the total opportunity cost of an individual operating a photocopier is not incurred so costs are probably very similar.

As people become more familiar with technology, users may no longer need print copies. This could lead to a net reduction in the cost of using information. The report of a recent study on the impact of electronic journals on networked printing suggested that one of the reasons for printing material from the Internet is to ensure future access; networked access is not always reliable.

In effect users create a personal print cache of networked resources. The report predicted that improved access to networked resources would 62 reduce the need to print but suggested that it may also increase use of the network, which in turn would increase the print load. The net effect of a combination of such changes is virtually impossible to predict. Another factor impacting on the economics of digital information is the pace of technological change; new technologies become obsolete at an alarming rate, making it expensive for organisations to meet the changing needs of users. However, technological advances are reducing some costs, for example the cost of storing digital resources.

It is not possible within the scope of this project to estimate the infrastructure costs associated with delivering electronic resources in such an unstable and unpredictable climate. Investment in infrastructure that effectively enables all stakeholders to conduct much of their business electronically will be required. The models described here will be based on the assumption that the HE sector will invest in sufficient infrastructure to support digital/hybrid library activities.

At present there is no coherent model of the digital library, nor is there yet any developed model of the hybrid library. Furthermore, economic issues tend to be tested after solutions have been found to the more pressing technical, cultural and legal issues. Many specific digital library activities are insufficiently mature to have generated economic models. Where a model exists it has been evaluated and where alternatives exist these have been compared.

METADATA INTEROPERABILITY FOR CATALOGUING OF E-JOURNALS

The content of digital libraries includes data and metadata that describe various aspects of the digital record that consist of links or relationships to other data or metadata, whether internal or external to the digital library. Interoperability, as defined by the IEEE is "The ability of two or more systems or components to exchange information and use the information that has been exchanged. This makes it necessary that every library has to examine the issue of data and metadata required for accessing their documents. Metadata is provided in order to provide richer searching than would be possible using standard free-text indexing. In particular it was desirable to allow users to search on a number of fields including Author, Title and Discription.In addition it was felt desirable to allow users to restrict searches by issues by article type.

METADATA

Metadata Expand the use of data embedded in the digital object or text, and find ways of integrating different kinds of metadata. Metadata has been defined as "data about data". It is information about an electronic resource which may be embedded in the resource. Currently work is being done to define a metadata record which adequately describes a wide range of electronic objects. The aim is to give the authors or information providers associated with electronic resources the means to describe the resource themselves, to a defined standard.

The idea is that in describing the resource you need something which is more informative than an index entry, but less complete then a formal cataloguing record. According to Gilliland-Swetland metadata is more than description; a more inclusive conceptualisation of metadata is needed as information professionals consider the range of their activities that may end up in incorporating it into digital information systems. Repositories also create metadata relating to the administration, accessioning, preservation and use of collections. Acquisition records, exhibition catalogs, and use data are all examples of these, even though they are largely still created in paper form." There are three main types of metadata

- Descriptive metadata: Describes a resource for purposes such as discovery and identification. It can include elements such as title, abstract, author and keywords
- Structural metadata: Indicates how compound objects are put together, for example how pages are ordered to form chapters
- Administrative metadata: Provides information to help manage a resource, such as when and how it was created, file type and other technical information and who can accesses it. There are several subsets of cataloguers decisions about whether a catalogue record should be created for a whole set of volumes or for each particular volumes in the set, so that the metadata creator makes similar decisions

Metadata is structured information that describes, explains locates or otherwise makes it easier to retrieve, use or manage an information resource. Traditional library cataloguing is a form of metadata and MARC21 and the rule sets used with it such as AACR2 are metadata standards. Metadata can be embedded in a digital object or it can be stored separately. Metadata will not be lost and obviates problems of linking between data and metadata, and helps to ensure that the metadata and object will be updated together.

HOW TO CATALOGUE E-JOURNALS USING METADATA

Metadata is used to improve the utility of data by providing a structure of framework for describing that data. Metadata elements are in effect fields of information that can be stored and manipulated in catalogue. Metadata is particularly useful for large collections of documents or other materials, it can be used for managing the resource and for finding specific items. A Catalogue becomes an found by some libraaries is an essential tool for retrieval. Libraries made a commitment to provide users with online access to full-text journals, found in publisher packages and aggregator databases, via Web lists and OPAC with details such as holdings coverage, embargo, source, open access, and local subject headings. The metadata of e-journals were first tracked on spreadsheets in EXCEL for Web lists and were also cataloged in the OPAC, a dual-maintenance system which later proved to be needing improvement as library electronic journal collection expanded. Libraries thus developed an interim solution and a long-term solution for managing e-journals access.

The interim solution is to replace EXCEL with Microsoft ACCESS in processing e-journal metadata, still a dual-maintenance system but with greatly reduced maintenance work and enhanced timeliness of ejournal metadata in the OPAC and on the Web lists. The long-term solution is to generate e-journal

Web lists from the OPAC with streamlined e-journal metadata batch-loading process using Innovative's Electronic Resources Management Module. The OCLC/ NCSA Meta Data workshop in Dubin, Ohio held in 1995 proposed the following core set of elements to appear in *Uniform Resource Characteristics* (URC):

- Title,
- Creator,
- Subject and Keywords,
- Description,
- Publisher,
- Contributor,
- Date,
- Resource Type,
- Format,
- Resource Identifier,
- Source,
- Language,
- Relation,
- Coverage and
- Rights Management.

Increasing size and complexity of the digital information available on the web demands for methods of its organization. Uniform and structured meta information which can effectively be employed to achieve this goal. Metadata support efficient and effective organization, access and retrieval of information contents in a digital library. Meta information is used in effective designing of browsing and search interfaces of a digital library. Describing a resource with metadata allows it to be understood by both human and machines in ways that promote interoperability. Most metadata schemes include elements such as standard numbers to uniquely identify the work or object to which the metadata refers. Metadata is key to ensuring that resources will survive and continue to be accessible into the future.

Metadata elements are in effect field information that can be stored and manipulated in a database or a stylesheet. Alternatively the data elements may be embedded in a document, delimited by tags. The marked up metadata tags may also include details of the metadata schema used and the encoding system that has been adopted. Information retrieval is through a combination of key words, menus, and graphic map interfaces. Descriptions include the data custodian, custodian location, data cost, data quality, confidentiality constraints, spatial coverage, time period and a short description of the data set. The next section discuss access to E-Journals via internet.

E-JOURNALS ON THE INTERNET

Using the Web, publishers can easily distribute hypertext documents with multimedia components to a global audience, and they have been actively experimenting with Web versions of new or existing electronic serials. The Journal of Internet Cataloging also looks at:

- Uniform resource identifiers and link-resolve services
- Usability testing
- Interoperability, crosswalks, and mappings among metadata schema
- Learning object metadata
- Using classification and automated assists for organizing Web resources
- Software and hardware for retrieving, reviewing, and describing Internet resources
- Managing the cataloging process of Internet resources
- The problems of maintaining catalogue records for remote electronic resources
- Descriptive and subject cataloging applied to Internet resources
- Education and training
- International issues in organizing/cataloging Internet resources.

The Journal of Internet Cataloging is an essential resource for practicing librarians and information specialists, library and information science educators and students, and systems administrators. The following sections describe individual library/group metadata for cataloguing e- journals

MARC 21

The Library of Congress' Network Development and MARC Standards Office is developing a framework for working with MARC data in a XML environment. This framework is intended to be flexible and extensible to allow users to work with MARC data in ways specific to their needs. The framework itself includes many components such as schemas, stylesheets, and software tools. Library of Congress ' Network Development and MARC Standards Office has developed a schema for a bibliographic element set that may be used for a variety of purposes, and particularly for library applicationsa.

An XML schema, the *"Metadata Object Description Schema"* (MODS) is intended to be able to carry selected data from existing MARC 21 records as well as to enable the creation of original resource description records. It includes a subset of MARC fields and uses language-based tags rather than numeric ones, in some cases regrouping elements from the MARC 21 bibliographic format. MODS is expressed using the XML schema language of the World Wide Web Consortium. Marc also provides url linking facility in its tag. Metadata recorded for Journal of the American Chemical Society.

CONSER PROGRAMME

CONSER is:

- A cooperative online serials cataloging programme
- A source of high quality bibliographic records for serials

- A source of high quality documentation and training materials for the cataloging of serials and the input of serial records
- A group of serial experts who work together in an atmosphere of collegiality and trust
- A promulgator of standards related to serials
- A voice for serials in the library community
- A component of the Programme for Cooperative Cataloging

CONSER began in the early 1970s as a project to convert manual serial cataloging into machinereadable records and has evolved into an ongoing programme to create and maintain high quality bibliographic records for serials. In keeping with its evolution, the name was changed in 1986 from the CONSER Project to the CONSER Programme. In October 1997, CONSER became a bibliographic component of the Programme for Cooperative Cataloging. now in process, serials catalogers will soon be in position to utilize all the computer file bibliographic record elements. CONSER has taken a major step in developing policies for these new elements with the publication. Describing electronic access information is another challenge for the cataloger due to the different areas of the record involved, including the new electronic location and access field. *AACR2* requires catalogers to "always specify the mode of access" for electronic serials in a note. The CONSER "mode of access" note now includes more general information to limit redundancy with the 856 field, which contains the detailed information needed to locate and access documents. Serials catalogers now use the note field 538 for the more general information as the field is newly available through format integration.

METADATA INTEROPERABILITY

Metadata as a tool to facilitate exchange of information between interoperating systems and interoperability of metadata schemas themselves which can help to facilitate systems interoperability. There are three different types of interoperability:

- Semantic interioperability: Achieved through agreements about content description standards
- Structural interoperbility: A data model that is used for specifying semantic schemas
- Syntactic introperbility: Which provides a syntax for expressing metadata: an example is XML

Metadata crosswalks

A crosswalk allows metadata created by one community to be used by another group that employs a different metadata standards. Crosswalks are important for virtual libraries where resources are being collected from a variety of sources and are expected to act as a whole, perhaps with a single search engine applied. While these cross walks are key they are also labour intensive to develop and maintain. Reconciling metadata created in different environments is a major challenge and some effort has been devoted to mapping equivalent metadata elements between different metadata schemas. These mappings can be displayed as tables and are known as crosswalks. They can be used within systems to effect transformations between metadata objects. Crosswalks are a starting point for assessing the suitability of data sources for import.

The library participates in a metadata harvesting protocol to provide extracts of local metadata in a common format to a service provider so that information about the collection is automatically included in a number of relevant tools such as catalogs and portals. The Web page is linked to the library's web site dedicated to resources. Where it is available to researchers in context with archival and visual materials, digitized secondary sources, etc. Administrative, structural, and descriptive metadata for web site also has been created to hold all of its pieces together to allow them to be managed and allow them to be accessed.

COLLECTION DEVELOPMENT AND MANAGEMENT POLICIES

The libraries are now functioning as Information or Knowledge Centers, resource centers, which disseminates required pinpointed information to the users. Libraries collect the information published in various forms *e.g.* books, periodicals, thesis, patents etc. and organise it in helpful sequence. The heart of the library is in its collection. The main purpose of the collection is to serve the needs of users and organisational aims in better ways. Libraries have to develop the collection keeping in view the users need and demands and hence the collection development in the library must be proper.

Traditional Libraries have some set of rules framed for the collection development but not operative, but now due use of ICT, revolutionary changes have been observed in the library practices including collection development. The framed rules are not appropriate and suits to the changing practices and hence majority of the libraries in the developed countries have formulated the collection development policies to build the proper and useful collection in the libraries which supports to the needs of the users. Similarly the change in format from print to digital made the issues to develop new policies or to amend the existing policies to suit the environment.

In digital media acquisitions the process is different due to change in format and pricing structure as compared to previous methods followed in libraries. Collection development is the main activity of any library and hence librarians are now focusing more in this area. To maintain the proper collection in libraries there is a need to develop policies or amend to the existing to suit the emerging trends in publications and acquisition methods. The increase in digital media publication and usage the collection development policies for the digital information resources are required to be developed.The process of the collection development covers selection and de-selection of the resources.

Collection development or management involves activities like collection management programme, collection development policy statement, collection assessment, funding and budgeting, selection and de-selection, preservation, and resource- sharing projects. It is very clear from the statement made by Verzosa that collection development process is a complex process involving various activities but its advantages are more to have a proper collection.

WHAT IS COLLECTION DEVELOPMENT

The purpose of collection development pointed out by Melvil Dewey was to provide 'The best reading for the largest number at the least cost'. ALA defined a very suitable definition for collection development as "A term which encompasses a number of activities related to the development of the library collection, including the determination and coordination of selection policy, assessment of needs of users and potential users, collection use studies, collection evaluation, identification of collection needs, selection of materials,

Planning for resource sharing, collection maintenance and weeding." ALA Glossary State that "Library Collections will contain all types of registered information, including printed materials of all formats, audio-visual materials, visual material, materials used with computers, graphs and three-dimensional materials and ways to access the electronic information" Harold Libraries Glossary defined "collection developments as the process of planning a stock acquisition programmed not simply to cater for immediate needs but to build a current and reliable collection over a numbers of years to meet the objectives of the services."

These definitions clearly indicate the need of collection development in information growing age. If libraries need to provide qualitative services then qualitative collection is to be made available in the library irrespective of forms and formats.

WHY PROPER COLLECTION DEVELOPMENT

Collection of the documents in the library is the prime task as it is the power house of information resources. There are many factors involved to have proper collection development like

- Information explosion and Information overload
- Limited and shrinking library budgets
- Increasing users demands for pinpointed qualitative information resources due to specialisation
- Multiple forms and formats of the information resources including digital
- Increase in prices of documents all the times
- Shift in demand of users from collection based services to information and access based services
- More usage of Internet based e-documents

Since digital, internet resources, databases and e-publications are increasing and simultaneously the use in academic and special libraries are also increasing continuously. Growth in literature made necessary to manage proper collection.

Objectives and Purpose of Collection Development

The main objectives and purpose behind collection development are:

- Fulfill the user needs by proper collection
- To support the teaching learning and research endeavors
- Periodically review the collection for weeding
- To provide nascent and relevant information
- To acquire the best and useful literature to the core group of the users

Collection Development policies allows the library personnel's to develop proper collection and based on this value added services can be provided to the users. The purpose of the collection development policy is to provide guidelines for day to day acquisition and withdrawal decisions, resource allocation and long range planning of collection needs keeping in mind the library mission, activities, organisational needs and interest etc.

TECHNIQUES FOR PROPER COLLECTION DEVELOPMENT

For proper collection development for any library, a detailed written collection development policy is necessary. The policy clearly specifies the organisational requirements, goals and the user needs in specific. The Library committee formed for the proper development and progress of the library consist of the expert members from the various faculties who can contribute in formulating the proper collection development and designing the policies. It is also necessary to look in to the policies formulated by the other libraries and the policies prepared by LC and ALA etc. Library collection development policy should be in clearly spelt out in a written form.

The American Library Association's collection development policies assumed that a written collection development policy is a desirable tool that enables selectors to work with greater consistency towards defined goals. The following aspects need to be considered basically while developing policy:

- Users needs and demands
- Review the organisational needs and objectives
- Review the standard, core, border and peripheral subject areas
- Conduct use and users studies for user behaviour and need analysis
- Try to cover the sources which disseminate maximum access to current information in the area
- Take the help of techniques like citation analysis, impact factor, bibliometrics and scientiometrics studies, information audit, information behaviour of users etc

- Resource Sharing practices be initiated at various level including consortium
- Evaluation techniques must be adapted
- Trial access for the databases for certain period and get the feedback from the users before subscription
- Initiate the OA and IR project for protecting IP of organisation
- Analyse strengths and weakness of the collection regularly
- Apply management techniques for quality procurement

Many libraries have developed collection development policies but these are informal in nature and no concrete policies are developed except larger organisations. The collection development policy is required due to multidisciplinary subjects, procurement of epublications. Policy is a guideline to act on. To prepare a policy for any library a review of different standard collection development policies becomes useful to draft a policy.

REVIEW OF EXISTING COLLECTION DEVELOPMENT POLICIES

The basic elements while formulating the collection development policy for any library was discussed in the conferences also and the output presented in the National Conference on 'Putting Knowledge to Work: Best Practices in Librarianship" 1-2 May 2009 151-152 highlighted following issues.

- *Organisational Objectives*: The nature of the organisation, its function, objectives and the purpose must be considered at the initial level.
- *Users*: It is necessary to review the needs of the users of the library especially from the organisation, their main area of concern, projects under taken, information resources covering the general aspect about the stream as well as the specialised needs of the users in the area of research. Real and potential needs of the users must be covered.
- *Level of collection*: The collection may satisfy the needs of the experts as well as a common man whose interest is to read for the entertainment and knowledge addition. (Maslow's need based triangle). There is a need to focus on the current and future needs of the organisations.
- *Subject Coverage*: It is necessary to fix the core subjects in which organisational collection must be deep and updated. The peripheral subjects can be developed based on the priority as well as need based collection or even can be shared with other organisations (Resource Sharing). Hence collection assessment must be evaluated based on the area and subjects of core importance.
- *Type of Information Sources*: While selecting the information recourses it is necessary to provide the access to the literature published in the area which is covered by the secondary information sources. It is necessary to provide maximum access to the users rather than owning the information resources. To make the collection economic on

demand acquisition can also be preferred in case of peripheral area or can be obtained from ILL.

- *Budget*: Allocation of the budget must be proper and as per the usage. The budget of any library is not adequate to get all the literature published and hence policies must be fixed keeping in mind the usage and cost effective factors. Resource sharing activity will also help in reducing the expenses in case of peripheral research area.
- *Forms in which material must be acquired*: It is necessary to fix the form in which documents can be acquired. A policy stating the forms (print, digital, Non- print etc) to be procured must be detailed. However the acquisition must always be cost effective to adjust in the budget allocated.
- *Services provided*: Many libraries provide services to the users from the organisation as well as from different institutions. For this purpose the acquisition must be qualitative.
- *Users and use studies at frequent Intervals*: It is necessary to evaluate the usage of the acquired material. If the material is less used it must be weeded or stacked in parallel.
- *Policies for the preservation of the resources*: Preservation of the literature is the objective of the library. The heritage of the knowledge is useful for the future generation and hence modern tools and techniques may be used.

IFLA POLICY FOR COLLECTION DEVELOPMENT

The IFLA suggested following points in its collection development policy:

- Must be a written Policy covering procedure for selection, de-selection planning (future), public relations, weeding, retaining, preservation etc
- Covers general, narrative and subject profiles
- Use of collection evaluation methods
- Use of collection depth indicators
- Language (English, Primary and predominantly used as per need and country language)
- Policy implementation and revision

The first elements of a collection development policy will be a mission statement of the library, the purpose of this policy and the audience to whom it is addressed. General area covers current focus or also retrospective acquisitions; the resource types (monographs, periodicals, theses, gray literature, maps, etc.); languages; formats (printed, nonprint or electronic); special sources of funding (a grant or gift from a donor); the policy regarding gifts and any special policies regarding maintenance (weeding, discarding, preservation) of the collection; and size of the collections. Collection evaluation is based on quantitative and qualitative measures:

- Quantitative Measures reveal size, age, use, costs and other numeric data. Examples of quantitative measures include inventory, or shelf list measures to determine actual title or volume counts, by segment or subject area. Median age or similar measures indicate the currency of the materials. Amount expended for acquisitions in a segment or subject area per year illustrates the ongoing commitment to develop that area. Percentage of titles owned by a library when compared to a standard list shows the breadth and depth of the collection. Use statistics (including internal library use and ILL) are both collection and client-centred.
- Qualitative measures are obtained through subjective evaluation and involve the professional Judgement of librarians, appraisal from subject experts, or the opinion of customers. These techniques include impressions of the condition, character and appropriateness of a section of the collection. Another qualitative technique is the Judgement made by comparison of one subject in the collection to a similar subject in another library, or to a subject bibliography.

Collection depth indicators indicated are: current collection level, acquisition commitment and collection goal. Indicators define out of scope, minimum information level, basic information level, study and instructional support, research level, comprehensive level etc Each institution, including its community and other constituents, is unique. Therefore, its policy statements will be unique. The policy statements should reflect this particular library and the community it serves.

ALA POLICY

ALA covers following standard elements in its policy developed for academic libraries (College)

- *Standards* 1: Mission, Goals, and Objectives of institution
- *Standard* 2: Collections: including print materials in all formats, audiovisual materials, sound recordings, materials used with computers, graphics, and three dimensional materials. A formula is also presented in terms of collection development in the policy
- *Standard* 3: Organisation of materials: Library collections shall be organised by nationally approved conventions and arranged for efficient retrieval at time of need. The processing methods need to be applied for this purpose.
- *Standard* 4: Staff: The staff shall be of adequate size and quality to meet the library's need for services, programmes, and collection organisation. A staff formula is also presented in the policy
- *Standard* 5: Services: The library shall establish, promote, maintain a range and quality of services that supports the academic programme of the institution and encourage optional library use.

- *Standards* 6: Facilities: The library building shall provide well-planned, secure and adequate housing for its collections and personnel; secure space for users and staff, and space for the provision of services and programmes. A formula is also presented to calculate the space for per vol/Per Sqft.
- *Standards* 7: Administration: The college library shall be administered in a manner which permits and encourages the fullest and most effective use of available library resources.
- *Standard* 8: Budget: The library director shall have the responsibility for preparing, defending, and administering the library budget in accord with agreed upon objectives. These standards provide the guideline for formulating the policy.

UNIVERSITY GRANT COMMISSION (UGC) COLLECTION DEVELOPMENT POLICY

The UGC policy stated following points for collection development:

- Library Committee and its constituents (Chairman, member secretary, members, student representative)
- Library Collection norms based on courses, students and faculty
- Technical Processing.
- Library Finance
- Library Services
- Library Personnel
- Physical Facilities

AICTE COLLECTION DEVELOPMENT POLICY FOR ENGINEERING COLLEGE LIBRARIES

All India Council for Technical Education (AICTE) has formulated norms or policy for development of library collection including number of titles and their volumes, number of national and international journals including e-resources made available through INDESTAICTE. The main elements covered with formulas are:

- Collection of Books and Journals (Print Reading Material)
- Collection of Electronic Resources (e-journals and e-books etc)
- Library Personnel and Library Building

LIBRARY OF CONGRESS. COLLECTION DEVELOPMENT POLICIES

The Library's Collection Development Policy is a guide for materials to be added to the Library's permanent collections.

The Collection Policy Statement (CPS) governs the Library's collection development and acquisition efforts. The statements implement the Library's responsibilities to serve. The policies provide a plan for developing the collections and maintaining their existing strengths.The highlighted points in to this policy are:

- *Collecting Levels*: Out of scope no need to buy, minimum level, basic information level, instructional level, research level, comprehensive level
- *Collection Overviews*: Scope, research strength,
- *Selection Guidelines for Electronic Resources*: Evaluate contents, add value, server reliability, judicious use of multimedia, adherence to copyright and fair use guidelines, provision of links to source for the plug-in-software, organisation and ease of navigation, presence of search and help features, procurement of Standard Fee based resources with permanent retention.

From the analytical study of the collection development policies it is understood that minimum components to be considered are:

- *Selection*: Covers purpose (free or purchased) teaching, learning, research and needs of staff and students; responsibility (Staff and librarian), Format (Print or digital), Language, special collections
- *Allocation of resources*: Considerations based on need based requirements and on demand procurement and provide more access to information than possession.
- *Collection maintenance*: Retention policies considering usage, main stack, parallel stacking, compact storage, weeding, retro-conversion etc are properly applied for better management and reduction in cost.
- *Preservation*: Rare and useful collection is to be retained for longer use and needs proper preservation manual or converting to digital
- *Access*: open access or authority permitted to consult in case of rare and confidential.
- *More use of e-publications*: The print media is shifting to e-publications and databases and more use is observed in the present generation.
- *Network based resources and consortium arrangement*: These are also to be considered while planning collection economically
- *Resource sharing and IR initiatives*: Open access and IR and resource sharing initiatives need to be considered

There is a need to develop proper collection in different forms. Collection development policies are to be framed for digital collection also as these documents may increase in the collection including acquisition and resource sharing policies.

The policies need to be revised regularly. Policy supports to customer-focused needs, so that library users have access to current, relevant and authoritative information in their preferred format.

3

Metadata at Digital Informative Era

Collection of Items are called Data. The additional Information's about the objects stored within our collections may be Traditional or e-format is represented in the form of Metadata, which is nothing but data about data. In General, metadata is machine understandable information. In Library environment, metadata is commonly used for any formal scheme of resource description, applying to any type of object, digital or Non--digital. From Computing Point of View, the content management system contains digital objects. Thus, Metadata is also one of the components of Digital Library. Both Digital objects and Metadata are components of Digital Library. Digital objects are described, structured, summarized, managed and otherwise manipulated in surrogate form through the use of "metadata", which literally means data about data. Metadata is usually produced through a process called "cataloging" that is often carried out by trained librarians. Collections of such information are commonly stored in "catalogs". In computerized environments, metadata may be automatically or semi-automatically extracted or derived from the original content or the "full text" may simply be indexed and searched.

WHAT IS METADATA

Metadata is "DATA ABOUT DATA" or "INFORMATION ABOUT INFORMATION" Metadata is structured Information that describes retrieval for managing Information Resource. Which states that most data is waste without Metadata. Metadata describes data elements and their attributes such as name, size, data type and also Data Structures like length, field, columns, etc. It also has information about the location of data, how it is associated ownership, etc. Also, metadata describes specific characteristics about spatial data, which provides guidelines with a Standard Format. The Information may includes Name, Ownership, Description, Currency, Status, Access, Quality, Contact Details, etc., It helps us to know where exactly Information locates, Information requirement, relevant Information where exactly locates, even with in another part of your Organization, etc., are the special features of Metadata. Metadata can be encoded in MARC in "keyword=value" pairs or in any other definable syntax. Many current meta data schemes use SGML or XML. XML is an extended form of HTML which allows for locally defined tag sets and the easy exchange of structured information. SGML is a superset of both HTML and XML and allows for the richest mark-up of a document.

PURPOSE OF METADATA

The purpose of metadata according to Haynes the Purpose may be expressed as information retrieval, management of information services, documenting ownership and authenticity, interoperability.

- Information retrieval is a dynamic process which involves the user, the system and the librarian. The system indicates the usage of the computers, but can also be the manual catalogue. To obtain proper retrieval of relevant documents, the metadata representation is most important and should satisfy the users.
- Metadata also helps in management of various information services like OPAC, SDI, etc.
- It is a vehicle for documenting ownership and authenticity of the information.
- It also focuses importance towards the interoperability of information across continents.

Also, the Purpose extends to:

- Resource Description
- Administration and Management of Resources
- Record of Intellectual Property Rights
- Documenting Software and Hardware Environments
- Resource Discovery
- Preservation Management of Digital Resources
- Providing Information on context and Authenticity.

TYPES OF METADATA

Metadata is divided into different types:

- Descriptive Metadata
- Administrative Metadata
- Structural Metadata and
- Subject Metadata

Descriptive Metadata

Descriptive Metadata are used in the Discovery, Indexing and Identification of Digital Resources by semanting means. It is visible to the User of a system. Descriptive Metadata refers to the author, title content, etc. Preservation information refers to the best way of preserving documents like air conditioning or preserving books in the form of files at Systems, which requires meta fields to maintain with.

Administrative Metadata

To maintain Collections, this Administrative Metadata is used. Administrative Metadata is Managing metadata. Rights management metadata is a form of administrative metadata dealing with intellectual property rights. This Administrative metadata pertains to acquisition, vendor, location, etc., Also, it encompass a variety of data related to viewing, interpretation; use and management of digital objects over time. It includes technical data on creation and quality control, which has rights management, access control and user requirements.

- Management Information: Managing Information according to User requirements and reflects the output.
- Technical Information: Technical Information expresses the Technical details such as Name of the file, its Type, Hardware, Software, Resolution of the Images scanned, Colour space, Pixel dimensions, File relationships, Compressions, etc., Using related Information provides User Tracing Information.
- Structural Metadata: Structural Metadata is nothing but interface which complies individual digital object into more meaningful units for the users. Structural metadata indicates how compound objects are put together. Structural Metadata is used for representing Physical Entity through Navigation, Information Display and Display. Searching Contents among them or with in them. Structural metadata has information about Physical forms of the resources.
- Subject Metadata: To have effective Searching this Subject Metadata is used. For Browsing structure this Subject Metadata is used, with Keywords, Classification Codes, Classification System, Terms from Thesauri and Subject Heading.

HOW METADATA IS USED IN TRADITIONAL LIBRARY CATALOGUING

Traditional Library Cataloging is a form of metadata, and MARC 21 and the rules sets in AACR2 are metadata standards. Other metadata schemes have been developed to describe various types of textual and Non--textual objects such as archival materials, visual materials, geographic information, and science and social science datasets.

In mid 1990's Schwartz mentions the term metadata, which is used with database management, began to appear in the LIS literature. However, within a short period the topic became very popular in the area of research concentration, giving rise to several hundred publications, including an ARIST chapter in 1998.

Lange and Winkler traced the history of the term metadata back to the 1960s, but noted that it began to appear more frequently in the DBMS literature in the 1980s. Vellucci notes that the term metadata transcends boundaries among various stakeholders in the development of the internet and provides a common vocabulary to describe a variety of data structures.

XML (EXTENSIBLE MARKUP LANGUAGE)

XML is a Markup Language in the world of Web Designing and Programming. The markup text is a methodology for encoding data with information about it itself. Examples of markup are universal in the real world. The systematic arrangement of data elements for machine processing contains metadata multiple applications. The *Resource Description Framework* (RDF) is developed under *World Wide Web Consortium* (W3C), which enables encoding exchange and reuse of structured Metadata. RDF is a language for representing information about resources of World Wide Web, which is particularly representing Metadata with Web Resources. RDF utilizes XML as a common syntax for processing of Metadata. XML is a simple and very flexible Markup Language with a great technology also runs in any platform with any Environment. The XML syntax is a subset of the International text processing *Standard Generalized Markup Language* (SGML) which is meant for Web. The XML syntax provides vendor independence, flexible framework, instant push technologies with *Channel Definition Format* (CDF), Electronic Commerce uses the *Open Trading Protocol* (OTP) and *Mathematical Markup Language* (MML), Pre-defined Tags, User Extensibility, Validation, Human Readability, etc., to indicate complex structures. By exploiting the features of XML, RDF focuses the structure of expression of semantics with machine processing standard Metadata.

WHAT DOES METADATA DO

An important reason for creating descriptive metadata is to facilitate discovery of relevant information. In addition to resource discovery, metadata can help organize electronic resources, facilitate interoperability and legacy resource integration, support digital identification and support archiving and preservation.

HOW TO CREATE METADATA

To encode Information the Data should be expressed in proper way. Create a Single disk file for each metadata record, that is, one disk file describes one data set. Then use some tool to enter Information into this disk file so that the metadata confirm to the standard. The procedure is,

- Assemble Information about the data set.
- Create a Digital file containing the metadata, properly arranged.
- Check the Syntactical Structure of the file. Modify the arrangement of Information and repeat until the syntactical structure is correct.
- Review the content of the metadata, verifying that the information describes the subject data completely and correctly.

DIGITAL IDENTIFICATION

Most metadata schemes include elements such as standard numbers to uniquely identify the work or object to which the metadata refers. The location of a digital object may also be given using a file name, URL, or some more persistent identifier such as a Persistent URL (PURL) or the Digital Object Identified (DOI). Persistent identifiers are preferred because file locations change frequently, making the URL invalid. In addition to the actual elements that point to the object, the metadata can be combined to act as a set of identifying data, differentiating one object from another for validation purposes.

ARCHIVING AND PRESERVATION

Recently created resources are the current metadata. However, there is a growing concern that digital resources will not survive in usable form into the future. Digital information is fragile; it can be corrupted or altered according to the requirement. It may become unusable as storage media and hardware and software technologies change. Format migration and perhaps emulation of current hardware and software behaviour in future hardware and software platforms are strategies for overcoming these challenges. Metadata is key to ensuring that resources will survive and continue to be accessible into the future. Archiving and preservation require special elements to track the lineage of a digital object to details its physical characteristics and to document its behaviour in order to emulate it on future technologies.

RESOURCE DISCOVERY

Metadata serves same functions in resource discovery as good cataloguing does by

- allowing resources to be found by relevant criteria
- identifying resources
- bringing similar resources together
- distinguishing dissimilar resources and
- giving location information

ROLE OF METADATA IN INFORMATION MANAGEMENT SYSTEM (IMS)

The role of Metadata in Content Management is something Interesting and worth interrogating. Metadata is used in variety of Situations and applications with widespread web applications. For "Searching" techniques, the metadata role is very very important. If the user started searching in the name of " Isolation and Purification" one can get number of references for the above said Topic. The associated keywords are analyzed and the related topics may also appear to satisfy the user needs. The terms can be grouped into associative and hierarchically subordinate or super-ordinate terms. This can be represented with the concept of Isolation and Purification. According to Dr. Ranganathan classification, the Personality, Energy, Matter may be defined.

The subordinate terms can be incorporated into the classification schedule and used in assigning subject headings or keywords. This will serve the purpose of the user and the classificationist. However, change of keyword into subject heading is a different procedure. These are all metadata contents. Also, it serves as a good example for Information Retrieval. Finally, the most important fact is that there should be facility in the software for upgradation of the metadata when required. The elements holds related detailed border schema for description, which is enumerated from narrower schema, to increase both recall and precision. This type of Principle is applicable to any type of Information Management System.

DC METADATA

It is very pathetic to observe the paradoxical attitude of some of the library professionals and information specialists who continue to believe that cataloging web resources is a waste of time, it is better to make web pages (essentially webliographies or lists) because many of the web resources are too ephemeral to be included in the library catalog. To make the maintenance of metadata for web resources much simpler, new tools such as URL link checkers are used. The users are suggested to start with the library catalogue as a single gateway to the universe of knowledge. The usage of DC refinements and principles advocated in this chapter is both integrative and time saving. It will save the time of the library cataloger and the user because it recognised the lessons learned by the library, archival and museum cataloging communities and tries to incorporate them into DC metadata creation. Cataloging is synonymous for the activity of metadata description. Resource descriptions are synonymous for DC records. Instead of 999 tags in library MARK, 16 elements of Dublin core have been used. The best of cataloguing practice, however, be captured in the following simple guidelines. Required information should be filled normally, failing which an element becomes meaningless.

GUIDELINES TO CREATE DC METADATA

There are three main guidelines to create DC metadata as discussed below:

- *Guidelines 1*: A comprehensive Resource description is required. The data should be absolutely complete to avoid confusing meaning of the element. For example, if there is no title, make up a title. Leave the element blank only as a last resort.
- *Guideline 2*: Consistent resource description should be provided taking into consideration the inconsistent nature of humans beings, the principles of consistency is used in cataloging and classification to avoid cognitive overload. There are many techniques for ensuring

consistency and the simplest is to use words from a predetermined and authoritative list whenever possible for controlled values.

- *Guideline 3*: All of the DC elements is optional, repeatable, and modified by qualifiers. All 16 elements are described in detail and each element includes the following categories of instruction and information. Main categories of Instruction for creating DC Metadata are shown in fig.

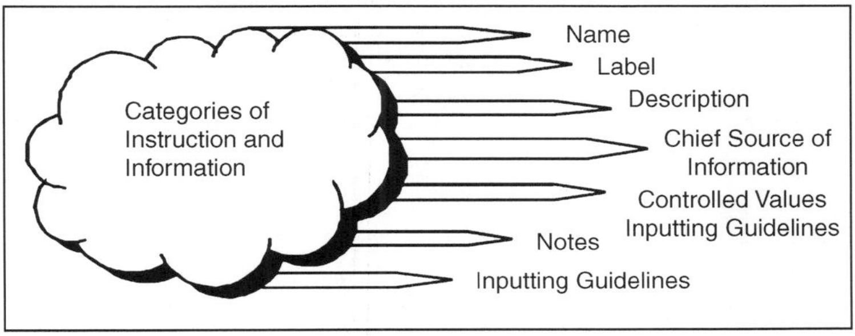

Fig. Categories of Instruction for Creating DC Metadata.

MAIN CATEGORIES FOR CREATING DC METADATA

The Main Categories for creating DC Metadata are Name, Label, Description, Chief Source of Information, Controlled Values Inputting Guidelines, Notes, and Inputting Guidelines.

- *Name*: Name is the name given to the element in DC standard.
- *Label*: Label as seen in an integrated library system or a bibliographic utility such as OCLC for entering this information. Somewhere elements name is same as the Label and sometimes it may be different
- *Description*: Description is the definition given in the DC standard Comments also come for the DC as appropriate.
- *Chief Source of Information*: Instruction modeled after the technical reading of the item for cataloguing practices, AACR2 is the chief source of information. The process of technical reading provides specific guidance to the sources of information the exact places in the resources from which the metadata for each element may be selected.
- *Controlled Values Inputting Guidelines*: Controlled values is also modeled after AACR2R and MARC to some extent and allows the metadata creator to know if the element uses a list of controlled values, a classification, or controlled vocabulary. These values may be made enforceable by the software or humanly selected from a given list or through consultation of an external list/source such as registers. Controlled vales help make meaning clearer and consistent. They do so by keeping the form of element vales, the metadata content for

each element describing the resource, the same across multiple resources. Precision, increased relevance of result retrieved in response to a query, is improved in subject information retrieval by the use of controlled vales and vocabularies.

- *Notes*: Metadata Creator Notes or creation guidelines discuss how much of the cataloguer's (metadata creator) judgement is involved in creating the metadata for each element. Metadata creation is often subjective rather than objective. Without clear rules and standards, two different catalogers may describe the same resource quite differently. The term subjective is used to indicate that a particular element can be described based on the personal judgement of the resource cataloger and objective is used on the personal judgement of the resource cataloger and objective is used to denote objectivity, when the data or content is found on the resource or may be identified in a similar manner by all resource metadata creators and catalogers.
- *Inputting Guidelines*: Inputting guidelines provide special directions that must be followed to enter the resource description. These illustrate the general principles of DC metadata creation.

ELEMENTS-BY-ELEMENTS DESCRIPTION OF DC METADATA

Description and how to create DC metadata (Notes) and inputting guidelines with examples for electronic (web) information resources for all DC elements are discussed below.

Element: Title

- *Description*: A name given to the resource.
- *Inputting Guidelines*: Enter the title information as found in the resource. Use capitalisation and punctuation as found in resource.
- *DC Creator Notes*: Generally, there should be no individual judgement involved as the metadata creator is merely transcribing the title, when the resource has a clearly presented title. Many electronic resources, however, may not have a title clearly visible or the title may be generic for the whole and not the specific part being catalogued. In these cases, creating the metadata for the title, where the cataloger must create or supply title, can become subjective. Follow the guidance prescribed in the Chief source of information and generally take title from the actual information resource whenever possible. Example: Title= "The Art of Music"

Element: Creator

- *Description*: An entity primarily responsible for making the content of the resource.
- *Inputting Guidelines*: Enter the Creator as found in the resource. Use

capitalisation and punctuation as found in resource. If Creator is an organisation, enter the name of the organisation.

- *Metadata Creator Notes*: Objective. Cataloging the creator becomes a subjective activity should the creator not be listed in the resource, while it is possible through extra research to find out this information, generally this would take too much time and hence, most cataloguing is only done based on actual examination of the resource. If creator can not be readily determined from this, leave this element blank. Many electronic resources do not have the creator easily identifiable. Example Creator= "Mishra, Rajeshver"

Element: Subject

- *Description*: The topic of the content of the resource.
- Inputting Guidelines: Input subject from LCSH or from resource as Keywords.
- *Metadata Creator Notes*: Objective when the terms are found on the resource. Subjective, if cataloger supplied. Most often will be cataloger supplied. Example: Subject="Library Automation"

Element: Description

- *Description*: An account of the content of the resource.
- *Inputting Guidelines*: Provide abstract, table of contents, or description of the resource.
- *Metadata Creator Notes*: Objective if taken from resource. The information in this element may be subjective if it is a summary provided by the cataloger. Example Description" The chapter defines metadata, examines the relationship between creating metadata and cataloguing, provides definitions for key metadata vocabulary terms and explores the topic of metadata generation. Cataloguing is for physical objects and metadata is exclusively for electronic resources"

Element: Publisher

- *Description*: An entity responsible for making the resource available in its present form such as Publishing House, a University Department, or Corporate entity.
- *Inputting Guidelines*: Enter the Publisher as found in the resource. Use capitalisation and punctuation as found in resource. If Publisher is an organisation,enter the name of organisation.
- *Metadata Creator Notes*: Objective, may become subjective. It is often difficult to find the name of the publisher for electronic resources. For example, consider the homepage. Who is the publisher? We generally consider the organisation or individual who is hosting the web page to be the publisher. Thus the

publisher of this author's home page is the University of Kanpur. Example Publisher="Kanpur University"

Element: Contributor

- *Description*: An entity responsible for making contributions to the content of the resource.
- *Inputting Guidelines*: Enter the Contributor as found in the resource. Use capitalisation and punctuation as found in resource. Contributors play different roles and can be indicated by using parenthesis, following the name. Thus, some roles are Editor, Translator, and Illustrator. Example Contributor= "Anand, Anoop (Editor)"
- *Metadata Creator Notes*: Objective. There are a great many more roles that Contributors can fall into. But, to keep the activity of metadata creation simple and save time, the three are sufficient.

Element: Date

- *Description*: A date associated with an event in the life cycle of the resource.
- *Inputting Guidelines*: Follow the YYYY-MM-DD format and choose from list what type of date is being recorded, whether the date is the date the resource was created or modified. If no date is available, leave blank, if multiple dates are found, enter the most recent only and indicate type. Enter 00-00 for month and date when it is not found on the resource easily.
- *Metadata Creator Notes*: Objective. Keep cataloguing simple and only specify one or two dates, when found, based on your local user needs. Example Date= "2007-07-27"

Element: Type

- *Description*: The nature or genre of the content of the resource.
- *Inputting Guidelines*: DCMI Metadata terms TYPE Vocabulary has a list, from which select as many as types. They are Collection, Dataset, Event, Image, InteractiveResource, MovingImage, PhysicalObject, Service, Software, Sound, StillImage and Text that can be found in the resource.
- *Metadata Creator Notes*: Objective. Example Type= "Image"

Element: Format

- *Description*: The physical or digital manifestation of the resource. Typically, format may include the media-type or dimensions of the resource.
- *Inputting Guidelines*: Select one or more of the formats.
- *Metadata Creator Notes*: Objective. Example: Format="Image/gif" or Format="2KB"

Element: Identifier

- Description: An unambiguous reference to the resource within a given context.
- Inputting Guidelines: Give full URL starting http://.....
- Metadata Creator Notes: Objective.

Element: Source

- *Description*: A reference to a resource from which the present resource is derived.Recommended best practice is to reference the resource by means of a formal identification or call number system.
- *Inputting Guidelines*: Enter the title followed by a comma and the URL. If no title or URL found or the original source is a print or other format, describe in own words. Many electronic resource are born-digital and have no print or other digital counterpart. Hence, source may often be left blank.
- *Metadata Creator Notes*: Objective. Example: Source="Image from page 34 of the 1922 edition of Romeo and Juliet"

Element: Language

- *Description*: A language of intellectual contents of the resource.
- *Inputting Guidelines*: Select the language of the resource.
- *Metadata Creator Notes*: Objective. Note that many learning resources are available in versions other than English, therefore record the language to match the object being catalogued. Do not use the language element to record version information. Example: Language= " en" for English and "fr" for French.

Element: Relation

- Description: A reference to a related resource.
- Inputting Guidelines: Select the appropriate relationship between two or more resources. A resource may have multiple relationships. Add Title and URL.
- Metadata Creator Notes: Objective. Example: Title="Electronic AACR2" Relation="Anglo-American Cataloguing Rules, 2nd edition"

Element: Coverage

- *Description*: The extent or scope of the content of resource.
- *Inputting Guidelines*: Select the appropriate spatial, temporal, jurisdiction coverage of the resource and use the words in the resources.
- *Metadata Creator Notes*: Objective. For some types of literary materials, this might be subjective.

Element: Rights

- *Description*: Information about rights held in and over the resource.

Typically a Rights element will contain a rights management statement for the resource, or reference a service providing such information. Right information often encompasses Intellectual Property Rights IPR, Copyright, and various Property Rights.

- *Inputting Guidelines*: May be either a text statement or URL pointing to a right statement, or a combination, when a brief statement and a lengthier one are available.
- *Metadata Creator Notes*: Objective. Example Rights="Access limited to teachers"

Element: Audience

- *Description*: Intended user for resource.
- *Inputting Guidelines*: Look for this information on the main resource page, if none is found, browse the resource and select one or more of the values from the Controlled values list - Elementary, Middle, High School, Undergraduate level,Graduate Level, Professional, General Education.
- *Metadata Creator Notes*: Subjective, if not found explicitly stated in resource. Example: Audience=" General Education"

METADATA–CATALOGUING IN THE DIGITAL CONTEXT

The shaping effect of the library tradition on digital libraries is perhaps most evident in the focus on descriptive metadata. This focus has its roots in cataloguing, one of the core functions of the modern library. The traditional catalogue developed for a number of reasons. At the simplest level, in a library of physical resources it gave users an easy and compact tool for finding information resources without having to traverse the shelves.

However, describing the catalogue as merely a compact shelf list trivializes its complexity and intellectual content. Underlying cataloguing is the concept of information entities having uniform attributes, such as author, title, or subject classification, and the utility of those attributes for logical organization of those entities. This organization presents multiple *access points* based on those uniform attributes, and allows users to search and browse within those access points.

For example, a user may search for information by author name and then traverse the resources associated with that author, or alternatively they may search for information by subject classification and traverse the resources associated within that class. As a result, the organization of the catalogue and the manner in which it is made available to the user (*e.g.*, cards in drawers or screens in an electronic catalogue) is independent of the manner in which the physical, or digital, resources are organized on shelves, or in repositories.

Furthermore, an individual information resource (*e.g.*, a book) may have multiple catalogue instances, each accessible through specific access points (*e.g.*, title, author, subject, etc.). Efforts to extend the practice of cataloguing into the context of online information reflects an ongoing belief that in a world where even the books that are part of library collections have been digitized and are available for full-text search, structured search over surrogates is more functional and ultimately preferred by users.

This is despite empirical evidence that users seem to prefer the "one text box" search paradigm of Google to the fielded-search paradigm employed in most digital library portals and online catalogs, and decades-old evidence of the frequent superiority in recall and precision of automated full-text search to human-assisted indexing and cataloguing.

Traditional library cataloguing is both complex and expensive, especially when applied to the rapidly expanding and diverse set of digital resources. The notion of metadata emerged as a simpler and less expensive alternative to traditional cataloguing records, perhaps making it possible for nonprofess-ionals to create structured bibliographic information.

The predominant digital library metadata effort is the Dublin Core Metadata Initiative. Ironically, the origins of Dublin Core lie in improving search and retrieval on the general web. However, this effort to develop easy-to-use bibliographic standards for networked information objects has been deemed irrelevant, ill-conceived, or even counterproductive by the mainstream web community and most notably the search engines that dominate it.

As I describe later, the attempts to translate the benefits of cataloguing to the online domain via metadata have been compromised by problems with ensuring the quality of the metadata records that are produced by Non--professionals and preventing so-called "metadata spamming" by unscrupulous agents trying to falsely lead information consumers to their sites.

DIGITAL OBJECTS — CONTAINERS FOR COMPLEX DATA AND METADATA

The content model of most digital library architectures is based on the notion of a *digital object*. an identified (first-class) information resource that is an aggregation of multiple information units consisting of multiple formats, multiple subsidiary units, versions, or document components (*e.g.*, the text, data, images, etc. of a scholarly paper).

These are generally known as *compound objects*. These object models reflect an ongoing effort by the library community to account for the complexity of information in both its abstract form and the physical or digital manifestations of it.

These efforts have focused on mechanisms to represent the various relationships among information resources. and to describe those resources at multiple levels of granularity, for various purposes, and in various descriptive formats. Access to compound objects and their components is frequently mediated by protocols unique to the particular repository architecture.

These protocols are usually embedded in the URLs that carry user requests from the digital library portal to the repository. These protocols allow operations such as access a digital object in a specific form, access a portion of a digital object such as its descriptive metadata, and the like.

The proliferation of these architecture-specific access protocols has spawned a virtual cottage industry of repository interoperability initiatives in the digital library community. In contrast, the web architecture includes a quite simple information model based on the atomic resource.

"Interoperability" is defined in the simple terms of the web architecture–resources, URIs, and HTTP. There is no architectural notion of a compound object, or aggregation of resources. Ad hoc and de facto aggregations exist, for example a logical document split into a set of interlinked web pages.

However, these aggregations are not first-class objects. they do not have a unique identity and are essentially ephemeral. There is, in fact, an increased awareness in the web community that more complex information models are appropriate in a number of instances. for example, scholarly publishing.

FEDERATION

The issue of federation arises because digital library systems are conceived as discrete institutionally-managed entities with distinct boundaries accessible to the user through branded portals. Sometimes, a user might want to search across multiple digital libraries when a selected resource is not available in their "local" library. In the physical library domain, this problem is solved by union catalogs such as WorldCat and by interlibrary loan.Digital library applications employ two mechanisms to allow users to search for and access information outside the confines of a single digital library. The first is federated searching or meta-searching, in which a single search query is multicast to several digital library search engines.

The query is then individually processed at those search engines. the individual result sets are then returned and integrated at the site from which the original query was multicast. Federated searching was the subject of substantial work in the early years of digital library research describes our own work in this area.Although instances of federated search still exist, the technique has fallen into some disfavour because of problems with dependence on the reliability of multiple search sites and the problems with the ranking of search results from several sources. The second is metadata harvesting, in which bibliographic records from several distributed institutional sources are combined at a single indexing site, which provides a search interface across the resulting "union catalogue". The most widely deployed mechanism for metadata harvesting is the Open Archives Protocol for Metadata Harvesting (OAI-PMH). That same chapter describes complica-tions with metadata harvesting. Neither of these techniques has achieved widespread deployment in the general web information space. Boundaries and the repositories that implement them are not a part of the web architecture. Web search engines such as Google crawl the web via graph traversal, ignoring the notion of the location of a webpage, except as a tool for optimizing graph traversal strategies. In addition, ranking algorithms such as PageRank are designed to operate over a centralized index, and are difficult if not impossible in the context of distributed methods such as federated search,

INFORMATION ACCESS IN DIGITAL LIBRARIES

A digital library (DL) system comprises a large, distributed information space, where the objects carrying the knowledge required by the users, live. Setting up and maintaining a DL would be entirely useless if users were not provided with the adequate tools to access the DL information contents. In defining the information access service of a DL, there are at least 3 areas of the information system field which can give significant contributions:

- *Information retrieval* (IR) can contribute content-based methods, that is methods that exploit the signal level of an information object. For textual objects, these include all classical methods based on the statistical properties of language, such as the vector-space method and the probabilistic method. For Non--textual objects, in the last decade there has been a fluorishing of methods for similarity-based retrieval of images, video and audio objects.
- The *database* area can contribute all methods for attribute-based information querying, ranging from traditional databases, to semi-structured databases; the methods falling under the last category are especially useful when ad- dressing the *structure* of objects.
- *Knowledge representation* can contribute methods for accessing objects by querying descriptions of their contents; these descriptions are typically couched in terms of representations of the underlying domain of discourse, or *ontologies* as these have come to be termed lately.

Putting the techniques found in the fields all together at work, requires a conceptual schema which integrates in a unique framework the different aspects of DL objects addressed by each of them. In what follows as suggested, try to sketch such a schema.

A CONCEPTUAL SCHEMA OF INFORMATION ACCESS

We characterise the space of information access by the following, orthogonal dimensions:

- The information access model, which establishes the basic terms of the system/user interaction;
- The information access mode, which establishes the role of the user and that of the system during their interaction.

Information access Models

Similarly to an information retrieval model, an information access model specifies:

- A representation of the objects to be accessed;
- A representation of the user information needs; and
- A function associating a set of objects to each user information need.

Information access models can be categorised according to the options available on each one of their dimensions. For object representation, following we distinguish between simple objects and composite objects. Simple objects cannot be further decomposed, and can be represented along the following dimensions:

- *Content abstractions*: these are representations used to access objects via IR techniques. They are created by IR indexers in an automatic way, by extracting low-level features from objects, such as the number of word occurrences in a text, or the energy level in a certain region of an image); content abstractions retain that part of the information originally present in the object content that is considered sufficient to characterise the object for access purposes;
- *Content representations*: these are symbolic representations of the meaning of documents, that is descriptions formulated in some suitable knowledge representation language, spelling out the truth conditions of the object. Content representations can be constructed manually, sometimes with the assistance of some knowledge extraction tool, or automatically, for instance via object classification methods. They can be precise or uncertain, depending on whether or not the content representation formulas are expressed in an un- certain logic, such as fuzzy or probabilistic logic.

Composite objects are structured set of simple objects, thus they are typically represented as mathematical *structures*, reflecting their internal organisation. Finally, objects, whether simple or composite, can have a *profile*, that is an attribute-based description of their external properties, such as the author and the publisher of a book, or the data and time at which an image has been taken, and the like. In the context of digital libraries, the 4 dimensions of object representation reduce to 3 only, since content representations and profiles are typically grouped together under the label of discovery metadata. The metadata associated to a DL object can therefore vary from simple records typically adhering to some standardised schema to very complex representations expressed in some knowledge representation language which must be coupled with a representation of the underlying domain of discourse, in order to be properly used for, *e.g.* information access. In summary, as suggested, therefore consider object representation as being categorised as:

- Content,

- Metadata, and
- Structure.

For information need representation, we have 2 options: formal language queries or natural language queries. For the retrieval function, we have 2 options: exact match or best match. Not all combinations of these options give rise to meaningful information access models. Considering the object representation options we have the following:

- Content is typically addressed via IR techniques, based on natural language queries and best-match retrieval function. For instance, users access the con- tent of an image base by providing as a query an image itself In so doing, users are implicitly asking the system to retrieve images which 'looks' similar to the image query, at least as far as the system can tell. For this reason, methods providing access by content are often called '*similarity-based*' access methods. An analogous pattern is found in access models for textual or for audio content. Notice that in some models of this kind, the query may not be expressed in the same medium as the sought objects. For instance, when accessing by content a video database, users may provide an image as a query, and the system is expected to retrieve the scenes sharing visual similarity with the provided image. Similarity-based access models are medium-dependent, in that different media require different techniques, and the possibility of using the same or a similar technique across different media is very limited. In addition, experience has shown that even within the same medium, the effectiveness of techniques is application-dependent: for example, retrieving by similarity sport images requires different techniques from those necessary to establish the similarity of X-ray images.
- Metadata is typically addressed via formal language queries, thus we are in the realm of databases or knowledge representation, depending from the degree of sophisticatedness of the involved representations. For instance, to query a Dublin Core scheme, one needs a very simple language allowing to state basic relational conditions on simple numeric- or string-based attribute values; instead, to query an OWL representation the ability to state conditions involving taxonomies and navigation of graph structures is required. In general, a query to metadata takes the form of a logical formula, and an exact match retrieval function is employed for query evaluation, grounded in some logical theory. We call these models *semantic* access models. Some retrieval engines allow to exploit information retrieval techniques when accessing objects via their metadata records. This is achieved by seeing metadata records as pieces of text whose words are the attribute values. Such a text is treated in the same way as textual content, and matched against a natural language query as in a

similarity-based textual access method. This kind of access model is widely employed on bibliographic records, as it frees users from the necessity of knowing the meaning of meta- data attributes.

- Also object structure can be queried in two different ways:
- Via exact match retrieval functions, such as the one underlying the query language XPath. In this case, the structural query is mostly embedded into a larger query addressing either content or metadata. We do not have therefore separate classes of access models but sophistications of similarity-based or semantic access models allowing also the specification of structural clauses in queries.
- Via best match retrieval functions, which express in a quantitative way the degree of similarity between the structure of each object and a user provided structure class. These models have been investigated in the con- text of XML, and are a structural variation of similarity-based models. We call the models falling in this class 'similar structure-based access models'.

In summary, we have the following information access model categories:

- Similarity-based access models, possibly with structural conditions;
- Semantic access models, possibly with structural conditions; and
- Similar structure-based access models.

Information Access Modes

Independently from the access model, the information access modes establishes the role of the system and that of the user. Each of these two can be either passive or active. Excluding the case in which they are both passive, we have the following 3 types of information access systems:

- *Query-answering systems*: in this case the user is active, that is, poses a query, while the system is passive, that is it just evaluates the user query and returns the result.
- *Filtering systems*: In which the user is passive, that is, does not pose any query, and the system is active, that is it selects on a stream of incoming objects, those that are deemed as relevant for the user; the relevance assessment is performed by relying on a user profile.
- *Personalised query-answering systems*: in which the user is active, that is, poses a query, and the system is active too, in that it alters the query evaluation process by taking into account the user preferences, represented as a profile. Recommendation systems also fall into this category, since they propose recommendations along with the answer to the query.

CHALLENGES OF DISTRIBUTED SEARCH ACROSS DIGITAL LIBRARIES

The peer-to-peer (P2P) approach allows handling huge amounts of data of digital libraries in a distributed and self-organising way. These characteristics offer enormous potential benefit for search capabilities powerful in terms of scalability, efficiency, and resilience to failures and dynamics. Additionally, such a search engine can potentially benefit from the intellectual input of a large user community.

However, recent research on structured P2P architectures is typically limited to exact-match queries on keys. This is insufficient for text queries that consist of a variable number of keywords, and it is absolutely inappropriate for full-fledged Web search where keyword queries should return a ranked result list of the most relevant approximate matches. This stage builds upon the MINERVA system architecture presented in and brings current challenges to ultimatively making distributed search across digital libraries feasible. MINERVA provides ranked search on data and an efficient query mechanism that adheres to reasonable space and bandwidth limits. Unlike the approach criticised in, we do not spread inverted lists across the directory, but use only pointers to promising digital libraries as compact metadata and utilise these pointers to efficiently answer multiple-keyword queries. We leverage the extensive local indexes to incorporate features that are impossible in the approach studied in, such as phrase matching or proximity searches. Our bandwidth requirements are well within the postulation that a query should send no more data than the size of the documents ultimatively retrieved.

RELATED WORK

Recent research on structured P2P systems, such as Chord, CAN, Pastry, or P-Grid is typically based on various forms of distributed hash tables (DHTs) and supports mappings from keys to locations in a decentralised manner such that routing scales well with the number of peers in the system. We briefly discuss some prior and ongoing projects towards P2P Web search. Galanx is a P2P search engine implemented using the Apache HTTP server and Berkeley DB.

The Web site servers are the peers of this architecture; pages are stored only where they originate from. PlanetP is a publish subscribe service for P2P communities, supporting content ranking search. PlanetP distinguishes local indexes and a global index to describe all peers and their shared information. The global index is replicated using a gossiping algorithm. The system appears to be limited to a few thousand peers. Odissea assumes a two-layered search engine architecture with a global index structure distributed over the nodes in the system. A single node holds the complete, Web-scale, index for a given text term. Query execution uses a distributed version of Fagin's threshold algorithm.

The system appears to cause high network traffic when posting document metadata into the network, and the presented query execution method seems limited to queries with at most two keywords. The paper actually advocates using a limited number of nodes, in the spirit of a server farm. The system outlined in uses a fully distributed inverted text index, in which every participant is responsible for a specific subset of terms and manages the respective index structures. Particular emphasis is put on minimising the bandwidth used during multi-keyword searches. considers content-based retrieval in hybrid P2P networks.

The peer selection for forwarding queries is based on the Kullback- Leibler divergence between peer-specific statistical models of term distributions. In addition to this recent work on P2P search, prior research on distributed IR and metasearch engines is also potentially relevant; see for overviews. However, their work has assumed a relatively small number of digital libraries or databases and a fairly static configuration.

SYSTEM DESIGN

As a detailed description of the system design has already been given in, we only present a brief overview here and refer the interested reader to this prior work. We view every library as autonomous. A conceptually global but physically distributed directory, which is layered on top of a Chord-style dynamic hash table (DHT), holds only very compact, aggregated information about the peers' local indexes and only to the extent that the individual peers are willing to disclose. Every peer is responsible for a randomised subset of the global directory.

The global directory consists of aggregated information (Posts) that contains contact information about the digital library who posted this summary together with statistics to calculate IR-style relevance measures that try to estimate the relevance of a particular digital library to a query. These measures are used to support the peer selection process, *i.e.*, determining the most promising libraries for a particular query. If, at query time, the local query result is considered unsatisfactory by the user, a library retrieves a list of potentially useful libraries. Using collection selection methods from distributed IR and metasearch, a number of promising libraries for the complete query is computed from these PeerLists. In we have studied promising and efficient techniques for this purpose. Subsequently, the query is forwarded to these libraries and executed based on their local indexes.

The results from the various libraries are combined at the querying peer into a single result list; this step is referred to as result merging. The goal of finding high-quality search results with respect to precision and recall cannot be easily reconciled with the design goal of unlimited scalability, as the best information retrieval techniques for query execution rely on large amounts of document metadata. Posting only compact, aggregated information about local indexes and using appropriate peer selection methods to limit the number of peers involved in a query keeps the global directory manageable and reduces network traffic. We expect this approach to scale very well as more and more peers jointly maintain the moderately growing global directory.

CHALLENGES

Our work is driven by the question of how a collaborative search across digital libraries can benefit from the unique nature of the P2P paradigm. We want to address the shortcomings of centralised search engines and further benefit from the intellectual input of a large user community.

Democratic Community Search

To overcome the danger of the infiltration of a centralised index by (commercial) interest groups we leverage the indexes from potentially thousands of digital libraries, making it harder to bias the final query results.

Implicit User Feedback

Additionally, we want to incorporate the fact that every library has its own local index, *e.g.*, by executing all queries first locally at the initiating library and using implicit-feedback techniques for automated query expansion.

User Recommendations

We want to incorporate local user bookmarks into our query execution. Bookmarks represent strong recommendations for specific documents. Also, user bookmarks can be considered as compact samples of peer indexes that describe their fields of interest. Queries could be exclusively forwarded to thematically related libraries with similarly interested users, to improve the chances of finding subjectively relevant pages.

Replication

In order to achieve service levels comparable to today's search engines and in order to actually benefit from the infrastructural advantage of a distributed system, we are going to introduce a certain degree of replication to the directory. Currently, as dictated by the DHT-style maintenance approach, a peer gracefully leaving the system forwards its share of the global directory to another peer. Analogously, a library entering the system asks for its appropriate share of the directory. While one approach to ensure a valid, complete, and up-todate directory is to simply rely on the libraries to regularly re-send their Posts to the directory, it is also necessary to replicate parts of the directory to avoid data loss as libraries ungracefully leave the system. Also, replication can serve as a load-balancing measure, relieving the burden from peers that host popular parts of the directory, and increases data availability. Adaptive, self-tuning strategies for choosing appropriate degrees of replication and placing replicas are an open issue in our ongoing work.

Caching and Proactive Dissemination

To further enhance query efficiency, statistical summaries and also the results of queries from across the network may be cached in a way that allows other peers not only to instantly benefit from the existing query results but also to benefit from click streamst that were recorded on the occasion of similar queries. Statistical summaries may also be disseminated proactively among thematically related peers. Finding good strategies to this end is a widely open issue.

Overlap-aware Query Routing

Peer selection has been a research issue for years. Most of the existing literature estimates the expected result quality of a collection, typically using pre-computed statistics, and ranks the collections accordingly. We believe that this is insufficient if the collections overlap, *e.g.*, in the scenario of digital libraries that share an arbitrarily large fraction of documents. We argue for the extension of existing quality measures using estimators of mutual overlap among collections. Preliminary experiments show that such a combination can outperform popular approaches based on quality estimation only, such as CORI. Taking overlap into account during collection selection in this scenario can drastically decrease the number of libraries that have to be contacted in order to reach a satisfactory level of recall, which is a great step towards the feasibility of distributed search across digital libraries.

Benefit/Cost Optimisation

Ultimatively, we want to introduce a sophisticated benefit/cost ratio when selecting remote libraries for query forwarding. For the benefit estimation, it is intuitive to consider such measures. Defining a meaningful cost measure, however, is an even more challenging issue. While there are techniques for observing and inferring network bandwidth or other infrastructural information, expected response times are changing over time. One approach is to create a distributed Quality-of-Service directory that, for all peers, holds moving averages of recent response times.

DIRECT—A DISTRIBUTED TOOL FOR INFORMATION RETRIEVAL EVALUATION CAMPAIGNS

Digital Library Management Systems (DLMSs) generally manage collections of multi-media digitalised data and include components that perform the storage, access, retrieval, and analysis of the collections of data. The evaluation of DLMSs is a Non- trivial issue that should cover different aspects, such as: the DLMS architecture, the DLMS information access and extraction capabilities, the management of multimedia content, the interaction with users, and so on. We are interested in the evaluation aspects concerned with the information access and extraction components of a DLMS ; this interest ranges from measuring and quantifying the performances of the information access and extraction components of a DLMS to designing and developing an architecture capable of supporting this kind of evaluation in the context of DLMSs.

EVALUATION ISSUES FOR THE INFORMATION ACCESS COMPONENTS OF A DLMS

Today, this type of evaluation is carried out in important international evaluation forums which bring research groups together, provide them with the means for measuring the performances of their systems, discuss and compare their work. The most important forums for Information Retrieval System (IRS) are:

- Text REtrieval Conference (TREC),
- Cross Language Information Retrieval (CLIR),
- NII-NACSIS Test Collection for IR Systems (NTCIR), and
- INitiative for the Evaluation of XML Retrieval (INEX).

A wide range of questions are covered by these forums like the quality of the information retrieved, the access of multi- lingual collections of documents, the retrieval of structured documents and the access to Asian-language collections. In general, these evaluation campaigns follow the Cranfield paradigm giving the participants one or more test-bed collections, a set of tasks to be performed, and a method by which evaluating performances of their systems with respect to the defined collections and tasks. A drawback of the approach followed during these evaluation forums is that huge chunks of textual files are shifted from side to side. Document collections usually reside on a single high-loaded server where all participants connect con- currently in a very short limited time in order to download the collections needed to carry out the experiments. The experimental results provided by participants to organisers usually consist of large text files, containing lists of retrieved documents together with their rank and score, that are numerical data.

The performance figures computed by organisers and returned to participants consist of text files full of numerical data; in particular, the presentation format adopted by TrecEval, the *de-facto* standard tool for computing the performance figures, is not very suitable for direct processing by a computer programme, since it is tailored to be human-readable. These file transfers often requires a mass-mailing between participants and organisers in order to acknowledge the receipt of the files or to correct errors. Moreover, if the performances figures are to be accessed in order to further process them, a lot of textual parsing is needed to transform chunks of text into numerical values, a process which is prone to errors. Another drawback is that while the performance of IRS are measured by means of traditional IR performance indicators, the analysis of the significance of this results is rarely performed by participants although statistical analysis is a fundamental step in the experimental evaluation, as pointed out by. We identify two main reasons for this: first, the analysis of the whole set of runs submitted is possible only by organisers that collect all the runs, and replicating experiments of other research groups is seldom possible for participants. Second, statistical tools are not easy to handle and the possibility to have Non- coherent results is high when participants make use of different tools. Moreover, the statistical analysis is burdened by all the textual parsing needed to transform chunks of text into numerical and processable data.

In this chapter, we want to tackle the problem of a new approach to evaluation campaigns, able to take into account the distributed nature of the entities involved during an evaluation campaign: data collections may reside on different servers, participants are scattered around the world, as well as assessors and organisers. Moreover, DLMSs themselves are distributed systems where the services under evaluation can be developed according to different architectural paradigms, such as Web Services (WS), Peer-To-Peer (P2P), and Grid. Finally, another innovative aspect of our approach is to provide participants with a uniform way of performing statistical analysis on their results.

In this way, not only participants benefit from standard experimental collections but also they may exploit standard tools for the analysis of the experimental results. This approach, that makes the analysis and assessment of experimental results com- parable, is quite innovative since up to now participants employed tools built on their own in order to analyse experimental results, making such analyses much more difficult to compare.

An innovative system named *Distributed Information Retrieval Evaluation Campaign Tool (DIRECT)* is being designed and developed to give an alternative to the management of data of these evaluation forums with the aim of integrating the activities among the different entities and giving the tools to make the activities themselves more interactive.

The goal will be to create a unified view of this kind of evaluation forums and to propose an innovative architecture able to provide dedicated services and tools to make available data and documents. In particular, the evaluation of information access components of a DLMS will not be calculated by means of standard IR measures only, but also with an integrated tools for statistical analysis available to all participants of evaluation forums. Since we are going to provide and manage the technical infrastructure, both hardware and software, for the *Cross-Language Evaluation Forum (CLEF)* 2005 ongoing evaluation campaign, the possibility of testing and evaluating the DIRECT system in real settings will be exploited.

DIRECT ARCHITECTURE AND FUNCTIONALITIES

Figure shows the architecture of DIRECT. It consists of three layers—data, application and interface logic layers—which allow us to achieve a better modularity and to properly describe the behaviour of DIRECT by isolating specific functionalities at the proper layer. Moreover, this decomposition makes it possible to clearly define the functioning of DIRECT by means of communication paths that connect the different components. In this way, the behaviour of the system is designed in a modular and extensible way. We briefly describe the architecture shown in figure, from bottom to top:

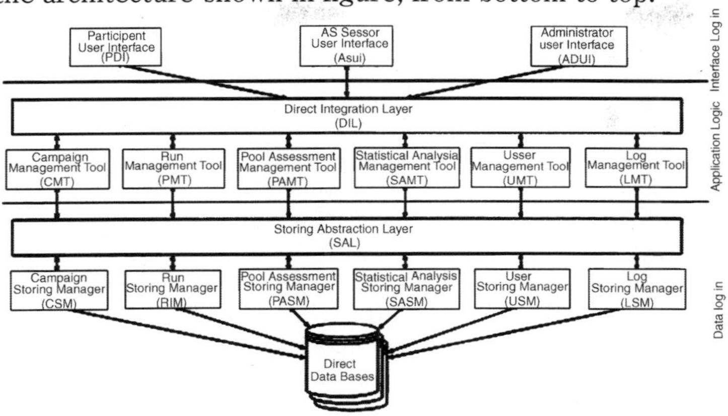

Fig. Direct Architecture.

Data Logic

The data logic layer deals with the actual storage of the different information objects coming from the upper layers. There is a set of 'storing managers' which translate the requests that arrive from the upper layers into *Structured Query Language (SQL)* statements to operate on the underlying *DataBase Management Systems (DBMSs)*. The heart of the data logic is an *Entity—Relationship (ER)* schema that is designed to fulfill the requirements to manage a complex evaluation forums. Note that, due to huge quantity of data to be managed, it may be necessary to split the underlying database across different DBMSs, thus dealing with a distributed database. Finally, on top of the various 'storing managers' there is the *Storing Abstraction Layer (SAL)* which hides the details about the storage management from the upper layers. In this way, the addition of a new 'storing manager' is totally transparent for the upper layers.

Application Logic

The application logic layer deals with the flow of operations within DIRECT. It provides a set of tools capable of managing high-level tasks. For example, the *Statistical Analysis Management Tool (SAMT)* offers the functionalities needed to conduct a statistical analysis on a set of runs; conducting a statistical analysis involves, in the data logic layer, both the *Run Storing Manager (RSM)* to have access to the experimental data, and the *Statistical Analysis Storing Manager (SASM)* to store the results of such analysis. Finally, the *DIRECT Integration Layer (DIL)* provides the interface logic layer with a uniform and integrated access to the various tools. As we noticed in the case of the SAL, thanks to the DIL also the addition of new tools is transparent for the interface logic layer.

Interface Logic

It is the highest level of the architecture, and it is the access point for the user to interact with the system. It provides specialised *User Interfaces (UIs)* for different types of users, that are the participants, the assessors, and the administrators of DIRECT.

P-INDEX — AN INDEX FOR GRAPH STRUCTURED DATA

In the context of the Semantic Web, *p*-operators are proposed in as a mean to explore complex relationships between entities. The problem of searching for the complex relationships can be modeled as the process of searching paths in a graph where entities represent vertices and edges the relationships between them. The notion of complex relationships can be also identified in bibliographic digital libraries, where entities could represent publications and the relationship can represent references or citations between them.

As proposed in, we recognise two kinds of complex relationships. The first one is represented by *a path* lying between two inspected vertices. Speaking in terms of publications this means that one publication indirectly cites or references the other publication — a chain of publications can be built so that one cites another. The second type of complex relationship is *a connection* between two inspected vertices. This symbolises a fact that the two inspected publications indirectly cite one common publication. The knowledge about complex relationships among publications can be used for example for ranking the result of the search for publications. Another use case can be an automated recommendation of publications based on the preferred set of publications. For that reason, this chapter presents an indexing technique called the *p*-index that enables efficient discovery of complex relationships in large collections of graph structured data.

MOTIVATION

The graph theory proved that a very handy representation of a directed graph is its adjacency matrix because using matrix algebra we can comfortably study the graph's properties. For instance, if the adjacency matrix is powered by two, each field in the resulting matrix contains a number of paths of length two lying between every pair of vertices in the original graph. If the computation continued, the result would contain amounts of all paths of an arbitrary length. The main difficulty of a matrix representation of a graph is that its use is limited to fairly small graphs, because the matrix grows in the quadratic space and the multisplication operation on matrices has even cubic time complexity. Therefore, we introduce graph transformations to enable the use of the matrix approach to graphs of arbitrary size.

OVERVIEW OF THE *P*-INDEX

The main idea of the approach introduced in this chapter is to identify certain units in the indexed graph such that when replaced by single vertices, they would form a new smaller graph that would be easier to navigate, but yet having the same properties as the original graph had. The aim is to enable the use of the matrix approach on $SG(G)$ while it is not possible to use it on G. And because $SG(G)$ is also a regular graph it can be again segmented.

Proposed Graph Transformations

The first graph transformation used is *a graph to a forest of trees* transformation. The result of this transformation is a set of trees together with a set of transitions among those trees. A lot of indexing techniques for trees have been developed for efficient navigation inside a tree. We have chosen the tree signatures. They enable fast navigation inside a tree using simple and cheap operation — a comparison of preorder and post order ranks of nodes in the particular tree. The ranks are represented by integer numbers thus the comparison of the particular ranks takes $O(1)$ time. If we take a closer look on the result of this transformation we see that the acquired trees form vertices and transitions among them edges in a new graph. This new graph represents the original graph but in a simplified way.

Certainly, any path that was in the original graph is also in the new graph and vice versa. If the size of the newly acquired graph is small enough to create the matrix representation of it, the job is done. The index would be then composed of the tree signatures and the matrix describing all paths among those trees. However, we would like to index a graph of an arbitrary size. An obvious idea is to use this graph transformation recursively onto the newly acquired graph as long as we get a graph of a desired size. But an evaluation of the recursive application of this transformation in showed that after few applications this method does not lead to a significant reduction of the amount of nodes in the new graph.

Therefore, another graph transformation has to be used to lower the amount of vertices in the new graph. The transformation that we have chosen for this is *vertex clustering*. It reduces the amount of vertices in a graph by collapsing subgraphs (segments) into single vertices. Also in the new graph acquired by this transformation is true that any path in the new graph is contained in the original one and vice versa. This graph transformation represents the graph segmentation, thus, the new graph is a segment graph of the original graph. The reason why the transformation of graph to forest of trees is used is to make more dense graph out of a sparse graph. The tree signatures can be applied to tree of any size. This kind of transformation is used only once as a first step in the process. In all following steps only the vertex clustering is used because the number of vertices in the transformed graph does not decrease in a linear way but rather converges to a certain limit.

Adjacency Matrix of Paths

A path type adjacency matrix is a modification of a usual adjacency matrix.

It is designed to represent a graph in a path oriented way. Initially, each field of our matrix contains a path consisting of a single edge whenever there exists such an edge between two vertices in the graph. The convenience it presents over the usual adjacency matrix is that after the transitive closure of the path type matrix is computed, the fields contain not just an amount of paths lying between any two vertices, but also the paths themselves. Naturally, the mathematical operations on numbers + and ¤ are replaced by the respective operations on paths - union and concatenation.

Outline of *p*-index's Structure

Let present a brief example of a three level *p*-index visualised in figure. Firstly, the graph to a forest of trees transformation is applied to the graph that is indexed. Subsequently, a tree signature is created to each acquired tree. The new graph, where vertices represent trees and edges represent transitions among trees, is then decomposed by the vertex clustering transformation.

For each collapsed subgraph, its path type adjacency matrix is created. After that a path type adjacency matrix is created to the newly acquired graph, where vertices represent collapsed subgraphs. Hence, the *p*-index has the following structure. On the lowest level, there are tree signatures of trees obtained by the first graph transformation. Above that is a set of path type matrices describing each collapsed subgraph. And at the topmost level is a single path type matrix used to navigate among the subgraphs. This particular example is visualised in figure.

PRELIMINARY EXPERIMENTAL EVALUATION

An experimental implementation of the *p*-index was built to evaluate its properties. The measurable aspects are the time necessary to build the *p*-index and the time consumed to discover the relationships. Furthermore, a proportion of accessible vertices from the inspected vertex in the indexed graph to the amount of actually accessed vertices in the *p*-index is measured. Also a total number of accesses to vertices in the *p*-index is recorded. The both graphs used to evaluate the *p*-index properties are a part of the Open Directory Project representing the connections among categories. They mostly differ in the size and density. We have run the tests on a usual desktop computer with a 3 GHz Pentium 4 processor and 2 gigabytes of RAM.

Table 6.1 Experiment Evaluation of *p*-index

The *p*-index was tested on two graphs that differed in the amount of vertices they contained. As the total number of edges in each graph proposes, the smaller graph is denser than the bigger one. The evaluation consisted of a set of executions of a path relationship search. Thus, we used the index to retrieve all paths lying between the two inspected vertices. The result of this search was either the empty set or all paths lying between the two vertices. During each execution the total number of accesses to vertices in the p-index was recorded to measure the efficiency of designed algorithms. The number of accessible vertices indicates the amount of vertices that can be accessed in the indexed graph from the starting vertex. Number of accessed vertices represents an amount of actually accessed vertices in the p-index.

The experimental evaluation concludes that the sparser the graph is the better results we get from the p-index. Why is that true indicates the total number of accesses to vertices in the p-index. We found out that not every segment sequence that is a product of the transitive closure computation of $SG(G)$ does represent some path on the lower level (in G). And this happens more often in the denser graph causing a huge amounts of these false segment sequences to be checked by the search algorithm.

4

Digital Library and Digitization

DIGITAL LIBRARY

Perception of the term "digital library" is a bit like perception of the elephant in the poem 'The Six Blind Men and the Elephant" where each of six blind men gives different descriptions of the elephant according the elephant's body part they touch. The library communities have also used different terms over the years to denote this concept. The idea of easy and fingertip access of information conceptualized as digital library begins with Vannenar Bush's MEMEX MACHINE and has continued to evolve with each advances in information technology.

Today people give different definitions of digital library in arrays of terms such as electronic library, virtual library, hybrid library, library without walls, cybrary, spatial library, digitize collection, library of the future etc. While these are not necessarily synonyms of digital library, they do have some aspects in common and the term digital library is one most widely accepted. Digital library may be treated as repositories of massive amount of information content in digital form in different servers on diverse format permitting access over different electronic networks.

According to Edward Fox (Editor of ASIS and commu-nication of ACM) a digital library is an assemblage of digital computers, storage and cummunication machinery together with the context and software needed to produce emulate and extend those services provided by conventional libraries based on paper and other material means of collecting, cataloguing, finding and disseminating information... A full service digital library must accomplish all essential services of traditional libraries and also exploit the well advantages of digital storage, searching and communication.Digital Library Federation in USA define digital library as "organizations that provide the resources, including the specialized staff, to select, structure, offer intellectual access to, interpret, distribute, preserve the integrity of ensure the persistence over time of collections of digital works so that they are readily and economically available for use by a defined community or set of communities".

A digital library "is that set of global internet worked libraries" that includes the following criteria:

- A collection of text, images, or data in digitized form
- A set of systems for indexing and navigating or retrieving in that collection.
- One or more defined community of users.

Christine Borgman opines that the term digital library has various meanings.

However, for her, it clusters around two themes:

- From research perspective, digital libraries are content collected and organized on behalf of users' communities,
- From library-practice perspective; digital libraries are institutions or organizations that provide information services in digital forms for the enhancement of information storage and retrieval system.

Similarly, Levy points out that "notably for librarians, digital library refers most directly to institutions that oversee digital collections. For the other professionals like computers and information scientist digital library refers to digital collections without regard to institutional settings in which they might be managed. More comprehensively, in digital libraries the information arrives as needed at the users' screen like the attending waiter ever filling the water glass before the glass is empty. However, these defined perceptions are likely to evolve as activities move research development endeavours to full scale practice.

Digitization, now a day, has become one of the key activities in libraries. These two terms Digital library and Digitization goes hand in hand, like the two sides of a coin, the elements that form both concepts can not be separated. Digitization can be defined as the digital conversion of library and other archival materials. Digitization is also a technique for data transmission at a very high speed.

It is the conversion of any fixed analog media – books, journals, and photos, paintings into electronic form through scanning, sampling, or even re-keying. Digitization provide solution to traditional library problems such as conservation, preservation, storage space, remote access to information collection, acquisition of original digital works created by other publishers, agencies, access to external digital materials and resources.

WHY DIGITAL LIBRARIES

Libraries have changed with time to time from mere static storehouse to dynamic service centers, serving all professionals and Non--professionals utilizing useful need base collection. The emphasis of the users has also shifted from micro document to micro piece of information with the changed of the medium from clay tablets to paper and now to electronic and optical media. The worlds of both communication and production of information are changing at a very fast pace and the conver-gence of these had huge impact on libraries. All this changes in libraries is due to the impact of information technology and this impact is seen in the form of digital library. Due to information explosion during the last few decades many techniques and technologies have emerged for handling the information more readily, speedily and effectively. Many computer specialists also succeeded in integrating text, graphics, audio, animations, and video converted into a digital media. People feel enthused to read from computer screens.

Varieties of software are now available which are capable of manipulating and rendering information. At the same time price of personal computers are getting cheaper and cheaper to a very affordable cost. Besides allowing remote access, bringing the diverse material together from scattered locations, solving space problems, raising the profile of institution, enhancing preservation, increasing in retrieval and dissemi-nation of information in digital libraries system, people in the library professionals shows increased concern in building digital library. Dwindling budgets of library and high information demand are also another factor.

NEED AND IMPORTANCE OF DIGITAL LIBRARY

We are in the midst of information explosion and information technology revolution leading to the emergence of electronics information era. Rapid advances in information processing, storage and communication technologies have revolutionized the role of libraries worldwide in disseminating information services to their users. Libraries therefore, are reconsolidating their services and information products, incorporating new technologies of upgrading information resources, changing information objects, models of communication and information delivery in order to add value to their services and to satisfy the changing information needs of user community.

In fact, impact of information technology on libraries and its users is an important factor for transformation of traditional organizational structure into new institutional entities. Infor-mation seekers are also no longer statisfied with the printed materials alone.

As a result the users demand for information delivery in digital form, considered more dynamic in electronics multimedia documents, at their desktop are increasing day by day.

Thus, there is a need to develop digital library and to adopt electronic media for its collection development so that it can fulfill the requirement of users. Libraries and other library professionals should make efforts for setting digital libraries and conversion of resources into a digitized format.

Some important features of Digital library can be summarized as:

- To introduce new service and material
- To provide remote access to information resources that are expensive and rare and easy searching that are impractical manually;

- To facilitate in the management of digital content
- To minimize in handling of rare and unique collection of traditional library
- To improve access to the latest information at a very high speed
- To support search and retrieval
- To provide users friendly interface
- To support formal and informal learning
- To reduce errors that would have occurred in the manual systems scientifically because of bar code
- Cost effectiveness and affordable and
- To raise library profile
- Digital libraries as global multilingual expository of data must attract people from all walks of life regardless of geographical locations.

Technical Architecture

Technical architecture is another factor that need enhance-ment for digital information service system. Therefore, libraries need to upgrade current technical architecture to accommodate digital materials.

The architecture includes the following components:

- Local Network with high speed and fast connection to internet
- Full text search engines to index and provide access to resources
- Variety of servers (FTP and Web server)
- Electronic documents management functions that will support digital resources
- A variety system functions to coordinate mange the entry and retrieve data
- Local Library system with adequate PCs having LAN
- Well trained and manpower
- Relational databases that support a variety of digital formats

Present Status of Library in Manipur in the present technological environment

In library information system, information technology has had a clear and persuasive impact in almost every area of the library. The most significant development in information technology over the last few years or so is digital technology. Digital technology is revolutionizing the traditional concepts of preservation and access in library and archive communities. The applications of digital system and computing system in the libraries have been a subject of interest to present day professional librarians.

More recently the libraries have sought to implement increasingly complex solution that involved distributed networking and access to remote information resources. During the eighties, the whole focus of the librarians shifted towards library automation but in the nineties it has shifted towards digitization. The phrase library automation has been generally accepted within the profession to encompass early automation activities, yet it does not do justice to the current state of affaires as libraries have move well beyond the automation of internal procedures. In Manipur, however, applications of technologies in libraries are lagging far behind.

There are two university libraries, 74 affiliated colleges, nine public libraries, one state central library at Imphal and others at different districts of Manipur and many high and higher secondary schools libraries. But most of the libraries function in the traditional way with conventional printed shelf collection except some libraries like Manipur University library, Central Agricultural Library, RIMS Library, DOEACC Library etc. These libraries have initiated automation. Manipur University Library started automation since 1989 in the areas such as cataloguing, serial control, information retrieval and circulation recently.

This library provides internet facility, OPAC and has become one of the important nodes in the academic libraries system. As far as college libraries are concerned collections of information resources which support the faculty and students are not up to the mark because of lack planned systematic approach to the development of resources. Many of college libraries built up their collection of printed materials as activities and services are yet to be automated. Only one college library *i.e.* Modern College library has started Data entry using CDS/ISIS.

Books are still the only important channel for dissemi-nation of information. The librarian and other supporting professional staff are not well qualified and trained with the new modern technology. As far as infrastructures are concern a large majority of libraries have not yet automated their activities as they are handicapped to switch over to computeri-zation and modernization because of lack of infrastructural facilities like computer hardware, software, and human-ware. And most of the libraries are not provided internet facility.

Regarding school and higher secondary school libraries, majority of school libraries are not able to provide even the facilities of a traditional library. From the discussion it is evident that the libraries in Manipur, except some, automation of the operations and services progressing very slowly.

Automation as well as conversion of digital library will not be possible within five year though plan for automation exist. In Manipur it is not an easy task to develop digital library system as automation in the library is totally absent. Keeping in views of the reasons, authority should take initiative for promoting library automation by implementing new IT in the libraries of Manipur so that users from different communities can get the universe of knowledge available in the digital format.

PROBLEMS

Problems faced while entering into a digital libraries systems in Manipur can be summarized as:

- Libraries exist only in the traditional form and there is no electronic library/digital resource;
- Most of the libraries function with inadequate number professional staff required for smooth functioning and there is a general unwillingness to develop digital library system;
- Even if the librarian and some professionals are qualified they certainly lag behind because of lack of awareness about value of information, cooperation and coordination in the resource building and sharing of information and poor communication skill;
- Libraries lack standardization of methods due to unwillingness to adapt to new requirements;
- Presently large majority of library have no computer and no internet facility and other infrastructural facilities required to exploit the opportunities provided by electronic media. Therefore, the best use of electronic publication on-line and network access are not possible;
- Total absence of hardware, software and trained human power is another reason;
- A highly irregular and unpredictable power supply; and
- Lack of financial support due to the acute financial problem the state is facing.

In fact, the main problems faced seem to be lack of financial resources and lack of computer education without which automation in the libraries are not possible.

PROSPECT

The dawn of information revolution is considered to be one of the marvelous achievements of the 20th century. The rapid growth and development of IT has resulted in the development of digital library, tools and skill relating to encoding information objects in digital format. The application of digital technologies within the library comes along with the development of computer technology. Keeping the points in view it is necessary to consider some perspective of digital library.

Digital library not only creates and develops modern libraries but also transforms many existing libraries. Digital Library introduced the concept of hypertext, facilitates networking in order to communicate and exchange digital information from source location to destination. It also facilitates preservation, storage, and communication of diverse multimedia objects but also provides intensive access from multiple locations and enrich teaching and learning environment which is not possible with the traditional library. Due to information explosion and existence of information society, everybody is aware of the newly developed technologies. This new developments are reflected in LIS education and in those libraries with existing infrastructure, services and network.

In fact, there is a complete change in activities, role of library, librarians and other professionals (staff). Most of the librarians in Manipur have now entered in the technological era of communication dominated by film and electronic media. The libraries are expected to be an automated information system having pervasive impact in almost every areas of library-be it the online catalogue, online database, online searching, document delivery, inter library loan, circulation etc. Clearly, the impact of automated system in libraries has been pervasive and significant.

ORIGINS OF THE "DIGITAL LIBRARY"

The decision in the early 1990's to extend the notion of the library forward into the emerging digital information context was the result of the collective and distinctive assumptions of three stakeholder communities: the funders, the technology-focused researchers, and the practitioner library community.

Each community responded to the opportunities offered by emerging networked computing technologies in a unique, opportunistic (and sometimes myopic) fashion. While they all agreed that "digital libraries" was an appropriate term for the new endeavour, they each had a different idea of the meaning of the term and different allegiances to the components of what they considered a library. The following parts demonstrate this "interpretive flexibility" by describing the different meanings attributed to digital libraries by the three major communities involved in the research effort.

PERSPECTIVE OF THE DIGITAL LIBRARY FUNDERS

The primary funders of digital library research in the U.S. were the NSF, within the Directorate for Computer and Information Science (CISE), DARPA, NASA, and NIH, with lesser contributions from NEH, IMLS (Institute of Museum and Library Services), and the Library of Congress. The notable characteristic of all the primary funders is their focus on technology-oriented science, in contrast to social science, humanities, or arts.

This focus is reflected in a research programme that funded mainly core computer science and its applications to networked information, with very little attention to network information as a sociotechnical phenomenon. In fact, the first phase of Digital Library Initiative (DLI) funding was exclusively technical.

This was moderated somewhat in the second phase. Influenced by the results of a 1996 NSF workshop that called for increased research on the social aspects of digital libraries, the NSF included social science research in the DLI-2 solicitation. An examination of documents published early in the digital library effort reveals the underlying assumptions and biases of the lead agencies that shaped the nature of the funding programmes and their vision of the digital libraries that would emerge from it.

Although it appeared in a visionary 1988 document from Kahn and Cerf, the term "digital libraries" was introduced into the national research agenda in February 1994 in a report from a task force on Information Infrastructure Technologies and Applications (IITA). This report was commissioned by the newly funded High Performance Computing and Communications programme, which was formed to leverage advances in computing and networking for the general social benefit.

The report defines digital libraries as follows:

> "[Digital libraries are] both technologies and applications which will lead to significant advances in the generation, storage, and use of digital information of different kinds across high speed networks. A digital library is a knowledge center without walls, open 24 hours a day and accessible by way of a network. Research areas range from advanced mass storage, online capture of multimedia data, intelligent filtering, knowledge navigation, effective user interfaces, system integration, to prototyping and technology demonstration".

The list of research areas enumerated in this statement is notable for its omission of the implications of eliminating the "walls", or a being open "24 hours a day." Clearly, the impression of the task force, or at least the only concern, was that the transfer of information to an online form raised only technical issues and that the larger social issues raised by this transfer were either inconsequential, unforeseen, or not worthy of study.

Another report from the same era, authored by Gladney and Fox, demonstrates prevailing thinking of the time that perhaps underlies this decision by the funders to focus only on technical issues:

> "The concept "library" has been refined over several centuries. It would be injudicious to depart from what people expect merely because a digital service is replacing a material one. Except where explicit reasons suggest an improvement that is easily explained to ordinary users (*e.g.*, in query services), library services should implement a familiar model".

Implicit in this text is the assumption that the nature of the institution and the information model it entails should remain as a stable overlay on a changed technical foundation. A digital library should, by nature, imply the same notions of integrity, trust, and quality, historically associated with libraries.

Books might turn into bits, the catalogue might become an online database, and shelves might turn into repositories, but the values, structures, and practices of the "institution" should be based on a "familiar model." Even as the web continue to grow in importance and scale, the notion that digital libraries were the focus for "serious" information-oriented activities persisted.

The web was relegated to a more lowbrow status–an unfiltered mishmash of questionable and frequently objection-able content. For example, a 2001 (U.S.) President's Information Technology Advisory Committee report called the web a "rudimentary" information environment that "only hint[s] at the future of digital libraries".

Even if the funding agencies had decided that the broader implications of the transfer of information to the online environment deserved investigation, it is doubtful whether they were structurally configured to handle such investigations. In a retrospective on the Digital Libraries Initiatives, Griffin takes note of the problem that agencies such as the NSF have with research that is by nature long-term: "The programme funding models did not work optimally, particularly for the mid-size, longer-term, interdisciplinary research and test bed projects."

PERSPECTIVE OF THE COMPUTER SCIENCE RESEARCH COMMUNITY

The computer science research community had every incentive to follow the funding agencies in this selective interpretation of digital library research. The DL initiatives were a new and relatively large stream of funding for extending their pre-existing database and information retrieval research into a new application area.

As stated by researchers: "The computer scientists] could see, or at least imagine, *how current library functions would be moved forward by an injection of computing insight*". The computer scientists who dominated DL research had little interest in examining the nature of "current library functions" or in understanding how the "injection of computing insight" might affect the foundations of these functions. The library was really only a convenient platform for technically focused work.

Indeed as researchers noted the computer science researchers had little patience for the less technically manageable aspects, and "nagging downsides" of digital library research. For example, issues related to copyright and intellectual property were perceived as an annoyance that interfered with work on more interesting technical problems.

Furthermore, the work often required collaboration with librarians who seemed overly focused on metadata "that the computer scientists felt would be replaceable by just another clever search algorithm improvement".

In hindsight, the attraction of the computer science research community to the field of digital libraries was really not based on special allegiance to the library notion, but was just a case of following the funding. When the funding disappeared and it became obvious that the web was a more attractive, and less restrictive environment for studying and exercising emerging computer science techniques such as machine learning, many of the former prominent members of the digital library community disappeared.

PERSPECTIVE OF THE LIBRARY COMMUNITY

The "real" librarians, those with over a century-long tradition collecting, curating, and preserving books and other materials, entered the realm of digital libraries with a consider-ably more institutionally-focused definition of the library and vision of what the digital library would look like. From their perspective the library, as an institution, had successfully managed previous transitions to new media (the transition of the printed form from scrolls to the codex book to the printed book, the inclusion of recordings, etc.) and had a track record of incorporating new technology into established practices, such as the computer-based catalogue.

The "digital" library would be just another library and through all, the venerable institution would prevail:

- The functions of the librarian have always been to select the material that his constituents will require. to catalogue it so that those who would use it can know what is available and where it is. and to preserve it so that both contemporary readers and those who will follow will be able to use it...none of these tasks will disappear with the emergence of the electronic library. Somebody will have to perform them: if not the librarian, then his replacement. The anarchy of the Internet may be daunting for the neophyte, but it differs little from the bibliographic chaos that is the result of five and a half centuries of the printing press.

Because of this allegiance to the institutional basis of the library and the belief that it was a necessary component of a useful information environment, librarians vigourously resisted the encroachment of the web on the domain formally dominated by the library. For librarians the intrusion of the web into the work on digital libraries was much more difficult to integrate.

Initially, they were largely dismissive and disdainful of the web as a serious information space, declaring that the "web is not a library" and likening it to a bookstore in which "the entire stock is just piled up in the middle of the floor". As the amount of valuable content increased on the web, they responded with efforts to fold the web into standard operations, such as cataloguing.

While these efforts to catalogue the web were ultimately abandoned, they demonstrate how persistent traditional practices can be even in the face of a rapidly changing technical landscape. In summary, the application of the library concept to the uncharted and unruly context of networked information reveals the distinctly narrow and flawed assumptions of the three parties responsible for its origin and use. The funding agencies mistakenly assumed that they could fund (and shape) the development of a new information infrastructure as a mainly technical endeavour. The computer scientists followed suit by framing digital libraries by-and-large as applications of familiar distributed database problems in which "predictable, repeatable ... access and retrieval is a prime value."In fact, the unpredictability of the web and its seemingly autonomous dynamism has not only affected our perceptions of information use and management, but it has had a far-reaching effect on computer science shifting it from its deterministic, algorithmic foundations to a more probabilistic and socially-oriented focus.

Finally, the librarians assumed that they could safely wrap radically new technology and traditional organizational values and structures in the same embrace. In combination, these flawed assumptions lead to a research area that by and large treads the middle ground. At a fine granular level, it produced a number of interesting research results and applications of those results. But, at the higher level, it failed to explore the more far-reaching questions of how putting information online and giving people power over their information might change the nature of the information and the way people use it. It is useful in closing this part to quote Agre who, "Information and institutional change", spoke of the dangers of naively mixing historical forms with innovations:

> A concept of "library" that is too fully rooted in past historical forms will make innovation impossible, but a superficial concept of "library" that draws out only a few aspects of those past historical forms (for example, a library as a big container of documents) will pass over phenomena whose absence in a newly designed system may be fatal. The middle ground between the maximal and simplistic conceptions of "library" is enormous and is not easily mapped.

READING AND DIGITAL LIBRARIES

The first and most fundamental document activity is reading. "Reading" encompasses a broad range of complex and poorly understood practices involving documents, including skimming, searching, browsing, speed-reading, surfing, reviewing, and rereading. Although we often take it for granted, reading can be hard work. We use the term *active reading* to distinguish this rich collection of activities from simply looking at words on a page.

Desktop computers do not support active reading. Once expected to create a paperless office, computers have instead produced ever-increasing quantities of paper documents. Dataquest predicts printers and copiers will generate over 1012 pages in the U.S. in 1997.

This statistic suggests that people do not use computers to read. The reason for this is obvious: paper supports extended, focused, deep reading practices better. Current research on digital libraries does not address a broad range of reading activities. Instead, as David Levy points out, digital libraries support shallower, more fragmented, and less concentrated reading.

The research focus in this field is on tools for search, selection, and distillation, tools that promote identification and extraction of information fragments. Because digital library interfaces do not support active reading, people search online and then print documents to read them. This "search and print" reality contrasts with the "search and read" ideal held by researchers.

Although a dual online/paper system is not *a priori* undesirable, we will show the many advantages of an online system that enables a variety of reading practices. The XLibris active reading machine supports a broad class of reading activities by employing a "paper document metaphor" (as opposed to the desktop metaphor) that imitates the physical experience of reading and marking on paper. The paper document metaphor follows lessons learned from a number of studies comparing reading online to reading on paper, summarized below.

TANGIBILITY

Readers often move paper documents to avoid glare, to speed up handwriting, or to adjust their perspective of a text. In contrast, most computer displays are stationary while in use, so that readers must move themselves—their heads, their bodies, and their arms— rather than their display. XLibris supports paper document-like tangibility by running on tablet displays. Although XLibris has not been deployed for real use, people say that holding a page-sized display in their lap and being able to easily reposition it changes their online reading experience. The tangibility of paper documents also supports navigation. Turning paper pages seems easy and natural, and the weight and thickness of a paper document convey length and location.

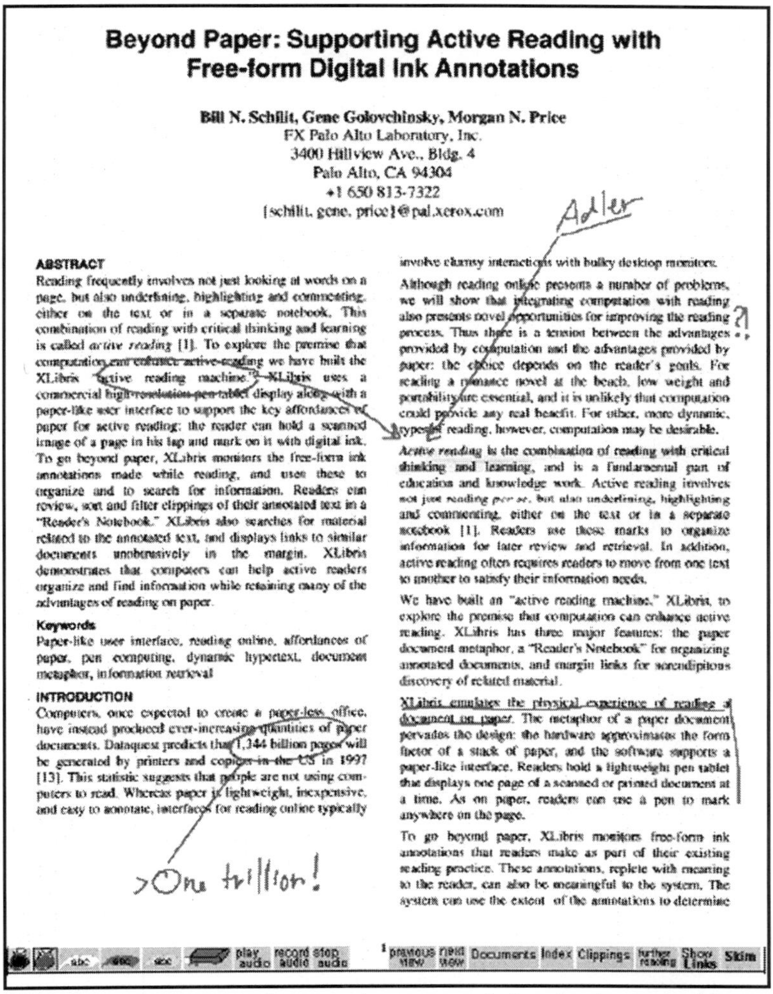

Beyond Paper: Supporting Active Reading with Free-form Digital Ink Annotations

Bill N. Schilit, Gene Golovchinsky, Morgan N. Price
FX Palo Alto Laboratory, Inc.
3400 Hillview Ave., Bldg. 4
Palo Alto, CA 94304
+1 650 813-7322
{schilit, gene, price}@pal.xerox.com

ABSTRACT

Reading frequently involves not just looking at words on a page, but also underlining, highlighting and commenting, either on the text or in a separate notebook. This combination of reading with critical thinking and learning is called *active reading* [1]. To explore the premise that computation can enhance active reading we have built the XLibris "active reading machine." XLibris uses a commercial high-resolution pen tablet display along with a paper-like user interface to support the key affordances of paper for active reading: the reader can hold a scanned image of a page in his lap and mark on it with digital ink. To go beyond paper, XLibris monitors the free-form ink annotations made while reading, and uses these to organize and to search for information. Readers can review, sort and filter clippings of their annotated text in a "Reader's Notebook." XLibris also searches for material related to the annotated text, and displays links to similar documents unobtrusively in the margin. XLibris demonstrates that computers can help active readers organize and find information while retaining many of the advantages of reading on paper.

Keywords

Paper-like user interface, reading online, affordances of paper, pen computing, dynamic hypertext, document metaphor, information retrieval

INTRODUCTION

Computers, once expected to create a paper-less office, have instead produced ever-increasing quantities of paper documents. Dataquest predicts that 1,344 billion pages will be generated by printers and copiers in the US in 1997 [13]. This statistic suggests that people are not using computers to read. Whereas paper is lightweight, inexpensive, and easy to annotate, interfaces for reading online typically involve clumsy interactions with bulky desktop monitors.

Although reading online presents a number of problems, we will show that integrating computation with reading also presents novel opportunities for improving the reading process. Thus there is a tension between the advantages provided by computation and the advantages provided by paper: the choice depends on the reader's goals. For reading a romance novel at the beach, low weight and portability are essential, and it is unlikely that computation could provide any real benefit. For other, more dynamic, types of reading, however, computation may be desirable.

Active reading is the combination of reading with critical thinking and learning, and is a fundamental part of education and knowledge work. Active reading involves not just reading *per se*, but also underlining, highlighting and commenting, either on the text or in a separate notebook [1]. Readers use these marks to organize information for later review and retrieval. In addition, active reading often requires readers to move from one text to another to satisfy their information needs.

We have built an "active reading machine," XLibris, to explore the promise that computation can enhance active reading. XLibris has three major features: the paper document metaphor, a "Reader's Notebook" for organizing annotated documents, and margin links for serendipitous discovery of related material.

XLibris emulates the physical experience of reading a document on paper. The metaphor of a paper document pervades the design: the hardware approximates the form factor of a stack of paper, and the software supports a paper-like interface. Readers hold a lightweight pen tablet that displays one page of a scanned or printed document at a time. As on paper, readers can use a pen to mark anywhere on the page.

To go beyond paper, XLibris monitors free-form ink annotations that readers make as part of their existing reading practice. These annotations, replete with meaning to the reader, can also be meaningful to the system. The system can use the extent of the annotations to determine

In XLibris, pressure strips on the case of the device provide a tangible interface for page turning: pressing on one side of a sensor moves to the next or previous page, and holding down initiates riffling through pages. The harder you press, the faster you move. A quick animated transition indicates the direction of turning.

Finally, "location guides" of varying thickness drawn in the top cor- ners of each page provide feedback about the length of the document and the reader's current location.

Page Orientation and Fixed Layout

Paper documents are laid out on fixed-size pages. The page layout often communicates the type of the document (*e.g.*,, business letter versus technical article) and where to find important information (*e.g.*,, a return address). The fixed layout also supports spatial memory and helps readers find old information.

In these and other ways, paper pages give readers an excellent "sense of the document." This sense of the document is often lost online.

Most CRT monitors cannot display a full page of text legibly, leading to awkward scrolling and zooming. Word processors and Web browsers commonly re-flow the text on a "page." And hypertext versions of paper documents can lead to disorientation and a sense of being lost. XLibris respects pages by displaying the image of a single page at a time.

Because the LCD panels we use are designed for landscape viewing, XLibris rotates the image 90° to approximate the portrait orientation of a typical printed page. XLibris stores the image of each page and the underlying text; this "image + text" file format is compatible with printed and with scanned documents.

Multiple Displays

People often work with multiple pieces of paper simultaneously, either with several pages from one document or with several documents. Most of today's computers provide multiple virtual displays through use of a windowing system. Unfortunately, the effort of managing window layout and switching among windows can interfere with reading.

Therefore XLibris displays a single page image and does not support windows. Since limiting the digital library information appliance to a single page image is problematic, we have considered a number of ways to address the need for collateral displays. Presenting two full-page images side by side, as in Book Emulator, makes text unreadable on current tablet displays, but may be feasible as LCD technology evolves. A form factor with multiple physical displays is another approach.

(Bush's vision of a Memex desk included multiple displays). In our case, to maintain mobility, a book (instead of a tablet or desk) with two opposable LCD panels may be appropriate. Weiser presents an enticing vision of ubiquitous computing with devices so cheap they can be scattered and used as paper. In the near term, however, a small number of pen computers in conjunction with nearby desktop displays or even paper may provide the most practical solution to the problem of collateral document work. In summary, XLibris employs tangibility, page orientation, and fixed layout to provide an online reading experience comparable, in many ways, to reading from paper.

FREE FORM INK ANNOTATION

"Until we provide support for smooth integration of annotation with reading, it is likely that people will continue to annotate paper materials, even as they read materials in a digital library." – Cathy Marshall The second key document activity is annotation. Knowledge work involves reading combined with categorizing, speculating, remembering, judging, or, more broadly, critical thinking. This active reading process is facilitated by underlining, highlighting and making notes on the text or in a separate notebook. Marking on paper helps readers "make the text their own" and is a common practice associated with deep understanding of written information. In a nutshell, readers write.

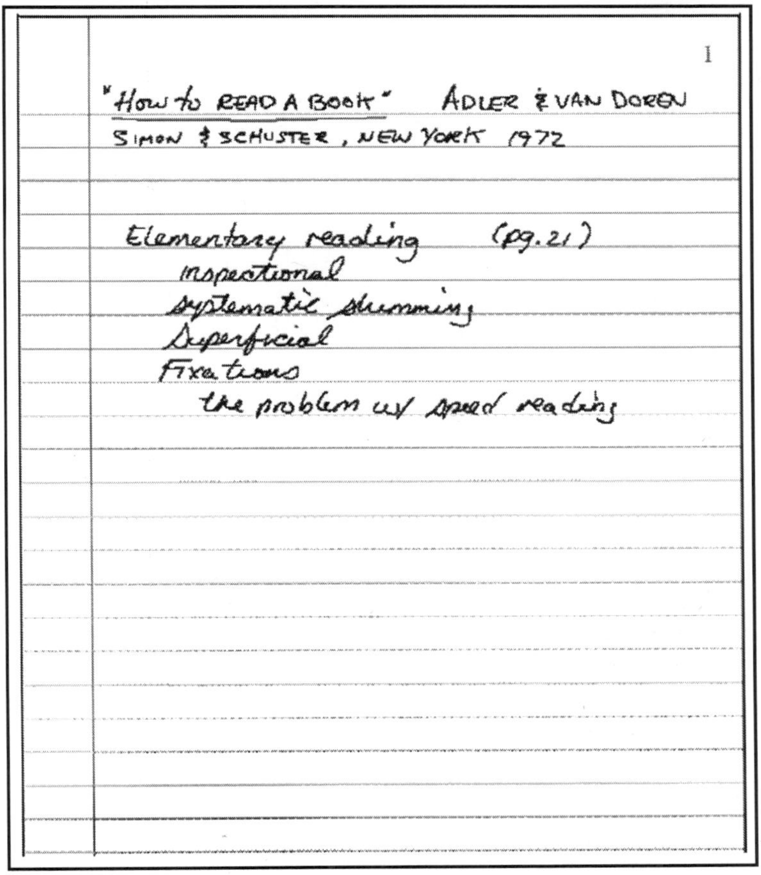

Fig. A Notebook page from XLibris.

Unfortunately, annotation online is quite different from its paper-based cousin. Interfaces for annotating often involve selecting a command, pointing with a mouse, and typing on a keyboard. They generally require much more effort than scribbling with a pen.

Text annotations are not as visually distinct as ink marks, and online annotations often cause changes in the layout of the document.

We believe that the ability to make unstructured, free-form, idiosyncratic ink marks is a crucial feature of any interface to digital libraries.

Although such marks may not have explicit meaning to the computer, they have rich semantic meaning, supporting visual and episodic memory. An essential aspect of ink on paper is its lack of modality: users can write anything they want, anywhere on the page.

In XLibris, we followed this principle by letting users scribble notes, draw figures, highlight, or annotate text, all without switching modes or applications. Readers highlight and mark-up document page images as they read or flip to a blank page in a lined notebook for more space. XLibris provides several colors of ink, several highlighter pens, and a stroke-based eraser.

THE SCOPE OF THE DIGITAL LIBRARY

INTRODUCTION AND BACKGROUND

The term "Digital Library" has a variety of potential meanings, ranging from a digitized collection of material that one might find in a traditional library through to the collection of all digital information along with the services that make that information useful to all possible users. As the WG discussed possible scenarios and challenge problems to drive our discussion of metrics, we found the need to come to at least a loose agreement on the scope of the digital library. This document is intended to serve that purpose.

Much of the question about the scope of the term is how broad a view should be taken of the digital library. Does it encompass all of information management or is a more tightly constrained view appropriate?

In this document, and for the purposes of the deliberations of the WG, we choose to take a very broad view. This is driven by the recognition that to do otherwise would require setting boundaries that are fairly artificial.

The structure of this document is as follows. In the first section, a brief definition of the term "digital library" is given, as a set of characteristics. The remainder of the document elaborates each of those characteristics.

At the kickoff meeting of the WG (held January 7-8, 1998 at Stanford University), the following definition was proposed:

The Digital Library is:

- The collection of services
- And the collection of information objects
- That support users in dealing with information objects

- And the organization and presentation of those objects
- Available directly or indirectly
- Via electronic/digital means.

The Collection of Services

A digital library is much more than just the collection of material in its repositories. It provides a variety of services to all of its users (both humans and machines, and producers, managers, and consumers of information). Thus we start our definition with the notion of the collection of services that the digital library represents.

There are a large and varied set of such services, including services to support management of collections, services to provide replicated and reliable storage, services to aid in query formulation and execution, services to assist in name resolution and location, etc.

The Collection of Information Objects

The basis for a digital library, however, must be the information objects that provide the content. A basic charact-eristic of the digital library is that the information objects are found in collections with associated management and support functions.

The types of information objects vary from traditional "documents" through to live objects (*e.g.,* sensor readings) or dynamic query results.

Supporting Users Deal with Information Objects

The goal of the digital library is to assist users by satisfying their needs and requirements for management, access, storage, and manipulation of the variety of information stored in the collection of material that represents the "holdings" of the library. Users may be humans or they may be automated processes acting on behalf of or in support of human needs.

Users also vary and include those who are "end" users (those not involved in the management and operation of the library but rather are the customers), library operators, and information "producers" who want their material available through the library.

The Organization and Presentation of those Objects

The key to effective collections management is to implement simple structural organizations and be able to present those organizations in a way that library users find useful and can understand easily.

In traditional libraries, books are primarily stored by subject, title, author, and date, and accessed by following signs to the appropriate floor, room, bookcase, shelf, and spine-labeled book. The size and relative celebration of each portion of the collection gives patrons information about the collection and can reveal the library's collection management objectives as well.

A library is created to serve a community of users. Users who participate in the digital library should be aware of its design and be able collectively to refine that design to better serve their own information needs.

Therefore, the ongoing human usability of a digital library depends on the clear and unobtrusive exposure of the library's design, its near-term goals, and its overall objectives.

Furthermore, digital libraries should continue the ongoing tradition of coupling utility with aesthetics in the organization and presentation of materials.

Available Directly or Indirectly

These information objects may be digital objects or they may be in other media (*e.g.,* paper) but represented in the library via digital means (*e.g.,* metadata). They may be available directly over the network (*e.g.,*, using a query service of the library to find and then retrieve electronically the information object) or indirectly (*e.g.,*, the result of the query may give instructions on how to obtain the object, but that is done outside the scope of the library itself.)

Electronic/digital Availability

Although the objects may not even be electronic, and although the objects themselves may not be available directly over the network, the objects must be represented electronically in some manner through, *e.g.,*, metadata or catalogs. Otherwise, we would not consider the objects to be part of the *digital* library.

The term *digital library* – denotes a collection of literature and its attendant metadata (data about data) stored electronically.

According to Herbert Samuel, a library is "thought in cold storage", and unfortunately digital libraries can be cold, isolated, impersonal places that are inaccessible to both machines and people.

Many scientists now organize their knowledge of the literature using some kind of computerized reference management system (BibTeX, EndNote, Reference Manager, RefWorks, etc.), and store their own digital libraries of full publications as PDF files. However, getting hold of both the data (the actual publication) and the metadata for any given publication can be problematic because they are often frozen in the isolated and icy deposits of scientific publishing.

Because each library and publisher has different ways of identifying and describing their metadata, using digital libraries (either manually or automatically) is much more complicated than it needs to be, and with papers in the life sciences alone (at Medline) being published at the rate of approximately two per minute, only computerized analyses can hope to be reasonably comprehensive. What then, are these digital libraries, and what services do they provide?

As far as computational Biologists are concerned, and for the purposes of this Review, we shall define a digital library more broadly as a database of scientific and technical articles, conference publications, and books that can be searched and browsed using a Web browser. As of early 2008, there is a wide range of these digital libraries, but no single source covering all information (in part because of the cost, given that there are some 25,000 peer-reviewed journals publishing some 2.5 million articles per year). Each library is isolated, balkanized, and has only partial coverage of the entire literature.

This contrasts with the historically pre-eminent library of Alexandria whose great strength was that it brought together all the useful literature then available to a single location. Like Alexandria, most digital libraries are currently *read-only*, allowing users to search and browse information, but not to *write* new information nor add personal knowledge. Other digital libraries are in danger of becoming *write-only* "data-tombs", where data are deposited but will probably never be accessed again.

Indeed, the literature itself is now so vast that most scientists 1choose to access only a fraction of it, at potentially considerable intellectual loss.

Digital libraries provide electronic access to documents, sometimes just to their abstracts and sometimes to the full text of the publication. Presently, the number of abstracts considerably exceeds the number of full-text papers, but with the emergence of Open Access initiatives (*e.g.*,, –), Institutional Repositories (*e.g.*,, –), and the like, this is set to change considerably.

This is very important, as much additional information exists in full papers that is not seen in abstracts, and, in addition, full papers that are available electronically are likely to be much more widely read and cited –. The format of the full text of such documents can vary significantly among publishers.

Such formats can be described using a Document Type Definition (DTD), *e.g.*,, that provided by the (U.S.) National Library of Medicine and, since not all publishers (especially those of Non--biomedical material) conform to the NLM DTD, this can considerably affect the types of analysis that can be done on such documents.In a similar vein, there is not yet a recognized (universal) standard for describing the metadata, although some such as the Dublin Core are becoming widely used.

Since all of these libraries are available on the Web, increasing numbers of tools for managing digital libraries are also Web-based.

They rely on Uniform Resource Identifiers (URIs or "links") to identify, name, and locate resources such as publications and their authors. By using simple URIs, standard Web browser technology, and the emerging methods of the next generation Web or "Web 2.0", it has become possible for digital libraries to become not just *read-only* or *write-only*, but both *read–write*.

These applications allow users to add personal metadata, notes, and keywords (simple labels or "tags",) to help manage, navigate, and share their personal collections. This small but significant change is helping to improve digital libraries in three main ways: personalization, socialization, and integration.The focus of this Review is largely about searching and organizing literature data together with their metadata. For reasons of space, we do not consider in any detail issues surrounding Open Access, nor structured digital abstracts, (note the recent initiative in FEBS Letters – and the RSC's Project Prospect for whole papers).

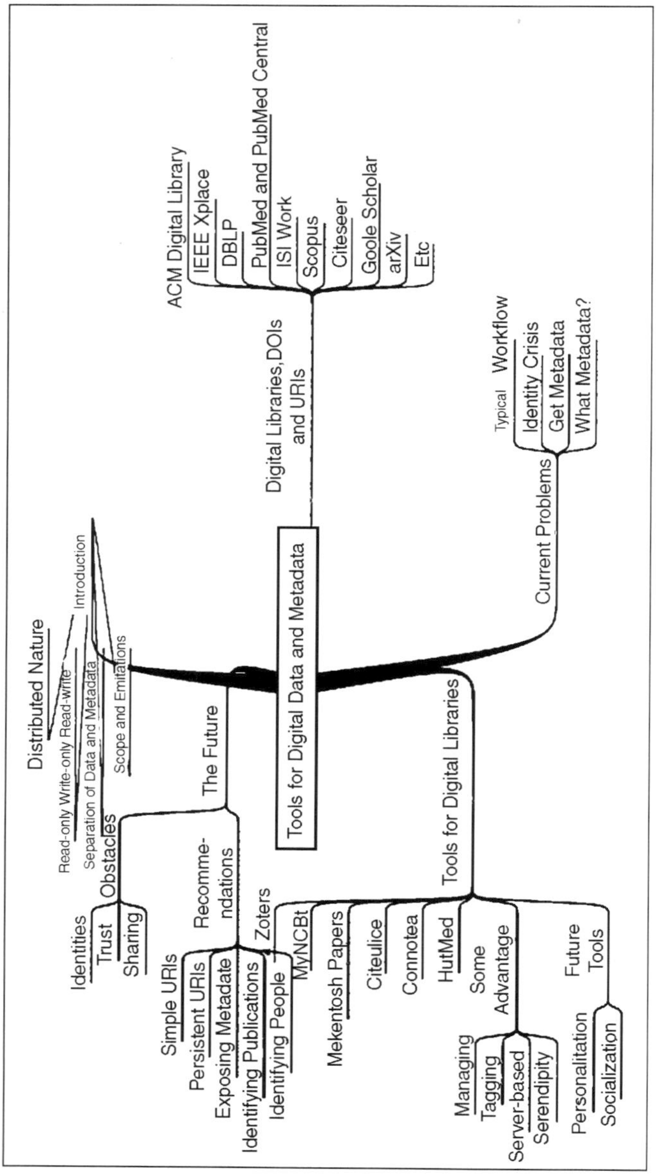

Fig. A Mind Map Summarizing the Contents of this Article in a Convenient Manner.

Neither do we discuss the many sophisticated tools for text mining and natural language processing, for joining disparate concepts for literature-based discovery, and for studies of bibliometrics literature dynamics, knowledge domains, detecting republication, and so on, all of which become considerably easier to implement only when all the necessary data are digitized and linked together with their relevant metadata.This Review is structured as follows: the section Digital Libraries, DOIs, and URIs starts by looking at the range of information in digital libraries, and how resources are identified using URIs on the Web.

In the section Problems with Digital Libraries, we consider a fairly standard workflow that serves to highlight some problems with using these libraries.

The following section, Some Tools for Defrosting Libraries, examines what Web-based tools are currently available to defrost the digital library and how they are making libraries more personal, sociable, and integrated places. Finally, the section A Future with Warmer Libraries looks at the obstacles to future progress, recommends some best practices for digital publishing, and draws conclusions.

Digital Libraries, DOIs, and URIs

Because computational biology is an interdisciplinary science, it draws on many different sources of data, information, and knowledge. Consequently, there exists a range of digital libraries on the Web identified by URIs and/or DOIs, that a typical user requires, each with its own speciality, classification, and culture, from computer science through to biomedical science.

DOIs are a specific type of URI and similar to the International Standard Book Numbers (ISBN), allowing persistent and unique identification of a publication (or indeed part of a publication), independently of its location. The range of libraries currently available on the Web is described below, starting with those that focus on specific disciplines (such as ACM, IEEE, and PubMed) through to libraries covering a broader range of scientific disciplines, such as ISI WOK and Google Scholar.

For each library, we describe the size, coverage, and style of metadata used. Where available, DOIs can be used to retrieve metadata for a given publication using a DOI resolver such as CrossRef, a linking system developed by a consortium of publishers. We illustrate with specific examples how URIs and DOIs are used by each library to identify, name, and locate resources, particularly individual publications and their author(s).

We often take URIs for granted, but these humble strings are fundamental to the way the Web works and how libraries can exploit it, so they are a crucial part of the cyberinfra-structure required for e-science on the Web. It is easy to underestimate the value of simple URIs, which can be cited in publications, bookmarked, cut-and-pasted, e-mailed, posted in blogs, added to Web pages and 1wikis –, and indexed by search engines.

Simple URIs are a key part of the current Web (version 1.0) and one of the reasons for the Web's phenomenal success since appearing in 1990. As we shall demonstrate with examples, each digital library has its own style of URI for being linked to (inbound links) and alternative styles of URI for linking out (outbound links) to publisher sites. Some of these links are simple, others more complex, and this has important consequences for both human and programmatic access to the resources these URIs identify.

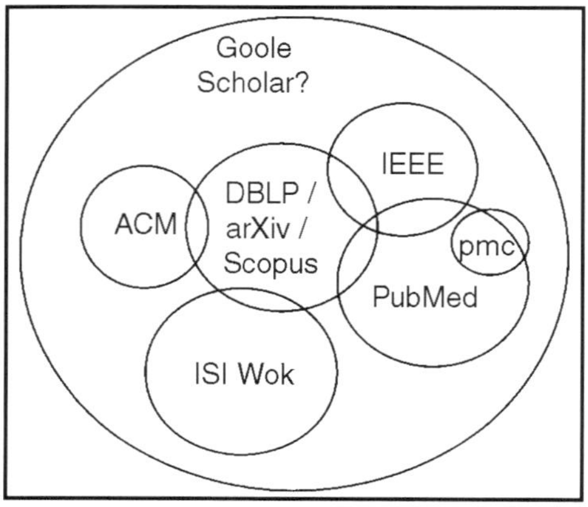

Fig. The Approximate Relative Coverage and Size of Selected Digital Libraries Described in the section Digital Libraries, DOIs, and URIs.

Of all the libraries described, Google Scholar probably has the widest coverage. However, it is currently not clear exactly how much information Google indexes, what the criteria are for inclusion in the index, and whether it subsumes other digital libraries in the way shown in the figure. Note: the size of sets (circles) in this diagram is NOT proportional to their size, and DBLP, Scopus, and arXiv are shown as a single set for clarity rather than correctness.

The ACM Digital Library

The Association for Computing Machinery (ACM), probably best known for the Turing award, makes their digital library available on the Web. The library currently contains more than 54,000 articles from 30 journals and 900 conference proceedings dating back to 1947, focusing primarily on computer science. Like many other large publishers, the ACM uses Digital Object Identifiers (DOI) to identify publications.

So, for example, a publication on scientific workflows from the 16th International World Wide Web Conference (WWW2007) is identified by the Digital Object Identifier DOI:10.1145/1242572.1242705. The last part of the DOI can be used in ACM-style URIs as follows: http://portal.acm.org/citation.cfmdoid12 42572.1242705. Metadata for publications in the ACM digital library are available from URIs in the style above as EndNote and BibTeX formats; the latter is used in the LaTeX document preparation system.

IEEE Xplore

The Institute of Electrical and Electronics Engineers (IEEE) provides access to its technical literature in electrical engineering, computer science, and electronics, through a service called Xplore. The exact size of the Xplore archive is not currently described anywhere on the IEEE Web site.

Xplore identifies publications using Digital Object Identifiers that are supplemented with a proprietary IEEE scheme for identifying publications.

So, for example, a publication on text-mining in *IEEE/ACM Transactions on Computational Biology and Bioinformatics* is identified by both the Digital Object Identifier DOI:10.1109/TBME.2007.906494 and an internal IEEE identifier 1416852. These identifiers can be used in URIs as follows: http://dx.doi.org/10.1109/TBME.2007.9064 94 and http://ieeexplore.ieee.org/search/wrappe r.jsparnumber 1416852.

Metadata for publications in IEEE Xplore are available from URIs in the style above in EndNote, Procite, and Refman. Alternatively, publication metadata are available by using a DOI resolver such as CrossRef. Currently, the IEEE offers limited facilities for its registered members to build a personal library and to share this with other users.

DBLP

The Digital Bibliography and Library Project (DBLP) created by Michael Ley, provides an index of peer-reviewed publications in computer science. Recently, DBLP has started to index many popular journals with significant computational biology content such as *Bioinformatics* and *Nucleic Acids Research*, and currently indexes about 900,000 articles, with links out to full text, labeled EE for electronic edition.

Thus an article by Russ Altman on building biological databases is identified by the URI http://dblp.uni-trier.de/rec/bibtex/jour nals/bib/Altman04. Metadata for publications in DBLP are available in BibTeX format only. Unlike some libraries that we describe later, DBLP is built largely by hand, rather than by bots and crawlers indexing Web pages without human intervention.

One of the consequences of this is that authors are disambiguated more accurately, *e.g.*,, where an author's middle initial(s) is not used or alternative first names appear in metadata. This kind of author disambiguation is particularly relevant to the naming conventions in some countries.

PubMed gov and PubMed Central

PubMed is a service provided by the National Centre for Biotechnology Information (NCBI). The PubMed database includes more than 17 million citations from more than 19,600 life science journals. The primary mechanism for identifying publications in PubMed is the PubMed identifier (PMID); so, for example, an article describing NCBI resources is identified by the URI http:/

/pubmed.gov/18045790. Publication metadata for articles in PubMed are available in a wide variety of formats including MEDLINE flat-file format and XML, conforming to the NCBI Document Type Definition, a template for creating XML documents. PubMed can be personalized using the MyNCBI application, described later in the section Some Tools for Defrosting Libraries.

PubMed Central, a subset of PubMed, provides free full-text of articles, but has lower coverage as shown in Figure. Related sites are also emerging in other countries, such as that in the UK. A URI identifying the NCBI resources article in the US PubMed Central is: http://www.pubmedce-ntral.nih.gov/article render.fcgiartid1781113. Metadata are available from URIs in PubMed Central as either XML, Dublin Core, and/or RDF by using the Open Archives Initiative (OAI) Protocol for Metadata Harvesting (PMH), a standard protocol for harvesting metadata.

For example, embedded in the page identified by the URI above, there are Dublin Core terms such as DC.Contributor, DC.Date, and DC.title, which are standard predefined terms for describing publication metadata. In addition to such standard metadata, PubMed papers are tagged or indexed according to their MeSH (Medical Subject Heading) terms, curated manually.

ISI Web of Knowledge (WoK)

ISI WoK is The Institute for Scientific Information's Web of Knowledge, a service provided by The Thomson Reuters Corporation, covering a broad range of scientific disciplines (not just computer science or biomedical science). The size of the library is somewhere in the region of 15,000,000 "objects" according to the footer displayed in pages of search results. Unfortunately, ISI WoK does not currently provide short, simple links to its content; so, for example, the URI for an NCBI publication in ISI WoK is hidden behind a script interface called cgi; this is usually displayed in the address bar of a Web browser, regardless of which publication is being viewed, as in this example: http://isiknowledge.com It is possible to extract individual URIs for publications, but regrettably they are usually too long and complicated and contain "session identifiers," which make them expire after a set period of time (usually 24 hours). Temporary and long URIs of this kind cannot be easily used by humans, and prevent inbound links to the content. ISI WoK also provides various citation tracking and analytical features such as Journal Citation Reports, which measures the impact factor, of individual journals. Metadata for publications in ISI WoK are provided in BibTeX, Procite, Refman, and EndNote. WoK provides citation tracking features, particularly calculating the H-index for a given author, as well as "citation alerts" that can automatically send e-mail when a given paper is newly cited.

Scopus.com

Scopus is a service provided by Reed Elsevier and seems to be the Digital

Library with individually the most comprehensive coverage, claiming (June 2008) >33,000,000 records (leaving aside Web pages). As far as linking is concerned, Scopus allows links <1?show=[to]?>to its content using OpenURL, which provides a standard syntax for creating URIs.

For example, the URI http://www.scopus.com/scopus/openurl/document.urlissn03029743volume3298spage350 identifes a publication from the Semantic Web conference, with the ISSN, volume, and page as part of the URI. The Scopus OpenURL link shown above is the simplest kind that can exist; many get much more complicated as more information is included in the URI, doubling the length of the one shown.

The longer and more complicated URIs become, the less likely they are to be useful for humans. Scopus also links out to content using OpenURL and provides citation tracking. Metadata can be exported in RefWorks, RIS format (EndNote, ProCite, RefMan), and plain text, etc.

Citeseer

Citeseer is a service currently funded by Microsoft Research, NASA, and the National Science Foundation (NSF), covering a broad range of scientific disciplines and more than 760,000 documents, according to Citeseer. The URI http://citeseer.ist.psu.edu/apweiler04un iprot.html identifies a paper about UniProt.

Publication metadata are available from Citeseer in BibTeX format, and citation tracking is performed annually in the Most Cited Authors feature.

Google Scholar

Google Scholar is a service provided by Google which indexes traditional scientific literature, as well as preprints and "grey" self-archived publications from selected institutional Web sites. A typical page from Google Scholar is shown in Figure.

The size and coverage of Google Scholar does not seem to have been published, and the exact method for finding and ranking citations has not yet been made completely public.

Google Scholar links out to external content using a number of methods including OpenURL, shown here by the "Find it via JRUL" (JRUL is a local library) links. Unlike, *e.g.,*, WoK, it is relatively easy to create inbound links to individual authors and publications in Google Scholar.

In contrast to some other digital libraries, Google Scholar provides simple URIs that link to different resources.

For example, http://scholar.google.com/scholarcites 98 56542662207029505 identifies citations of a publication by Tom Oinn.

At the time of writing, Google Scholar does not currently offer any specific facilities for creating a personal collection of documents or sharing these collections with other users, other than using simple links such as the one above.

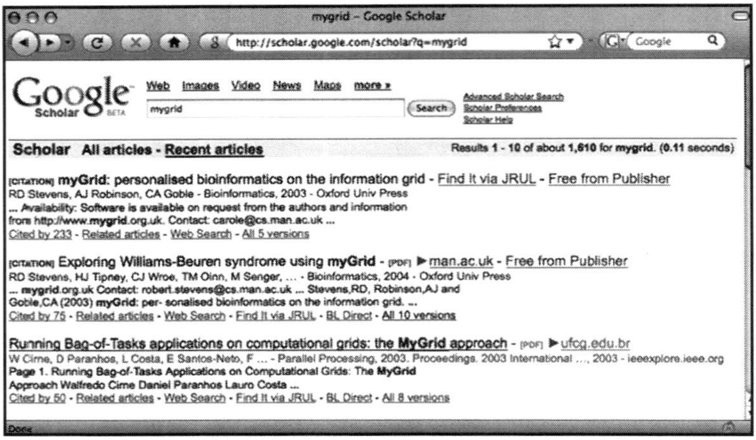

Fig. Google Scholar Search Results, Identified by http://Scholar.google.com/scholar?q = mygrid.

Publication metadata can be obtained from Google Scholar where OpenURL links are found in its search results; otherwise, metadata can be obtained by clicking through the links to their original sources.

ArXiv.org

ArXiv provides open access to more than 44,000 e-prints in physics, mathematics, computer science, quantitative biology, and statistics, and was created by Paul Ginsparg. It is a leading example of what *can* be done, although it is presently little used by biologists.

The arXiv has a different publishing model from that of the other digital libraries described in this paper, because publications are peer-reviewed *after* publication in the arXiv, rather than before publication. (A related but Non--identical strategy is pursued with PLoS ONE, where papers are peer reviewed before being made accessible, but if they do not pass peer review they do not appear.)

The arXiv is owned, operated, and funded by Cornell University and is also partially funded by the National Science Foundation. arXiv uses simple URIs to identify publications that incorporate the arXiv identifier. Because arXiv acts as a preprint server, some of its content eventually becomes available elsewhere in more traditional peer-reviewed journals. For example, an article on social networks published in *Science* is also available from http://arxiv.org/abs/cond-mat/0205383. Metadata for publications in arXiv are available in BibTeX format, with various citation-tracking features provided by the experimental citebase project. This alternative approach to manual citation counts works by calculating the number of times an individual paper has been downloaded, as with the Highly-accessed feature on BioMedCentral journals.

In a short review such as this one, it is not possible to describe every single library a computational biologist might use, because there are so many.

Also, it is surprisingly hard to define exactly what a specific digital library is because the distinction between publishers, libraries, and professional societies is not always a clean one. Thus, we have not described the digital libraries provided by Highwire, WorldCat, JSTOR, the British Library, the Association for the Advancement of Artificial Intelligence (AAAI), the Physical Review Online Archive (PROLA), and the American Chemical Society (ACS) (*e.g.,*, SciFinder).

Neither do we discuss commercial publisher-only sites such as SpringerLink, Oxford University Press, ScienceDirect, Wiley-Blackwell, Academic Press, and so on here, since *most* of this content is accessible, typically via abstracts, via the other libraries and databases described in the section on digital libraries with links out to the publishers' sites.

Summary of Libraries

Although they differ in size and coverage, all of these digital libraries provide similar basic facilities for searching and browsing publications. These features are well-documented elsewhere, so we will not describe them in detail here. With the exception of arXiv and PubMed Central, which provide full free access to entire articles, all other libraries described here provide free access to metadata (author, year, title, journal, abstract, etc.) and link to data (the full-text of a given article), which the user may or may not be licensed to view. The approximate relationship between the different libraries, as far as coverage is concerned, is shown in Figure.

Where these libraries differ is in the subscription, personalization, and citation-tracking features. So, for example, ISI WoK is a subscription-only service, not freely accessible, but which offers more extensive citation tracking features (such as ranking papers by citation counts, the impact factor and h-index) than other libraries. Other services, such as the NCBI, are available freely, and provide additional features using custom tools to freely registered users.

Other services such as Google Scholar and Citeseer are free, but currently offer no personalized view. Both ISI and Google Scholar provide services for counting and tracking citations of a given paper, which are not provided by most other libraries.These libraries also differ considerably in the nature and power of their indexing by which users can search them on specific topics of metadata. Most permit Boolean searches on the basis of authors, keywords, words in a title or abstract, and so on, though none does this in real-time, and comparatively few allow sophisticated combinations.

All of this reflects the fact that these libraries and the means of searching them evolved independently and largely in isolation. Consequently, it is generally difficult for a user to build their own personalized view of *all* the digital libraries combined into one place, although tools described in the section Some Tools for Defrosting Libraries are now beginning to make this more feasible.

Before we describe these further, we shall look at some of the current issues with using these digital libraries, as it is exactly these kinds of problems that have motivated the development of new tools. These tools, and the digital libraries they are built on, have to manage two inescapable facts:

- *Redundancy*: any given publication or author can be identified by many different URIs;
- *Representing metadata*: there are many different ways of identifying and describing

Problems Using Digital Libraries

The digital libraries outlined in the previous section all differ in their coverage, access, and features, but the abstract process of using them is more standard.

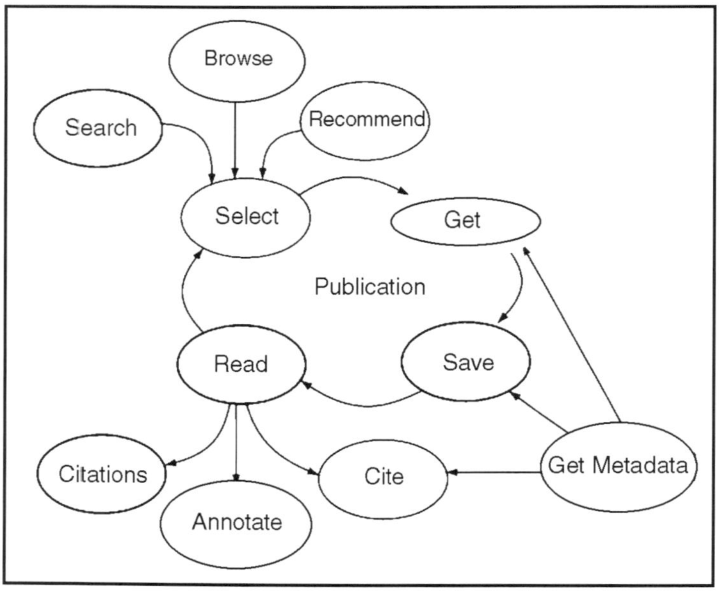

Fig. A Typical Workflow for Using a Digital Library Representing a Subset of the Literature.

Figure shows an abstract workflow for using any given digital library. We do not propose this as a universal model, which every user will follow, but provide it to illustrate some of the problems with managing data and metadata in the libraries described in the previous section on digital libraries.

Tasks represented by white nodes are normally performed exclusively by humans, while tasks shown in blue nodes can be performed wholly or partly by machines of some kind. The main problematic tasks that make digital libraries difficult to use for both machines and humans are "GET" (publication) and "GET METADATA". These are shown in bold and discussed further in the Identity Crisis section of this paper.

To begin with, a user selects a paper, which will have come proximately from one of four sources:

- Searching some digital library, "SEARCH" in Figure;
- Browsing some digital library ("BROWSE");
- A personal recommendation, word-of-mouth from colleague, etc., ("RECOMMEND");
- Referred to by reading another paper, and thus cited in its reference list ("READ").

Once a paper of interest is selected, the user:

- Retrieves the abstract and then the paper (*i.e.*,, the actual paper itself as a file), "GET" in Figure)
- They save the paper, for example by bookmarking it, storing on a hard-drive, printing off, etc., ("SAVE"). Saving often involves getting the metadata, too, ("GET METADATA"). By metadata, we again mean the basic metadata about a publication, such as the author, date, journal, volume, page number, publisher, etc. In practice, this means any information typically found in an EndNote or BibTeX entry;
- They read the paper, "READ" in Figure;
- They may annotate the paper, ("ANNOTATE");
- Finally, they may cite the paper ("CITE"). Citing requires retrieving the metadata, if these have not been retrieved already.

This abstract workflow is idealized, but highlights some problems with using current digital libraries, for both humans and machines.

- *Identity Crisis*: There is no universal method to retrieve a given paper, because there is no single way of identifying publications across all digital libraries on the Web. Although various identification schemes such as the PubMed identifier (PMID), Digital Object Identifier (DOI), ISBN, and many others, exist, there is not yet one identity system to "rule them all."
- *Get Metadata*: Publication metadata often gets "divorced" from the data it is about, and this forces users to manage each independently, a cumbersome and error-prone process. Most PDF files, for example, do not contain embedded metadata that can be easily extracted. Likewise, for publications on the Web there is no universal method to retrieve metadata. For any given publication, it is not possible for a machine or human to retrieve metadata using a standard method. Instead there are many inadequate options to choose from, which add unnecessary complexity to obtaining accurate metadata.
- *Which metadata?* There is no single way of representing metadata, and without adherence to common standards (which largely already exist, but in a plurality) there never will be. EndNote (RIS) and BibTeX are common, but again, neither format is used universally across all libraries.

We describe each of these issues more fully in the following sections.

Identity Crisis

We are suffering from an acute identity crisis in the life sciences. Just as sequence databases have trouble managing the multiple identities of sequences, digital libraries also suffer from being unable to identify individual publications and their authors.

These are essential pieces of information that make libraries easy to use, and also help to track citations, but in the present implementation they create considerable barriers to users and machines. Any single publication or author is identified by numerous different URIs.

An important task for managing these disparate collections involves reconciling and normalizing these different identity schemes, that is, calculating if two different URIs identify the same resource or not.

For example, a human can fairly easily determine that each of these URIs identify the same publication, but writing a generic programme to automate this for arbitrary URIs is more challenging: http://nar.oxfordjournals.org/cgi/conten t/full/36/suppl_1/D13; http://www.ncbi.nlm.nih.gov/pubmed/18045 790; http://www.pubmedcentral.nih.gov/article render.fcgiartid1781113; and http://dx.doi.org/10.1093/nar/gkm1000.

Where DOIs exist, they are supposed to be the definitive URI. This kind of automated disambiguation, of publications and authors, is a common requirement for building better digital libraries. Unlike the traditional paper library, machines play a much more important role in managing information.

They come in many forms, typically search-engine bots and spiders such as Googlebot, but also screen-scrapers, feed-readers workflows Programmes, Web services,, and ad hoc scripts, as well as semantic Web agents and reasoners.

They are obviously of great importance for text-mining, –, where computer algorithms plus immense computing power can outperform human intelligence on at least some tasks. Publication metadata are essential for machines and humans in many tasks, not just the disambiguation described above. Despite their importance, metadata can be frustratingly difficult to obtain.

Metadata: You can't Always GET What you Want.

As well as the problem of extracting metadata from PDFs, getting metadata for any given URI which identifies a publication is also problematic. Although the semantic Web has been proposed as a general solution to this –, it is currently a largely unrealised vision of the future.

The Open Archives Initiative mentioned previously provides a solution to this problem, though it is not adopted by all publishers. So, given an arbitrary URI, there are only two guaranteed options for getting any metadata associated with it. Using http, it is possible to for a human (or machine) to do the following.

- *Http GET the URI*: Getting any URIs described in the previous section Digital Libraries, URIs, and DOIs will usually return the entire HTML representation of the resource. This then has to be scraped or parsed for metadata, which could appear anywhere in the file and in any format. This technique works, but is not particularly robust or scalable because every time the style of a particular Web site changes, the screen-scraper will probably break as well. Some Web sites such as PubMed Central make this easier, by clearly identifying metadata in files, so they can easily be parsed by tools and machines.

- *Http HEAD the URI:* This returns metadata only, not the whole resource. These metadata will not include the author, journal, title, date, etc., of the publication but basic information such as the MIME type which indicates what the resource is (text, image, video, etc.), Last-Modified date, and so on.

The lack of an adequate method for retrieving metadata has led to proposals such as the Life Sciences Identifier (LSID), and BioGUID (Biological Globally Unique IDentifier).

These may be useful in the future if they become more widely adopted, but do not change the current state of the digital library.

As it stands, it is not possible to perform mundane and seemingly simple tasks such as, "get me all publications that fulfill some criteria and for which I have licensed access as PDF" to save locally, or "get me a specific publication and all those it immediately references".

Metadata for Publications

Even if there were a standard way to retrieve metadata for publications, there is still the problem of how to represent and describe them. In addition to EndNote (RIS) and BibTeX, there are also various XML schemas such as the U.S. Library of Congress Metadata Object Description Schema (MODS) format and RDF vocabularies, such as the Dublin Core mentioned earlier.

Having all these different metadata standards would not be a problem if they could easily be converted to and from each other, a process known as "round-tripping".

However, some conversions gain or lose information along the way. Lossy and irreversible conversions create dead-ends for metadata, and many of these mappings are Non--trivial, *e.g.*,, XML to RDF and back again.

In addition to basic metadata found in EndNote and BibTeX, there are also more complex metadata such as the inbound and outbound citations, related articles, and "supplementary" information.

The identity crisis, inability to get metadata easily, and proliferation of metadata standards are three of the main reasons that libraries are particularly difficult to use and search as automatically as one would wish. These are challenging problems to overcome, and the tools we describe in the next section tackle these problems in different ways.

Some Tools for Defrosting Libraries

Although libraries can be cold, the tools described in this section could potentially make them much warmer. They do this in two main ways. Personalization allows users to say this is my library, the sources I am interested in, my collection of references, as well as literature I have authored or co-authored.

Socialization allows users to share their personal collections and see who else is reading the same publications, including added information such as related papers with the same keyword (or "tag") and what notes other people have written about a given publication.

The ability to share data and metadata in this way is becoming increasingly important as more and more science is done by larger and more distributed teams rather than by individuals.

Such social bookmarking is already available on the Web site of publications such as the Proceedings of the National Academy of Sciences (http://www.pnas.org) and the journals published by Oxford University Press.

The result of personalization and socialization is integration of a kind that cannot be achieved by machines alone. First, we look at personalization-only style tools, then we examine tools that also allow socialization of the library through sharing.

Zotero.org and Mendeley

Zotero is an extension for the Firefox browser that enables users to manage references directly from the Web browser. As with most Web-based tools, Zotero can recognise and extract data and metadata from a range of different digital libraries. Users can bookmark publications, and then add their own personal tags and notes.

Currently, Zotero does not allow users to share their tags in the same way that more "sociable" tools such as CiteULike and Connotea do, although enhancements to the current 1.0 version of Zotero may include this feature. Zotero bookmarks cannot be identified using URIs, so it is not possible to link in from external sources to these personal collections.

Mendeley is a similar application that helps to manage and share research papers, although as well as having a Web-based browser version it is possible to store bibliographies using a more powerful desktop-based client that automatically extracts metadata from PDF files, but it can only do this where metadata is available in an amenable format.

MyNCBI

MyNCBI allows users to save PubMed searches and to customise search results. It also features an option to update and e-mail search results automatically from saved searches. MyNCBI includes extra features for highlighting search terms, filtering search results, and setting LinkOut, document delivery, and external tool preferences.Like Zotero, MyNCBI currently allows personalization only, with no socialization features. It is also limited to publications in PubMed. As we have previously seen, computational biologists frequently require access to many publications outside PubMed, so they cannot capture their entire library in MyNCBI alone. Like Zotero, it is currently not possible to link to personal collections created in MyNCBI.

Mekentosj Papers

Papers, is an application for managing electronic publications, originally designed by Alexander Griekspoor and Tom Groothuis. Although it is not a typical browser-based Web application, it can be closely integrated with several services on the Web-like Google Scholar, PubMed, ISI Web of Knowledge, and Scopus mentioned in the Digital Libraries section of this paper.

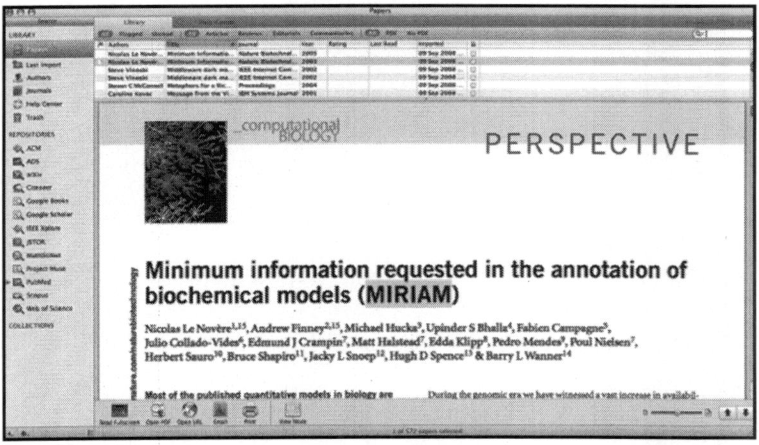

Fig. Mekentosj Papers can Organize Large Collections of Locally Stored PDF files, with their Metadata.

The Papers application demonstrates how large collections of PDF files can be managed more easily. Papers provides a simple and intuitive interface shown in Figure to a collection of PDF files stored on a personal hard drive. It looks and behaves much like Apple's iTunes, an application for managing music files, because the user does not have to know where the data (PDF file) is stored on their hard drive. Unfortunately, Papers is only available for Apple Macintosh users, and there is no version for Windows, which limits its uptake by scientists.It looks and feels much like the popular iTunes application, allowing users to manage their digital libraries by categories shown at the top. It is presently available only under Mac OS/X.

The personalization of libraries is nothing especially new or groundbreaking, and scientists have been creating personal libraries for years, for example by having their own EndNote library or BibTeX file. Tools such as Zotero, MyNCBI, and Papers just make the process of personalization simpler.

However, socialization of digital libraries *is* relatively new, in particular the ability of *multiple* users to associate arbitrary tags with URIs that represent scientific publications. This is what CiteULike, Connotea, and HubMed all allow, thereby capturing some of the supposed "wisdom of crowds" in classifying information.

CiteULike.org

CiteULike is a free online service to organize academic publications, now run by Oversity. It has been on the Web since October 2004 when its originator was attached to the University of Manchester, and was the first Web-based social bookmarking tool designed specifically for the needs of scientists and scholars. In the style of other popular social bookmarking sites such as delicious.com it allows users to bookmark or "tag" URIs with personal metadata using a Web browser; these bookmarks can then be shared using simple links such as those shown below.

The number of articles bookmarked in CiteULike is approaching 2 million, indicated by the roughly incremental numbering used. While the CiteULike software is not open source, part of the dataset it collects is currently in the public domain. Publication URIs are simple: http://www.citeulike.org/article/1708098.

CiteULike normalizes bookmarks before adding them to its database, which means it calculates whether each URI bookmarked identifies an identical publication added by another user, with an equivalent URI. This is important for social tagging applications, because part of their value is the ability to see how many people (and who) have bookmarked a given publication.

CiteULike also captures another important bibliometric, *viz.,* how many users have potentially *read* a publication, not just cited it. It seems likely that the number of readers considerably exceeds the number of citers and this can be valuable information. Time lags matter, too.

This is particularly the case with Open Access, where the "most-accessed" *Journal of Biology* paper of 2007 had in June 2008 been accessed in excess of 12,000 times, but has been cited just nine times (note that early access statistics can provide good predictors for later citations).

CiteULike provides metadata for all publications in RIS (EndNote) and BibTeX, providing a solution to the "Get Metadata" problem described in the previous section Metadata: You Can't Always GET What You Want, because every CiteULike URI for a publication has metadata associated with it in exactly the same way.

Connotea.org

Connotea is run by Nature Publishing Group and provides a similar set of features to CiteULike with some differences. It has been available on the Web since November 2004. Connotea uses MD5 hashes to store URIs that users bookmark, and normalizes them after adding them to its database, rather than before.

This post-normalization means Connotea does not always currently recognize when different URIs (such as the examples in the section Identity Crisis) identify the same publication, a bug known as "buggotea", which also affects CiteULike to a lesser extent. Like CiteULike, URIs in Connotea are simple. A publication about Connotea, for example, is identified by the URI http://www.connotea.org/uri/685b90ae66cf bc3fc8ebeed0a5def571. Metadata are available from Connotea in a wider variety of formats than from CiteULike, including RIS, BibTeX, MODS, Word 2007 bibliography, and RDF, but these have to be downloaded in bulk only, rather than individually per publication URI.

The source code for Connotea is available, and there is an API that allows software engineers to build extra functionality around Connnotea, for example the Entity Describer.

HubMed.org

HubMed is a "rewired" version of PubMed, and provides an alternative interface with extra features, such as standard metadata and Web feeds which can be subscribed to using a feed reader. This allows users to subscribe to a particular journal and receive updates when new content (*e.g.,*, a new issue) becomes available.An example URI for a publication on HubMed is http://www.hubmed.org/display.cgiuids168 45111. Like CiteULike, HubMed also solves the "Get Metadata" problem because metadata are available from each HubMed URI in a wide variety of formats not offered by NCBI. This is one of HubMed's most useful features. At the time of writing, HubMed provides metadata in RIS (for EndNote), BibTeX, RDF, and MODS style XML. Users can also log in to HubMed to use various personalized features such as tagging.

Advantages of using CiteULike and Connotea

Both CiteULike and Connotea require users to invest time and effort learning how to use them, and importing or entering bibliographic information. Why should they bother? Managing bibliographic metadata using these tools has several advantages over the common scenario of storing un-indexed PDF files locally on a personal computer.Both CiteULike and Connotea provide a single place (a Web server) where data (PDFs) and metadata can both be shared and more tightly coupled; this has the following benefits.

Searching

Easier and more sophisticated searching is possible. Conversely, given a collection of PDFs on a hard drive, it is typically difficult (or impossible) to make simple queries such as "retrieve all papers by [a given author]".

Managing

When authoring manuscripts, managing references in a Web-based repository can save some of the pain of re-typing metadata (*e.g.*, , author names) for a given publication. Provided the publication has a URI that is recognized by these tools, metadata are automatically harvested on behalf of the user, saving them time.

Tagging

Tags are just keywords, but these allow both persona-lisation and socialisation of bibliographic data, see for papers cited in this Review as an example.

Tagging of papers by other users allows Non--expert users to explore related papers in ways that may not be possible through traditional reference lists, since exploring a subject of research in which you are not expert is made easier by following links added by other potentially more expert users.

Server-based

Hosting a bibliography on a Web server means that, if and when the user moves computer, the library is still accessible. However, keeping local and remote versions requires appropriate synchronisation, which can be problematic.

Serendipity

Many serendipitous discoveries or intellectual linkages that may be determined via co-occurrences (*e.g.*, , –) exist in science, and these can be assisted by browsing links provided via social tagging.

Future Tools

The tools described here are the first wave of Web 2.0, Library 2.0, or even Science 2.0 style tools that are helping to defrost the digital library. There will certainly be plenty more in the future; for example, the Research Information Centre from the British Library is investgating innovative new tools in this area, backed by Microsoft.

Some are calling it "Web 3.0", but, whatever the name, it seems likely that we will see many digital library applications that will exploit the novel social features of platforms such as Facebook, and OpenSocial. Here they can exploit the identity mechanisms already built into those systems.

Personalization and socialization of information will increasingly blur the distinction between databases and journals, and this is especially true in computational biology where contributions are particularly of a digital nature. Scientific contributions to digital knowledge on the Web often do not fit into traditional scientific publishing models. This is usually because they are either too "small" or too "big" to fit into journals. Web logs or "blogs" are beginning to fill the "too small" gap and can be used for communicating preliminary results, discussion, opinion, supplementary material, and short technical reports – in the style of a traditional laboratory notebook. Biological databases, such as those listed in the annual NAR database review, have long filled the "too big" gap in scientific publishing.

They are clearly more significant than their publications alone. As we move in biology from a focus on hypothesis-driven to data-driven science, it is increasingly recognized that databases, software models, and instrumentation are the scientific output, rather than the conventional and more discursive descriptions of experiments and their results.In the digital library, these size differences are becoming increasingly meaningless as data, information, and knowledge become more integrated, socialized, personalized, and accessible. Take Postgenomic, for example, which aggregates scientific blog posts from a wide variety of sources. These posts can contain commentary on peer-reviewed literature and links into primary database sources. Ultimately, this means that the boundaries between the different types of information and knowledge are continually blurring, and future tools seem likely to continue this trend.

A Future with Warmer Libraries

The software described in the section Some Tools for Defrosting Libraries are a promising start to improving the digital library. They make data and metadata more integrated, personal, and sometimes more sociable. While they are a promising start, they face considerable obstacles to further success.

Obstacles to Warmer Libraries

We suggest that the main obstacles to warmer libraries are primarily social rather than technical in nature. Identity, trust, and privacy are all potential stumbling blocks to better libraries in the future.

One Identity to Rule them all?

The basic ability to identify publications and their authors uniquely is currently a huge barrier to making digital libraries more personal, sociable, and integrated. The identity of people is a twofold problem because applications need to identify people as *users* in a system and as *authors* of publications.

The lack of identity currently prevents answering very simple questions such as, 'show me all person *x* publications', unless the authors concerned are lucky enough to have unique names. Both the NCBI and CrossRef have initiatives to identify authors uniquely in digital libraries, but these have yet to be implemented successfully. The use of Single Sign-On (SSO) schemes such as Shibboleth and OpenID (the latter is used in projects such as myExperiment.org and Connotea) could have a huge impact, enabling identity and personalization, without the need for hundreds of different usernames and password combinations. It remains to be seen what their impact on scientific literature will be. Technically, there are also tough challenges for creating unique author names such as synonymy, name changes, and variable use of initials and first names, which are ongoing legacy issues.

Passing valuable data and metadata

Passing valuable data and metadata onto a third party requires that users trust the organization providing the service. For large publishers such as Nature Publishing Group, responsible for Connotea, this is not necessarily a problem.

That said, many users are liable to distrust commercial publishers when their business models may unilaterally change their data model, making the tools for accessing their data backwards incompatible, a common occurrence in bioinformatics. Smaller startup companies, who are often responsible for innovative new tools, may struggle to gain the trust of larger institutions and libraries.

Most of the software described in the section Tools for Defrosting Libraries require a considerable initial investment from users to import their libraries into the system. Users have to trust service providers that this investment has a good chance of paying off in the longer term.Scientists also have to decide how much to trust and rely on commercial for-profit companies to build and maintain the cyberinfrastructure they require for managing digital libraries. Not all commercial companies provide the best value-for-money services, and this is often true in scientific publishing.

Paul Ginsparg, for example, has estimated that arXiv operates with a cost that is 100 to 1,000 times lower than a conventional peer-reviewed publishing system. If the market will not provide scientists with the services they require, at a price they are willing to pay, they need to build and fund them themselves. The danger is that too much electronic infrastructure will be owned and run by private companies, and science will then be no better served than it was with paper-based publishing.

data Scientists want to Share

Although the practice of sharing raw data immediately, as with Open Notebook Science, is gaining ground, many users are understandably cautious about sharing information online before peer-reviewed publication.

Scientists can be highly secretive and reticent at times, selfishly not wanting to share their data and metadata freely with everyone and anyone, for fear of being "scooped" or copied without proper credit and attribution. Some tools provide security features, *e.g.,*, both CiteULike and Connotea allow users to hide references. However, this requires users to trust external providers to respect and protect their privacy, since the information is on a public server, and out of users' control.

Recommendations

Warmer digital libraries cannot be achieved by software tools alone. The digital libraries themselves can take simple steps to make data and metadata more amenable to human and automated use, making their content more useful and useable. Only with proper and better access to linked data and metadata can the tools that computational biologists require be built. We make the following recommendations to achieve this goal.

Simple URIs

URIs for human use should be as simple as possible, to allow easy linking to individual publications and their authors. Short URIs are much more likely to be used and cited than longer, more complicated URIs.

Persistent URIs

It has been noted many times before but it is worth repeatedly restating: persistent URIs make digital libraries a much more useful and usable place. Although URIs will inevitably decay many (but not all) will be preserved by the Internet Archive and every effort should be made to keep them persistent where possible.

Exposing Metadata

Publication metadata, in whatever style (EndNote, BibTeX, XML, RDF, etc.), should be transparently exposed and readily available, programmatically and manually, from URIs, HTML, and PDF files of publications.

Identifying Publications

URNs (such as Digital Object Identifiers) should be used to identify publications wherever possible. Most large publishers already do this, although there are still many confounding exceptions.

Identifying People

This problem is twofold: people need to be identified as users of a system and as authors of publications. To tackle the first issue, tools and libraries should use Single Sign On (SSO) schemes, such as OpenID to provide access to personalized features where possible, as this prevents the endless and frustrating proliferation of username/passwords to identify users in Web applications. The second requires unique author identification, an ongoing and as yet unsolved issue for digital libraries. By following these recommendations, publishers, scientists, and libraries of all kinds can add significant value to the information they manage for the digital library.

Conclusions

The future of digital libraries and the scientific publications they contain is uncertain. Rumours of the death of printed books and the death of the journal have (so far) been greatly exaggerated. In scientific publishing, we are beginning to see books and electronic journals becoming more integrated with databases, blogs, and other digital media on the Web.

These and other changes could lead to a resurgence in the role of nonprofit professional societies and institutional libraries in the scientific enterprise as the cost of publishing falls. But the outcome is still far from certain.

What is certain is the fact that we can look forward to a digital library that is more integrated, sociable, personalized, and accessible, although it may never be completely "frost-free".

Ultimately, better libraries will be a massive benefit to science. The current breed of Web-based tools we have described are facilitating this change, and future tools look set to continue this trend. Ultimately, data and metadata will become less isolated and rigid, moving more fluidly between applications on the Web. There are still issues with trust, privacy, and identity that may hinder the next generation of Web-based digital libraries, and these social problems will need addressing.

It has frequently been observed that scientists lag behind other communities in their use of the Web to communicate research, and that this is ironic given that the Web was invented in a scientific laboratory for use primarily by scientists.

Most scientists are painfully familiar with the shortcomings of the databases and software described in this Review, because these tools are at the very heart of science. Digital libraries are, and always will be, fundamental components of e-science, and of the "cyber-infrastructure", –, necessary for both computational and experimental biology in the 21st century.

DIGITAL LIBRARY AND ITS IMPACT

The origin of ICT has changed the performance and service pattern of every institution and organisation, library is not excluded from it. Impact of ICT has transformed the 'traditional library' into 'automated library'. 'Digital library' and 'virtual library' are also the gift of ICT. Many libraries have been serving as hybrid libraries. A library digital is an organised collection of electronic resources. Digital library is a very complex and dynamic entity.

It has brought phenomenal change in the information collection, preservation and dissemination scene of the world. It is a complex entity because it is completely based on ICT systems and the concept is of recent origin. Its main aim is to provide ready access to the required information at a right time to the right user with right information. The collection of digital library are not limited to document surrogates they extend to digital artifacts which cannot be represented or distributed in printed formats. Therefore, digital library is not a single unit, but a complex of multiple units that provide instant access to all information, for all sectors of society, from anywhere in the world.

Therefore, in this context, the digital library must cope up with the changing technology, information seeking behaviour of its user, user needs, etc. The day has come to adopt change management at par with information management in the library.

CHANGES IN LIBRARY AND INFORMATION CENTRE MANAGEMENT

Due to fast-paced technological change and new skill requirements, information professionals are increasingly required to renew their skills and practice in order to gain an awareness of technological advances. As a result, the profession itself exists in a state of flux alongside these emerging technologies, with traditional roles being increasingly subsumed by new skills and working environments, and, therefore, job descriptions. Thus, information professionals are now expected to be aware of and capable of using and demonstrating emerging ICTs. There is a need for additional training to augment the traditional skill and knowledge base with a competency in ICT use. Information professionals must be flexible, and adopt traditional skills to incorporate the requirements of technological advances.

Given the current situation, wherein ICTs are being continuously updated or introduced and traditional formats are being replaced or supplemented by digital formats, it seems likely that there will continue to be a need for regular training for information professionals. There is also an increased focus on communication skills, with more people involved in the electronic information environment. Information professionals are being called upon to work closely with ICT users and providers - including IT staff - and to work in collaboration with others in the profession. Some groups of users lack the necessary IT skills to obtain quality information and information professionals will therefore be called upon to act as both educators and intermediaries.

Given these circumstances, information professionals are required to have additional teaching and communication skills. Thus, it is vital for those in management positions to recognise the imperative of *continuing professional development* (CPD) and ensure that the staff is proactive in maintaining up-to-date levels of expertise. The significance of CPD in this milieu has been acknowledged by both the United Kingdom's *Chartered Institute of Library and Information Professionals* (CILIP) and the United States' *American Library Association* (ALA).

Certain active roles are necessary for change management to:

- *Establish the quality goals of the library:* Library and Information Centres (LICs) should aim to establish the quality goals for qualitative service to its user community.

- *Provide the resources to their library:* LICs should provide all necessary resources suitable in the ICT era to manage the LICs in a better way.
- *Provide the quality-oriented training to the library staff:* New generation library staff are almost trained with ICT applications to LICs but old staff and others who are novices in such applications need quality training because without quality training library staff are unable to provide automated services.
- *Stimulate quality improvement in the day to day activities of library:* This is the age of competition. Like other organisations, to survive the LICs, top management should stimulate the staff for quality improvement in the day to day activities of LICs.
- *Review progress of the library activities:* Higher management should review the progress of library activities to maintain the quality and quantity of assigned job to the staff.
- *Give recognition to library staff:* Top level management should recognise the operational level library staff for quality performance, without which they will be demoralised to perform the job in a better way.

With the change in environment the objectives need to be revised to face the challenges of future. Over a period of time, due to the impact of technological advances, research and development, economic, social and political factors, the objectives also tend to change. To adopt these changes, it is essential to state objectives and functions of information system in changing context. For this purpose the following steps should be followed.

Structure Related Changes

The structure related changes in libraries and information centres may include:

- *Change in the work design:* The work design of a traditional library is not similar to modern automated library, so a change in the work design is compulsory for the success of automated library.
- *Change in the basis of departmentalisation:* There are various departments in university and research libraries. In case of automated library, book acquisition, classification and cataloguing, circulation, serial control assignments are being done through computer with specific software instead of doing manually. Besides these departments, modern library has other departments like barcoding, RFID tagging, OPAC/web-OPAC, e-journals, e-books, CD-ROM, digital library, touch screen kiosk, server maintenance etc.
- *Change in the number of operation levels to perform various activities, routine work of library staff:* As there is a major change in the processing and service departments a change in the number of staff

in the lower level or operational level management has become essential.

- *Change in the plans, programmes, policies and procedures to and improving integration among various sections:* Due to changse in the pattern of service; plans, programmes, policies and procedures and integration within various departments it is very essential to cater to the service in a better way.
- *Change in the span of management and levels of management for effective co-ordination mechanism and flow of task:* Since the nature of job of modern automated library is more complex than traditional library, it is very difficult to manage large number of operational level staff under one middle level manager. In view of this span of management should be narrow and levels of management should be changed because top and middle level management have to be directly linked with every department to perform each department's functions in a better way as well as for effective co-ordination mechanism with every department.
- *Change in line-staff and functional authority, work group relations between people and functions to improve their ability:* Line positions are responsible for accomplishing the organisation's primary objectives; they have final authority to make decisions.

  Staff positions, on the other hand, provide suggestions and advice for the line positions but cannot, theoretically make decisions for the line positions.

  An organisation seeks to keep authority for decision making in the positions accountable for results and to preserve a clear chain of command from the top to the bottom of the organisation.

  But in the automated library system there should be no hurdle between line and staff position because anyone who is aware about a particular system can give his advice.

  It helps to improve the work group relation as well as the ability of the all levels of management. Structural changes affect relationships among the organisational positions and in the interactions among internal departments, the reporting mechanism, interactions of all sections in the library and the functional relationships.

Changes for Technological Advancement

The technology refers to the sum total of human knowledge providing ways to do the things in a better way with the help of techniques. It may include inventions and techniques affecting the ways of doing things.

Thus, technology related changes may include:

- *Use of new machines and equipments for developing new services or modifying existing services:* Many new machines and equipments, *e.g.*, computer, server, barcoding equipments, RFID tools are necessary

for developing new services or modifying existing manual services. So the awareness about the use of new machines, equipments and tools is very essential.
- *The procedure of doing things which may result in change of work process:* The methods and procedures of doing new tasks should be changed in context of old library system. So that the work process is not disrupted.
- *Introduction of technological devices like computers and computer related technologies:* Introduction of technological devices like computers and computer related technologies is necessary for automated library. Without computers and related technologies, we are unable to cater to services in automated library system.
- *Change in the existing techniques for making or doing the things in effective way or adoption of new techniques for creative work:* Automated library is ICT oriented and some technique is involved in every work. So existing techniques of traditional library management should be changed and adoption of new techniques is very essential to carry out every task and service in automated library environment.
- *Change in the methods of using new tools equipments and products:* In the traditional library system, there are only a few equipments like fumigation chamber, catalogue cabinet, book rack, cardex, journal display rack, etc. But now computer terminals, server, barcoding equipments, RFID tools, etc., equipments and products are being used, so it is very natural to change the methods of using new tools, equipments and products.

The change in the technology affects the nature of work and activities, organisational structure, the processes and the people's behaviour.

Task-related Changes

Technology related changes determine the ways to complete the task effectively and efficiently. Task related changes helps to achieve major gains in terms of cost, service and time.

Task related changes may include:
- *Identifying the steps involved in performing tasks:* It is very necessary to organise meeting with library staff at all levels to identify the steps to perform the tasks effectively.
- *Task identification:* Every task should be identified to depute the staff who is efficient in that work. So, proper task identification is the key factor to perform the task properly and to serve the user community in a better way.
- *Significance of task related changes in attaining the organisational and institutional objectives:* As the nature of library has been changed so

it is very significant to change the task which is relevant in changed atmosphere to attain the organisational and institutional objectives.

- *Identifying the skills and abilities required for the changed task:* It is very natural to identify the skills and abilities required for the changed task and to assign the specific job to the specific staff that is suitable for that particular job.
- *Improving both quality and quantity of work/ service:* For the satisfaction of our customer we should improve our quality as well as quantum of day to day work/service.
- *Bringing cost-effective solutions through maximum use of available resources:* Cost-effectiveness is concerned with the value. It asks, "This is what the service costs. Is it worth it?" So effectiveness of the resources is the key to maximum use of available resources.
- *Improving the work performance:* Quality training of staff is very essential to aware the task of each and every personnel effectively which improves the work performance.

People-related Changes

Change in any factor has an impact on human resources and human behaviour.In the context of Library and Information Science, the people-related categories include:

- *The library staff:* In case of library staff, it requires the corresponding changes to be made in the skills, abilities and the performance of the employees.
- *New investment in training and development activities so that employees acquire new skills and activities:* New skills and activities are required in automated library system so new investment in training and development is essential. Library can get the fund from UGC for this purpose by making a systematic and comprehensive proposal
- *Socialising employees into the organisational structure so that they learn the new routines on which organisational performance depends....':* Top management should meet with middle and operational level management to become aware about the every bit of work with theory and practical and to assign the job to every personnel as well as time required for this purpose. Through socialising the employees organisational efficiency can also be increased. Accordingly the change may also include –
- *Change in skill levels of the workforce:* Skill levels of each and every employee should be changed to cope up with new task.
- *Change in the training programmes to improve performance levels:* Training programme should be organised in a scientific way to sensitise the employee about every practical aspect of work and

service. So change in training programmes is essential to improve performance levels of the staff.

- *Change in attitude and values:* Change in attitude and values is a must for better performance in work and service in the changed library environment.
- *Change in behaviour and interaction pattern:* As the library scenario has changed from traditional to automated one, behavioural and interaction pattern regarding work and service should also be changed.
- *Change in technology requires different skills of the operator:* Presently, library is technology controlled. To cope up with this change, the library personnel requires different skills to carry out their own task because it is very difficult to work properly for a unskilled staff.
- *Change in the structure requires change in their position, their authority, responsibility, etc.:* Due to shift from traditional to automated library, structural change is required. For this purpose positional, authoritative and responsibility change is necessary for better performance.
- *The readers:* Readers/users/customers are our prime focus. To serve the right user to the right information at the right time, we have to organise our resources systematically through which they can collect their information himself/herself. Such a systematic arrangement helps us to work and serve the users with less human resources.

Any change in the processes demands that it should be communicated to the readers to enable them to adjust to these changes. Readers are ultimately getting the benefits of all the technological advances, procedures, services, activities as well as other resources for their satisfaction in the libraries and information centres.

Changes in Library Policies

Change in the objectives and functions of the library and information system by the planning body would directly impact the existing plans and policies of the library. Accordingly, change in plans and policies become essential. The developmental plans and policies should be in conformity with the objectives and functions of library and information system as well as the institution it serves.

Changes in Objectives and Functions of Information System

The information system in the changed environment shall aim at:

- *Ensuring maximum use of all available resources:* Top management should ensure maximum use of all available resources through cost-effective solutions.
- *Promotion and development of all units in the library:* In the automated library, to cater the service to the users in a right way, it is very essential to develop all units in a proper way.
- *Better communication of ideas to achieve the objectives in an ever*

changing environment: To communicate every new ideas to all levels of management is essential to achieve the objectives in constantly changing environment of library work and service.
- *Minimising the time, cost and efforts involved in all the activities, processes and functions:* Top level management should plan with with staff at middle and operational level for proper coordination of every function with minimum time, cost and efforts because duplicity of activities, processes and functions increases the time, cost and efforts.

In order to achieve the newly stated objectives as per the requirement of changing circumstances, certain functions are to be carried out. These functions may relate to adoption of latest technologies, use of modern tools and techniques, updating professional skill, ability and knowledge through education and training, future prospects of change in goals, objectives and functions, etc.

Librarians will need to be ready for competition and prepared to find new ways to make their skills and services distinct from those offered by the competition from media companies, publishers, internet companies, intermediary service providers and also from technologists parking on traditional library territory with technical names for old fashioned library ideas.

PROCESS OF MANAGERIAL CHANGE IN LIBRARIES AND INFORMATION CENTRES

The various steps involved in a planned change are:
- *Identifying need for change:* In the changing scenario of library, it is very essential to identify every need of users for effective planning and execution.
- *Elements to be changed:* It is very natural that the elements in traditional library and automated library are different. So top level management should foster awareness about every element of change and communicate the relevant elements to every unit.
- *Planning for change:* Every organisation/institution plans the total work procedures for proper execution. So, for the sake of efficiency all the steps for success in the changing scenario.
- *Assessing change forces:* It is very essential to assess the change forces for success of the new project/assignment.
- *Change actions:* Each and every action should be changed for proper functioning of every unit for better work and service.
- *Feedback:* This is very important aspect of every organisation/institution. Without feedback system, an organisation/institution cannot assess their customer needs and information seeking behaviour as well as their satisfaction level.

Above steps in a planned change can be applied for managing the changes in libraries and information centres.

Identifying Need for Change

Various external and internal factors necessitate change in libraries and information centres. This change may be made in staff, library building or internal layouts with infrastructural facilities, the hardware and software requirements, activities and services, etc.

While identifying the need for change, the following should be considered:

- How the change will have an effect on the system, space, staff, services, activities, etc.
- What will be the frequency and nature of change.
- How it will impact use of information sources for study, research and development.
- How it will impact users information requirements.
- How it will have an effect on the procedures, policies and programmes.

Identification of need for change depends on:

- Readers' expectations;
- Changing objectives of libraries and information centres according to changing environment;
- Policies and programmes to be implemented to achieve these objectives; and
- New challenges created by change in technology.

These steps will determine the rationale why change is essential and if change will be made, whether it will create problems or not?

Elements to be Changed

What elements of the libraries and information centres should be changed is to be decided for managing the change. It will be decided on the basis of the need for the change as well as the objectives of the change. The identification of need for change will determine the base for why change is essential whereas this step will specify what elements in the system are to be changed.Generally change is required in the structure, technology, hardware and software requirements, database design, IT infrastructure, skills of the staff, and nature of library services, etc. The nature and extent of change in the elements will further depend upon the nature of problems being faced by the libraries. Sometimes a change in one element may require change in another element, *e.g.*,, a change in any activity from manual to machine may require change in staff and their skills but at the same time change in the structure of the libraries may also be required.

Planning for Change

Planning for change includes deciding in advance about:

- When to bring change.
- Who will bring change and
- How to bring change, etc.

In the libraries and information centres change is usually required in the structure, technology, staff and services. Careful planning for bringing change in these elements is essential because "Planning looks at how the librarians and information scientists can develop the means to locate the resources which are most relevant to the need of users community, integrate these resources into their infrastructure, adopt the necessary technology and finally to anticipate the future trends in changing circumstances".

Accessing Change Forces

Various internal and external forces enable us to bring change. To manage the change effectively, it becomes necessary to ensure the co-operation of the people to create an environment in which change will be accepted by all. Change force, both internal and external, is an important consideration to anticipate and respond properly for the problems in the existing system.

Success in managing the change is possible only when we assess change forces and their impact on the efficiency and effectiveness of the existing system. If the effect of these change forces can be accessed, it becomes possible to take necessary actions for change.

Actions for Change

A distinguished social psychologist, Kurt Lewin, developed what he called 'Action Research' which happens to be a more motivational approach and a more evolutionary one.

According to him 'since most change efforts flounder because carefully expected plans are ignored or sabotaged', this first step is critical:

- Seek change when the people who are going to have to effect the changing are distressed and feel they have a problem.

The next step involves getting them to accept some procedure for exploring how the problem can be solved.The manager . . . gets the department to establish a study or mini research project on the problem:

- What kind of information is needed?
- Who will collect it?
- Who should analyse it and how; what is secret and what can be openly discussed?

The manager may have to help to get the project underway. It may require some outside technical aid, a survey, a review of old records, interviews with people in the departments.

This step means the manager must:

- Get consensus on what kinds of data and what method of collection and assessment the group will accept as valid for evolving a solution to its problem.
- Make feedback then, the critical element; it becomes a catalyst to

the people who will have to change, emphasising the discrepancy between what they believed and the reality of the situation.

- Aid people in coping, skill transfer, experimenting with new methods.
- Then the cycle is repeated.

Usually, the initial efforts won't be roaring successes; there will still be unresolved problems, and some innovations won't work as planned or hoped.

So the group which is the focus of change is encouraged to continue:

- Research/study the work flow problems – by collecting data.
- Evaluate and feedback.
- Consider further innovations.
- Get help in implementing these.
- Then check how these are working.

The manager's role is one of felicitato, so that the individuals will be motivated to change, in contrast to being told to change; Further, the process is, or ought to be, a continuing one'. The Lewin model has suggested that every change requires three steps – "the first step is unfreesing - individuals who will be affected by the impending change must be laid to recognise why the change is necessary. Next, the change itself is implemented. Finally, refreesing involves reinforcing and supporting the change so that it becomes a part of the system.

These steps can also be effectively applied in library and information centres to manage the change. At first step, the library staff as well as the reader community have to be informed about why change is essential to improve efficiency of services. At second step, they have to be made aware about new methods of working, new procedures adopted, their expected roles in changed environment, etc. We have to conceive them to recognise the basic purpose of change and ensure that they fit into the new organisational change for the benefit of all. At third step, integrating change into actual practice, the staff as well as readers has to adapt to the new environment with improved performance. They have to be protected from reverting back to the old and traditional behaviour.

Feedback

Feedback is essential to ensure that changed pattern is going to achieve the objectives with minimum time, money and energy and determine whether follow-up action is essential to ensure success of change in management. The impact of change is to be measured in terms of attainment of objectives, improvement of services, readers' increased satisfaction, employee motivation and increased level of efficiency and effectiveness of each activity, product and service.

ADVANTAGES OF DIGITIZATION

The most promising strategy for saving the intellectual and artistic content of endangered volumes is to transform or convert it to a different medium by copying it to a film or digital form. Digital archiving is a recent work of digital libraries and ensures long term storage and access. By digitizing the documents, lots of space can be saved-a stack of CD's will take much lesser space compared to the space occupied if the same information was to be stored as hard copies. In addition, Electronic-files can be accessed from any where, at any time and at a cheaper price.

MIGRATION OF DIGITAL INFORMATION

Refreshing digital information by copying it from medium to medium and the possibility of maintaining a complex set of emulators describe two distinct points on a continuum of approaches to preserving digital information. It is a periodic transfer of digital material from one hardware and software configuration to another or from one generation of computer technology to a subsequent generation.

CREATION OF INFORMATION IN DIGITAL FORM

Information objects in digital form have to be created, edited described and indexed, annotated, revised, re-created, modified, disseminated and retained for future use, by a complex interwoven community of creators and other owners, value-added services and institutional and individual users. The process of preserving digital information will vary with different kinds of objects like textual, numeric, image, video, sound, multimedia simulation etc.

ORGANIZATION OF DATA

Before scanning the documents for digitization, one has to organize the data, that is to be archived, so that the process will go on in a smooth way and the scanned data can be retrieved properly.

The most important steps which are to be followed are given below:

- Organize the data that is to be archived in to files.
- Decide how to organize the scanned file, for example-by subject, by code number, by chrono-logical order, by keyword, by author, by title etc.
- File names should be clearly identified, so that one can easily recognize the contents of the file.
- All the files or documents which are to be scanned should be kept in order.
- All the staples and paper pins, if present, should be removed.
- The paper folds and creases in the paper should be smoothened out.

Scanners

Different scanners are available for scanning the docu-ments but one has to select the scanner on the basis of materials, like

- Vacuum-fed belt scanners–can be used for fragile and odd shaped material.

- Plane-protected wide-angle scanners–can be used for book scanning.
- High-volume scanners can be used for–architectural drawings and other oversize materials.
- Flat-bed scanners can be used for–delicate and fragile materials.

METHOD OF SCANNING

After deciding the type of scanner and type of material to be used, one has to decide whether to scan the documents as images or with OCR (Optical Character Recognition).If the document is scanned with OCR, the files need to be saved in the form of application for easy editing. The benefit of OCR is that the documents are converted to an editable format. If the document is to be archived to maintain the integrity of the records for preserving, they should be scanned as images. The documents should be scanned at a minimum resolution of 150 ppi, through 300 ppi, for future use or print.

The choices available for saving the documents as images are:-

- *BMP:* Bit Map is the native image format for the windows operating system and will provide high quality images.
- *TIFF:* Tagged Image File Format is very detailed and it is supported by many operating systems.
- *JPEG:* Joint Photographic Experts Group format comprises the data, but it is enough for normal use.

STORAGE METHOD

When all the documents are scanned, they should be saved on CD zip disks or floppy disks or tape drives. For storing the files on the disks, labeled folders should be created, the disks as well as the disk cases should be labeled. In digital archives there may be many levels of storage on the basis of expected use for the retrieval. Seldom-used material may be stored offline, usually in tape media, which is less expensive. The data which is in high demand and where retrieval time is at a premium, online storage in magnetic media may serve best.

An intermediate solution is near-line storage, where the data can be stored on optical or tape media and loaded in jute box, which is more responsive to users demand than offline storage. The most promising strategy for saving the intellectual and artistic content of endangered volumes is to transform or convert it to a different medium by copying it to a film or digital form. Paper documents can be transferred to microfilms, DVD's (Digital Video Data) and CD-ROM's (Compact Disk Read Only Memory).This process is known as Archiving. Digital archives can use any of the three methods.

RETRIEVING DIGITAL ARCHIVES

Digital archives must maintain the information in a form, so that the users can access the information over the net through search engines, print, audio etc. If the archives are saved on CD's, floppies or tape mediums they should be checked periodically for content redundancy. If the digital archives need to be accessed in a distributed network environment, the digitized data should be connected to networks using proper protocols and bandwidth suitable for retrieving the information.

ARCHIVING IN INDIA

Preservation of Indian culture and literature is one of the oldest traditions of India. Thousands of years ago, Indian philosophers, scholars and poets have expounded their knowledge through treatises, sacred songs, commentaries on scriptures etc. which were recorded on specially treated palm leaves and birch barks, in the form of engravings on brass and copper plates etc. for future use. Before the invention of the printing press, the texts were handwritten by the craftsmen so that the universal knowledge can be preserved for future use. This proves our theory that Archiving has existed since long in India.

Indian National Archives

Indian National Archives department, which is located in Delhi is making efforts through various conservation methods and photo duplication processes to preserve the important documents of Indian cultural art, political and economical and literature. Department of Indian National Archives is using a unique method of rejuvenating and repairing the old documents with the help of "Cellulose acetate foil and tissue paper", which is known as "Solvent of Hand lamination". The Conservation Research Laboratory is a department of Indian National Archives has been successful in retrieving palm leaves that have gone dry since the last three decades. The National Archives is trying to ensure the longevity of documents by microfilming and reprographing.

Preservation of Indian Art

C-DAC–Center For Development of Advanced Compu-ting is trying to digitally preserve and disseminate Indian Art in the form of paintings. By using HP (Hewlett Packard) equipment to capture, store and make available via internet to the researchers and art lovers.

In this project, using comprehensive suite of H.P. Technologies, the scientists capture images in extraordinary details using digital cameras to store and process the images on workstations and to develop new colour pallets and drivers to make the individual works and print realistic reproductions on large prints. By digitizing Indian art in this way not only the art is preserved but is also made available to a larger audience.

Muktabodha Institute-Archiving of Indian Manuscripts

Muktabodha institute is working in collaboration with libraries and institutions around India to make digital images of specific, rare manuscripts and texts. The institute recognizes the importance of saving the spiritual knowledge and preserved around 871 works in microfilm format. Around 262 of these works were converted to digital image format. The institute is launching the "On-line digital library" Web site with 74 volumes of the Kashmir series of texts and studies. These volumes were originally published in Sanskrit language.

The main contribution of this institute is in the preser-vation and accessibility of photographic images of rare manuscripts and religious scriptures, so that the valuable information is more easily available to scholars around the world. At present Muktabodha discontinued the practice of microfilming the manuscripts and started producing digital images directly from the manuscripts. Since the main objective of the institute is in the dissemination of old religious literature by digitizing and preserving them, the institute decided not to face the hassels of microfilming and adopted the process of digital imagery.

COMMERCIAL ARCHIVING ORGANIZATIONS

Many commercial organizations have come up and made it easy to have any time anywhere, to access to information. These organizations provide electronic publicizing, content management, digital archiving etc. for the E-Publishers, individual purposes and institutions like libraries etc. Some of the organizations of India are the following.

DPS (Digital Publishing Solutions)

The Digital Publishing Solutions (DPS) is a Pune based organization, which has digitized so far 3.5 million pages and made digital archiving a reality. It scans the data from paper, photographs, negatives, microfilm, microfiche, transparencies and then the data digitized using the OCR and stored the digitized data in E-book format. Now the data is sold online using DX Reader, online XML reader. This organization is a approaching the libraries interested in preserving the rare books, manuscripts etc. In India DPS is working for 15 libraries, National research Institute, Indian national science academy etc.

JALVA

Mumbai based Jalva Media provides solutions for media management, indexing, content archiving data distribution, with partnership of other companies like mediasite, Ibeam Broadcasting, Madge.web, microsoft, Real and Apple. Jalva and SGI are offering better technologies like MPEG2 (moving picture experts group 2) which allows archiving data in DVD (digital versatile disk) by providing longer storage like and cross-platform compatibility.

Sampradaya

SAMPRADAYA Which means *handling down of tradition*. It serves as a resource centre by documenting the various aspects of the South Indian (Karnatic) music. It was founded in 1980, by two students of South Indian music Michael, Nixon of Veena and Ludwig, Pesch of Flute, under the guidence of late Savitri

Rajan with the purpose of documenting Sampradaya Sangeetam. The main contribution of this organization is to bring to light and preserve this music tradition by documen-tation, archiving of recordings, music books, journals, manuscripts etc. This organization is conducting in-depth taped interviews of eminent Carnatic musicians, and organizing seminars and workshops on important topics of South Indian Music. Sampradaya Audio listening library is only one of its kind in South India, where the public has free access to music recordings and archival collections. It has 8 separate music listening stations.

5

Digital Library Services

INTRODUCTION

Always library services are followed by library works. But now the advancement in information technology has brought changes in the concept of traditional library work as well as service. The recent trend and change in the information related field especially in collection, storing, processing and dissemination of information have resulted in to the evolution of digital libraries. Now most of the reference books like encyclopaedias, dictionaries, directories, hand books, etc. are published in electronic form.

Similarly about 50% of the existing secondary resources like abstracting and indexing services are available in electronic form for example, Chemical Abstracts Service, Index Medicus, Engineering Index. At present most of the digital libraries have been highlighted mainly on providing access to diverse digital information resources. The provision of personalized reference and information services is considered as one of the important characteristics of the library and information profession.

However reference services include:

- Either finding the required information on behalf of users, or assisting users in finding information themselves;
- Instruction in the use of library resources and services, and
- User guidance in which users are guided in selecting the most appropriate information sources and services.

In this changing scenario, reference works of modern libraries are influenced by a set of related technical and economic factors, especially the increasing use of technology and techniques. To cite some examples, the recent developments in the INTERNET and in Web Technologies have brought significant changes in the concept of traditional reference services and a number of web-based "expert services", that are now offered by many Non--library organisation.

Information services are provided to the users on demand as well as anticipating the user needs including various forms of current awareness and selective dissemination of informa-tion services. Such services are provided to the users to keep them abreast of the latest developments in their field of interest through on-line search services in digital information environment, even by the Non--library organisations like Dialog.

DIGITAL REFERENCE SERVICES OF ACADEMIC LIBRARIES

Web based reference services are also now being provided by academic libraries, Recently a study report on web-based reference services reflects the current practices of digital library services in seventy academic libraries of USA. The study shows that university libraries allow their patrons to put reference questions in a variety ways: 99% offer e-mail reference, 96% offer reference services by appointment while 29% of the libraries offer real-time virtual reference. These libraries use *customer relationship management* (CRM) software packages for providing web-based reference services in the virtual reference environment.

ROLE OF TECHNOLOGICAL INNOVATIONS IN IMPROVING LIBRARY SERVICES

Once librarians were considered only the custodians of the library collection, but the change in information media from print to electronic has shown the new sunrise in the life of librarians. The basic aim of a library is to meet the teaching, learning, scholarly-research and other information needs of its faculty, students and research scholars and that too effectively and with efficiency. Medical library and information professionals ensures that health care providers have access to reliable, relevant, accurate, up to date and timely information that enhances the quality of health care.

The migration of information from paper to electronic media has changed the whole nature of research. With the easy availability of office computers and the transformation of media, the popularity and usage of digital and virtual libraries has been increased. World Wide Web has totally changed the meaning of a library. Physical presence has been decreased rapidly with the invention of virtual library. There is a universal assumption that man was born innocent or ignorant and should actively seek knowledge. "Information seeking is thus a natural and necessary mechanism of human existence". Information seeking behaviour is the purposive seeking for information as a consequence of a need to satisfy some goal. In the course of seeking, the individual may interact with manual information systems or with computer-based systems.

Information seeking behaviour involves personal reasons for seeking information, the kinds of information which are being sought and the ways and sources with which needed information is being sought. Information seeking behaviour is expressed in various forms, from reading printed material to research and experimentation. Scholars, students and faculties actively seek current information from the various media available in libraries, *e.g.*

encyclopedias, journals and more currently, electronic media. In this era of 'E', a sea change can be seen in the information-seeking behaviour of the users of library. In the phase of print media, users had no choice except going to the library and search for the material in books, journals and archives for hours. Search was very time consuming in print phase. Changing needs of users have changed the role of a librarian, which has transformed a librarian into information professional. Librarians have always acted as a link between knowledge source and its users.

In this era of 'E', librarians are playing the role of an electronic middleman. They are now helping the readers in the best possible way by using the latest technology and searching techniques. Users are being connected to the information resources via Internet for hyper-links and for many more options and choices for advance search. The change in the information-seeking behaviour is the result of the invention of E-resources. Readers felt relaxed with this invention and inclination towards these resources was natural.

There are many types of E-resources like Ebooks, E-journals, various open sources, gateways and databases. Chronologically we can divide these resources specifically journals as, in-print journals, on-line journals free with print, only on-line journals, on-line databases. In the era of 'E', readers demand has become significant as they ask for an article or topic in place of a book or journal and at the same time they prefer to search online databases to fulfill their needs. With the invention E-resources quantity and quality of research both have been affected. Different search techniques are undertaken by library users to search and locate relevant information. To understand how users of libraries search and locate relevant documents, we librarians, need to understand the search techniques and what resources and sources of information they generally use and require. Information professionals and users both suffer from the problem of exhaustive information, from a wide range of sources and shortage of time to find, manage and evaluate.

Sometimes users search internet indiscriminately without knowing the facts. Here librarian plays an important role by making the users aware of the importance of the evaluation of the retrieved information by guiding them, how to retrieve, what to retrieve and how to further use that retrieved information, which is called evaluation of information. The challenge posed by the information explosion is being successfully met by electronic information sources. Further this information explosion, diversity of user need, financial crunch and impossibility of self-sufficiency has led to the formation of consortia at local, regional, national and international level.

REVIEW OF RELATED LITERATURE

The literature of understanding and meeting information needs of library users available is greatly broad ranging. An attempt has been made to cover number of works that go beyond discussions of the information seeking behaviour itself and its direct applications to closely related topics such as information seeking. Rafiq and Ameen have investigated information seeking behaviour and satisfaction level of teachers at the National Textile University, Pakistan. Respondents heavily rely on Google, yahoo and MSN, while hotmail and yahoo are preferred e-mail servers, followed by Gmail. NTU webmail is less preferred. Callen satisfying the clinical information needs of doctors in less developed countries is particularly challenging and even though improvements in IT can facilitate access to knowledge, there still exist barriers. Jackson have conducted a study to identify the sources of information currently received, information seeking behaviours, information requirements and preferences for future information provision amongst health and social care professionals. Authors assumed that print and online both formats of resources of information can prove effective in meeting information needs.

In a paper Urquhart has reported a research conducted under the JISC User Behaviour Monitoring and Evaluation Framework. Work was conducted in two strands, by two project teams, JUSTEIS and JUBILEE. It was found that information skills and experience develop across work, home and study. There is a growing use of EIS in curriculum, but practice varies between institutions and disciplines. Tutors express concern about students' ability to evaluate and use the information that they find. Assignments can promote EIS use. Ziming found that with an increasing amount of time spent reading electronic documents, a screen-based reading behaviour is emerging. The screen-based reading behaviour is characterized by more time spent on browsing and scanning, keyword spotting, one-time reading, Non--linear reading and reading more selectively, while less time is spent on in-depth reading and concentrated reading. Suriya carried out a research work to investigate how faculty members seek information from the library. Authors have concluded that that most of the respondents visited the library several times a week to meet their information needs.

Regarding the type of search made by the respondents the majority of the respondents made their search by subject. Shokeen and Kushik studied about information seeking behaviour of social scientists working in the universities located in Haryana. They reported that most of the social scientists visited the library daily. Authors further reported that social scientists of Haryana universities most frequently used current journals, textbooks and reference books. Challener investigated artists and art historians teaching in five liberal arts colleges and three universities.

It was found that they need information for teaching. The participants visit libraries frequently, usually more than one library and unlike previous reports, the majority of them are willing to ask the librarian for help. The present study is an attempt to fill some gap in literature on information-seeking behaviour in the local context.

OBJECTIVE

The main objective of this study is to know the changing needs and information-seeking behaviour of the users and further various methods and resources being adopted by the librarians to fulfill these needs, which is the result of various technological innovations. Information seeking is a fluid and situation dependent activity where a seeker's actions are influenced by access to information, perceived quality and trust in the information source. This reminds the necessity of regular study and development of information system and management information services in North Indian Medical Institutes.

This work intends to study followings in libraries as a prototype of North Indian Medical Institutes:

- To examine information seeking behaviour of library users of North Indian Medical Institutes.
- To study the problems faced by the library users of North Indian Medical Institutes while seeking and using information.
- To explore the role of the library consortia's for providing service to the library users.
- To review the use of E-databases in this era of information explosion.

HYPOTHESIS

In this study it is hypothesized that:

- Physical visit to the libraries has been declined.
- Preference of users has been shifted to online documents from print one.
- Lack of knowledge about IT is the main problem the user face in the information searching process.

METHODOLOGY AND SCOPE

There are many ways to get information. The most common research methods are: literature searches, talking with people, focus groups, personal interviews, telephone surveys, mail surveys, e-mail surveys and internet surveys. A survey has been conducted on North Indian Medical Libraries through a questionnaire to know the changes in the information-seeking behaviour and needs of the users in this era of 'E'. So the medical professionals who were enrolled as member in the various medical libraries of Chandigarh and adjoining areas were considered for the study in hand. Further it can be stated that there were about 720 active library users of these libraries, so these users were taken as the subject for the study.

Through the stratified random sampling technique 72. Questionnaire method was used as it can be completed in one of the two basic ways. Firstly, respondents were asked to complete the questionnaire with the researcher not present and thus data was collected from 72 medical professionals, out of which 33 were students and 39 were senior residents, Assistant professor and professors. Secondly, respondents were asked to complete the questionnaire by verbally responding to questions in the presence of the researcher. This variation is called a structured interview and this method was applied on 28 librarians to know their observations.

FINDINGS (USERS)

Visits to the Library

Twenty-nine respondents (40%) reported frequently visiting a medical library, 18 (25%) rarely visited and 24 (33%) never visited; one respondent did not answer this question. Respondents in their first year reported frequent visits to the library more often than those did in their second year. In the overall group, those who never or rarely visited a library indicated that E-resources are not sufficient; documents that they needed were not available or libraries were not needed because of the Internet.

So the main observation regarding visit to the library is that students visit library more frequently in their initial years of college/ institute. Overall group of users prefer to search Internet as they are not satisfied with the available E-resources in their library. They only visit the library after making sure that this required information is available in the library. This service is being provided through WEB OPAC in most of the libraries today. So hypothesis 1 stands proved.

Preference of Information Sources

Most respondents reported performing database searches independently. Among those who did their own searches, MEDLINE and PUBMED was the bestknown and most frequently used database: only 1 of 72 respondents did not know of MEDLINE. HINARI is being used by some users but the main problem with this database is that site is very slow. When asked about criteria for selecting references, the most important feature was free full-text availability with the demand of online database and formation of consortia. Regarding access to the full text, few respondents said they visited a library to check document availability and ordered articles through a library. More than half of respondents preferred electronic tools for literature searching.

Yet most indicated they preferred to print documents rather than read them online. Respondents were further asked about their preferences about the form of the document. An online database is the most preferred format (39%) in contrast to the print only format that is the least preferred one (10%). This observation directly shows the shift of the preferences of the users from print to the online formats. It is strongly supported by the findings in which online journals and databases have become the most preferred form of document as 75% users need only online resources in form or the other. Further users prefer taking print of the required information as they feel discomfort in reading directly from the screen. So hypothesis 2 stands proved.

Problems in Information Seeking

Several problems were identified in the information searching process. Many respondents found difficulties in choosing among the large number of documents retrieved in searches and lack of time was also noted as a problem. Common obstacles in the information-seeking process identified by respondents include lack of time, doubt about the existence of relevant information, retrieval of too much information and difficulties with navigation and searching. Since latest innovations have made the search easier with the latest options like E-mail alerts, send articles etc., but problem in information searching still persists due to the lack of knowledge of I.T. So the hypothesis no. 3 also stands proved.

OBSERVATIONS (LIBRARIANS)

According to the librarians, Internet search engines, E-print services, author Websites, full-text databases, electronic journals and print resources are all used to some extent by most of the users. Convenience remains the single most important factor for information retrieval. Speed of access, ability to download, print and send articles are top advantages of electronic journals for all groups. All these services and facilities are possible with the application of IT.

These observations reaffirm that important opportunities remain for librarians and libraries in providing both access to information resources and educating clinicians in how to effectively utilize such tools. Determining the relevance of a document or source is solely an individual's perspective, so the library or librarian is not a determining factor in differentiating sources. It would, however, be advantageous for a library to know and have the relevant material available for use. Library users expect their libraries to obtain new electronic resources while simultaneously maintaining or growing traditional print collections until the electronic resources are fully stable. Libraries are expecting to do this with no additional funding. Research has also concluded that information sources like electronic databases are of fundamental importance in a clinical environment giving their direct contribution to decision making in health issues, often making the difference in patient survival. Increasing demand of E-databases can be met with the formation of consortia only, as E-databases are the main feature of consortia these days. Important observation is that these databases have become addiction for the users.

Library Consortia

Information explosion, diversity of user need, financial crunch and impossibility of self-sufficiency has led to the formation of consortia at local, regional, national and international level. A library consortium is an association of a group of libraries to achieve mutually the common objective. Working in an atmosphere, which is fully affected by *Information Communication Technology* (ICT), librarians are mastering the use of electronic resources to better understand and meet the information needs of the users and further train them in using new searching tools for better search.

Consortia provide the following common benefits to the libraries involved:

- Access to otherwise un-subscribed reading materials.
- Scope for electronic archives.
- Getting deep discounts through joint pricing negotiations.
- Developing common resources databases.
- Effective document delivery system.
- Enhanced search facilities
- Better scope for developing a union catalogue among participating libraries.
- By forming consortia, librarians are contributing to the economy of their country by saving Government revenue to a great extent. Following are some of the big and successful consortia's of India.

E-DATABASE

Understanding the user needs play an important role in growing the libraries and librarians; otherwise the library profession may grey in future. To meet the increasing and advanced demands of the user, consortia are playing an important role. Secondly to avail full fruit of consortia a very sincere suggestion to library professionals is to be in touch with whole of the new technology, bridging the libraries through I.T and ICT. One should know the inside out of all the E-databases and involved I.T application.

An E-database is an organized collection of information, of a particular subject or multidisciplinary subject areas; Information within an Edatabase can be searched and retrieved electronically. Edatabase can be full-text or bibliographic. Full-text databases contain the whole content of an article such as citation information, text, illustrations, diagrams and tables. Bibliographic databases contain only citation information of an article, such as author name, journal title and publication date and page numbers. There are many Edatabases and all these databases have various features of searching techniques and tools, which are being used by the librarians to help the users in finding best information in less time.

Some of the popular medical E-databases are mentioned below:

- Academic Search Premier:
  - BMJ
  - MEDLINE
  - OVID
  - PROQUEST
  - PUBMED

- SCOPUS
- WEB OF SCIENCE
- HINARI

Almost all the reputed publishers have come up with the Edatabases like Oxford University Press, American academy of Pediatrics, Cambridge University press and many more. All these e-databases can be considered as the latest technological innovation in the field of information.

CO-OPERATIVE DIGITAL LIBRARY SERVICES

The rising cost of digital reference sources and its proper processing by the trained manpower and also the initial infrastructural investment for introducing new services in libraries have influenced different organisations to choose a co-operative model of digital reference services. As a result some co-operative projects have been launched for providing web-based reference services to the users who can ask for such services from a remote location at any time.

The Library of Congress, USA has launched the collaborative digital reference service with a mission to provide the users, anywhere anytime through an international digital network of libraries.

This network has three main components consisting of:

- Member Profiles
- Request Manager-Software for entering, routing and answering reference queries; and
- Knowledge Base-a searchable database of questions and answer sets.

In this network a participating library sends a question to the system on behalf of a user and the system looks in to the knowledge base for a match. Then a reply is sent to the relevant library through e-mail. Incase the question and its corresponding answer is not found in the knowledge base, then it is passed on to the Request Manager where using the profiles of participating libraries and their information resources collection, expertise etc, relevant query is passed on to an appropriate library.

This library receives the query, finds an answer and sends back reply to the results store and answer to the knowledge base. Thus the Knowledge Base and Request Manager become able to provide reference service in digital environment. However, the Library of Congress and OCLC have developed a co-operative "Question Point" the advanced generation of *collaborative Digital Reference Service* (CDTS) in June 2002 which integrates local as well as global electronic reference networks.

PERSONALIZED SERVICES

Most of the researches on digital library development have focused on access to and retrieval of digital information but they have overlooked the personalized service aspects, as primary goal of library information services.

However the technology and information resources, on their own, can not make up an effective digital library. On priority basis the personalized services in a digital library environment would help the users to find information resources available in a digitally chaotic world.

In a Delphy study it was revealed that:

- The primary roles library professionals play in digital libraries include organization of macro and micro-documents, selection and acquisition and acting as gateways to the provision of information services, and
- The best reasons of developing a digital library include: increasing access to information serving and users needs and bringing organization to the unstructured universe of electronically available information.

However there is a demand for end-user instruction on the use of digital libraries and the digital library professionals who are subject specialists should help users to formulate disciplinary search strategies and provide assistance in developing new digital information resources.

Web-based reference and information services

Several reference and information services are now available on the web and many of these services are provided by Non--library organization. Also a web site that provides a categorized listing of libraries that offer real-time reference services using specific software, live interactive communication tools, call centre management software, bulletin board services and other INTERNET technologies.

Of course, most of these services are designed for registered users of some specific libraries in-digital information environment. HodgKin has made an aggregation approach to reference and information services. According to which more than one reference sources is made accessible digitally and also it is more practicable in terms of visibility and profitability than a single reference source.

Further:

- It's reference service becomes much better known to professional users and thus easier to find, by providing access to several reference works,
- By tackling a number of reference works at a time, the publishers can achieve economics of scale in production and development
- The user's search session is likely to be much more powerful and fruitful.

Online reference and information services can be broadly categorized into three groups:

- Those from publishers, database search services and specialized institutions
- Those provided by libraries and/or experts through the INTERNET and

- Where the users need to conduct a search and find information through the web.

Also they have listed several online information services that belong to the first category comprising various current awareness, and SDI services, for example:

- Contents pages services from commercial publishers, such as Elsevier's Contents Direct Service and IDEAL Alert from Academic Press.
- Information on new books available for free from publishers and vendors, such as Wiley Book, Notification Service from Wiley, and Amazon.com.
- SDI services from online search services providers, such as Dialog (Dialog Alerts)
- Current contents and ISI Alerting Services from ISI and so on.

However some of these services, particularly the contents page services from publishers of journals, are free, while for others, such as Dialog Alerts, or Current Contents from ISI, users need to register and pay for the services. There are also some web-based reference services where users need to conduct a search in order to answer their reference query.

For example:

- The Internet Public Library,
- Britannica,
- The Electric Library and
- The Internet Library for librarians.

Most of these web-based reference services are available free of charge but some charge a small amount as fee. For example, the Electric Library charges an annual subscription fee.

SEARCH ENGINE SERVICES

Sherman made a comparision among three web-based reference services like:

- Ask Jeeves basically a search engine, is useful for complex questions and is a good choice for searchers who lack Boolean or other searching skills, because of its strong natural language parser and question-and-answer template structure. The users can ask a question on a given topic and it comes up with a list of questions on the same or similar topics; the users can select any of those predefined questions and then it provides further answers. It processes each query syntactically and semantically and then its answer processing engine provides the question template response. When the users click on a response, the answer-processing engine retrieves the answer template that contains links to the answer locations. Thus Ask Jeeves can help users to select a query from a pre-defined set of queries on a given topic. So it is considered as a useful model for reference and infor-mation services in digital libraries.

- The Electric Library is an excellent choice for a serious researcher in need of timely content from a wide array of otherwise unavailable sources. It provides access to various on line reference sources and allows users to either select a specific source or conduct a search on a range, or all, of the sources.
- Information please is a suitable tool for students and other researchers, as an authoritative source of facts and pointers for further investigation.

Moreover Chowdhury and Chowdhury have suggested some other useful search engine services like:

- Web help.com that claims to offer real time search assistance with a real live expertany time, day or night,
- About.com is a service that shows a number of pre-defined categories related to a search topic given by the user.

For example, a simple search on 'e-commerce' not only produces a list of sites, but also provides a set of topics related to e-commerce, such as e-commercedefinition, e-commerce security, the advantages and disadvantages of e-commerce, e-commerce statistics and so on.

DIGITAL LIBRARY INFRASTRUCTURE

A digital library has certain technological requirements such as:

- Locally developed database
- Local library system with adequate personal computers having LAN and CD-ROM Drives.
- Electronic mail service
- Network connection to have access to other data bases
- Various functions to coordinate, manage the entry and retrieve data.
- Multimedia Kit
- Well trained manpower
- Computer Hardware with Audio-Visuals, Video Conferencing Kit, Pentium Web Server, Laser Printer, Scanner, Barcode Scanner, Barcode Printer, Digital graphic printer and UPS.
- Software and its accessories.

The super structure of digital library rests on some important factors like:

- The human need for information especially that is timely and relevant and
- Accumulation of information, and all the supporting infrastructure that includes research community, professional associations, libraries and publishers, advances in methods and technology leading to developments in net working, information science, information storage and retireval, hyper-media, human-computer interaction, artificial

intelligence and other areas of computer science that make digital libraries a possible proposition.

DIGITAL REFERENCE SERVICES FOR GENERAL PUBLIC

Today web-based digital reference services are being provided by a network of public libraries. The users make their query on an enquiry page and it is automatically routed to one of the participating libraries which records it as an e-mail message to the user containing necessary and available information.

For example, the British Library, London provides special reference services for business, scientific, technical, medical, patent and environmental information which range from answering simple queries up to complex questions involving on line data base searches. Of course some of these services are free if users put simple queries, but for complex queries users need to pay at the prescribed rate which covers the costs of staff time, on-line searching and value added tax (VAT). The British Library provides STM (Science, Technology and Medicine) Search Service for which users need to pay. Similarly New York Public Library (Digital Library), American Library of Congress, Alexandria Digital Library, Berkeley Digital Library, Bibliotheque Nationale de France, Victoria State Library, Vatican Library, etc. are some other libraries which provide digital reference services for users.

PRESENT SCENARIO IN INDIA

All the six IITs (Indian Institute of Technology) created as centres of excellence for higher training, research and development in science, engineering and technology, have automated their libraries and now they have access to more than one thousand electronic journals. The Central Library IIT, Delhi has switched over to the Silver Platter's Electronics Reference Library (ERL) technology for providing access to bibliographic databases subscribed on CD-ROM.

The technology facilitates simultaneous and integrated access to ERL complaint reference databases to multiple users across the LAN/WAN Via TCP/IP. This library offers network-based CD-ROM search services from the CD-ROM databases subscribed in the central library. Most of its databases have now been transferred to ERL technology and its CD-NET system has been installed for searching of CD-ROM databases on the campus intranet. This Library has started subscribing to the web-based full-text electronic journals with availability of high speed INTERNET connection and about 1330 electronic journals are accessible full text.

In most of the higher learning and research institutes in India such as:

- The Regional Engineering Colleges (RECs),
- Tata Institute of Fundamental Research (TFIR),
- Indian Institute of Science (IIS),
- Indian Statistical Institute (ISI),

- Indian Agricultural Research Institute (IARI),
- Institute of Veterinary Research of India (IVRI),
- All India Institute of Medical Science (AIMS),
- Indian Institute of Management (IIMs),
- Institute of Physics, Institute of Life Science,
- Shaha Institute Nuclear Physics,
- The Medical College Libraries etc., have automated their library systems.

Some of them are in the process of digitization of rare and valuable documents. Digital library services in India are in developing stage. At present most of the university libraries have taken steps to provide web-based reference and information services in digital environment in addition to their traditional library services.

These services include:

- Access to library catalogues and union catalogues.
- Access to bibliographic databases
- Access to subject gate ways in specific disciplines
- Providing links to web sites
- Accessing and procuring e-reference sources
- Subscribing to e-journals
- Reference services provided by librarians and experts on the web
- Document delivery services
- On-line current awareness services
- Digitization of library resources, considering their intellectual value.

The University Grants Commission (UGC) of India has launched the major initiative for setting up nation wide communication network for Indian universities called UGC-Infonet. Each university was to establish a LAN in its campus linking all the teaching departments including library. ERNET of India and INFLIBNET Centre, Ahmedabad are conducting a series of training programmes for technical staff of each participating university library for managing and maintaining the network at their premises. The INFLIBNET Centre will administer and monitor the E-Journal programme and will have independent electronic access to all the publications to help with the process.

The INFLIBNET Centre has carried out training programmes in various places to spread awareness and to develop expertise in the University community in the use of E-Resoures under the networked environment. The INFLIBNET Centre has developed and also recently released library automation software package new version for university libraries (SOUL) for building up digital library services. Soul is Windows based user friendly software, based on client server architecture with multi-user and multi language facilities which supports internationally known standards such as CCF, AACR-II andMARC-21, etc.

Thus INFLIBNET centre is patronizing for digitization of college and university libraries and encouraging e-subscription and e-learning in Indian

Universities and colleges. The DELNET (Delhi Library Network) created as a metropolitan network in 1988, has changed its name to Developing Library New Work (DELNET) in 2000. The main objectives of DELNET are to promote resource sharing among its member libraries, develop a network of member libraries, collect store and disseminate information, offer computerized information services in digital environment

The DELNET presently avails the high speed satellite communication facilities of NIC spread across the country and its 620 member libraries can access about 35 lakh bibliographic records in machine readable form. Also it maintains an online union catalogue of books available in its member libraries in CCF format. Its union catalogue is continuously updated. DELNET has been networking the libraries of about 400 affiliated institutes of AICTE, New Delhi. DELNET presents two management software packages *i.e.* DELMARC and DELPLUS.

DEFINITION OF DIGITAL LIBRARIES AND PERSONALISED SERVICES

While reviewing the definitions of digital libraries, Borgman noted that "in general, researchers (who primarily come from computer science and/or engineering backgrounds) focus on digital libraries as content collected on behalf of user communities, while librarians focus on digital libraries as institutions or services'". She further stressed that the current state of digital library research and development, especially in the USA, is influenced by the research definition of digital libraries.

The emphasis on the "enabling technologies" for access to digital resources rather than on the services traditionally provided by libraries becomes quite evident when one looks at the two special issues of the *Journal of the American Society for Information Science*, The two issues contain excellent articles reflecting the state of digital library research but none focus on digital library services *per se*. Even the editor of the two special issues did not discuss reference and information services. He mentioned that "digital libraries have the ability to provide a previously unattainable level of service". He emphasised access to information and suggested the various methods, tools and techniques that facilitate improved access to information in digital libraries. However, this is in sharp contrast to the views of the two editors of the special issue of *Information Processing and Management* on digital libraries. Marchionini and Fox in their editorial stated that "digital library work occurs in the context of a complex design space shaped by four dimensions: community, technology, services and content".

The fact that digital libraries should not be regarded only as point of access to digital information was emphasised by a definition of digital libraries given by Borgman as early as in 1992 whereby she contended that a digital library are:

- A service;
- an architecture;
- A set of information resources, databases of text, numbers, graphics, sound, video, etc. and
- A set of tools and capabilities to locate, retrieve and utilise the information resources available.

The definition of a digital library that came up in the March 1994 Digital Library Workshop emphasised that a full service digital library must accomplish all the essential services of traditional libraries and also exploit the well-known advantages of digital storage, searching and communication.

There are many other definitions of digital libraries that mention the services aspect, either explicitly or implicitly. Pointing out the lack of emphasis on reference and information services, Sloan lamented that "human interaction in the digital library is discussed far less frequently. One would almost get the impression that the service tradition of the physical library will be unnecessary and redundant in the digital library environment". He emphasised the point that "technology and information resources, on their own, cannot make up an effective digital library". Emphasising the need for personalised services in digital libraries, Lombardi mentioned that, "helping clients find resources in a digitally chaotic world is the first priority". In a Delphi study of digital libraries it was revealed that "the primary roles librarians play in digital libraries include organisation, selection and acquisition and acting as gateways to the provision of services involving information". This study also revealed that "the best reasons for developing a digital library include: increasing access to information, serving end users' needs and bringing organisation to the unstructured universe of electronically available information".

Thus, this study shows the importance of "serving end users' needs", and the need for the librarians to act as "gateways to the provision of services involving information" in a digital library. Another study conducted by Downs and Friedman indicated that "in the absence of human intermediaries, there is a need for end-user instruction on the use of digital libraries". Covi pointed out that "digital libraries will be used only when workers can readily integrate into social legimitated and legitimatable ways of working". She further suggested that subject specialists, as digital library service providers, help users formulate disciplinary search strategies and provide assistance in developing new resources.

Arms, while trying to answer the question "whether or not we need reference librarians in a digital library", pointed out that automatic tools are steadily reducing the need for reference librarians in fields like medicine that required a significant amount of intermediation in information searching. The essence of Arms' paper is that while computers can do a lot in performing most of the traditional jobs of reference librarians, their skills may be required in case of complex information searches.

Arms, however, believes that there have been significant improvements in the end-user search facilities, provided by electronic database search services and Web search engines, and hence, the need for human intermediaries in information searching has reduced significantly. Perhaps the most comprehensive view of the need for and the nature of personalised services in a digital library has been delineated by researchers.

They maintained that:

- Services reflect the functionality afforded by systems serving the community of users. Access services that facilitate search and browsing have been central to digital library research thus far, but there is great need for attention to reference and question-answering, on-demand help, and fostering of citisenship and literacy and mechanisms to simplify participatory involvement of user communities.

REFERENCE AND INFORMATION SERVICES ON THE WEB

A number of reference and information services are now available on the Web. Interestingly, many of these services are provided by Non--library and commercial organisations. While some are free, others need payment.

Detailed discussions on such services are available in a number of publications, McKiernan maintains a site that provides categorised listing of libraries that offer real-time reference services using chat software, live interactive communication tools, call centre management software, bulletin board services and other Internet technologies. Most of these services are designed for registered users of the libraries concerned.

Researchers categorised online reference and information services into three broad groups:

- Reference and information services from publishers, database search services, and specialised institutions;
- Reference services provided by libraries and/or experts through the Internet; and
- Reference and information services where users need to conduct a search and find information through theWeb.

Researchers discussed several online information services that belong to the first category.

They have listed various current awareness and SDI services such as: the contents page service from commercial publishers, such as Elsevier's

- Contents Direct Service, IDEAL Alert from Academic Press, and so on;
- Information on new books available free from publishers and vendors, such as the *Wiley Book Notification Service* and Amazon.com;
- SDI services fromonline search service providers, such as Dialog;
- *Current Contents* and *ISI Alerting Services* from ISI, and so on.

Some of these services, particularly the contents page services from publishers of journals, are free, while for others, such as *Dialog Alerts* or *Current Contents* from ISI, users need to register and pay.

Table 5.1 provides a quick overview of some online reference and information services currently available. This is not an exhaustive list, but the table shows the different types of services and some of their characteristics. It provides the following facts about theWeb-based reference services listed there:

- The listed Web-based reference services are offered by dotcom companies;
- These services use the Web only for communication between the user and the system/answer provider, while the information service is provided by a human expert;
- While most services are free, some charge as high as $250 per question;
- in many cases services are provided by (self-proclaimed?) volunteer experts;
- There are some services offered in specific subject fields.

In addition to those in table, there are also some Web-based reference services where users need to conduct a search for a reference query. Such services provide free access to various online reference sources, and allow users either to select a specific source or conduct a search on a range, or all, of the reference sources.

Examples of such services include the following:

- Internet Public Library.
- Infoplease
- Britannica
- Bartleby Reference.
- Internet Library for Librarians.
- Electric Library.
- Mediaeater Reference Desk.
- ReferenceDesk.
- Xrefer.

While most of these Web-based reference services are available free, some charge a small fee. For example, the Electric Library charges $79.95 for an entire year of unlimited access. Janes *et al.* reported a study of 20 Web-based "expert services". By asking 240 questions to 20 selected expert services, they noted that the sites gave verifiable answers to 69 per cent of factual questions. An interesting observation of this study was that the kind of reference interview that takes place in traditional reference service environments is Non--existent in Web-based reference services. In fact, the sites did not come back for any discussion or clarification after receiving the initial queries. As a justification, the authors suggested that Web-based information services have been built mainly to answer factual questions, and therefore the experts concerned do not need to go through the reference interview process. Nevertheless, the high rate of success of factual questions shows that more and more end-users will move towards these expert services rather than to libraries for answers to simple types of questions.

SEARCH ENGINE SERVICES

Although Ask Jeeves is basically a search engine, many researchers also see it as aWeb-based information service because of two reasons:

- Unlike in other search and metasearch engines, users can ask a question in Ask Jeeves, and in many cases can get an answer right away; and
- Users can ask a question on a given topic, and Ask Jeeves comes up with a list of questions on the same or similar topics; the user can select any of the those predefined questions, and then Ask Jeeves provides answers to that.

This is an interesting service and may be considered as a useful model for digital library reference and information services.

The Ask Jeeves site maintains that:

- Ask Jeeves is a unique question-answering system that allows users to ask questions in plain English, and then delivers the answer. As one of the most sophisticated navigation systems on the Internet, Ask Jeeves combines a unique natural language engine with a proprietary knowledgebase.Taken together, this mechanism processes the meaning and grammar of real questions in plain English; provides intelligent responses for user confirmation; links directly to relevant, high-quality answers; and, perhaps most exciting of all, becomesmore intelligent as its knowledgebase expands with each question asked and each answer delivered.

The site further says that Ask Jeeves processes each query syntactically and semantically, and then Ask Jeeves' answer-processing engine provides the question template response. When the user clicks on a response, the answer-processing engine retrieves the answer template that contains links to the answer locations. Thus, Ask Jeeves helps users select a query from a pre-defined set of queries on a given topic.

However, there is a debate on whether the kind of service provided by Ask Jeeves matches reference services provided by libraries. Kresh reported an interesting finding: "One consortial system in northern California conducted an informal test of Ask Jeeves by sending it 12 questions its libraries had answered. There were no trick questions, none were arcane, just questions typically received by those libraries. Jeeves was unable to answer any of the questions".

Nevertheless, the techniques and the technology used by Ask Jeeves may be very useful for introducing reference services in digital libraries.

Webhelp.com is another service that claims to offer "real-time search assistance with a real live expert I any time, day or night". About.com is a service that shows a number of pre-defined categories related to a search topic given by the user. For example, a simple search on "e-commerce" not only produces a list of sites, but also provides a set of topics related to "e-commerce", such as e-commerce definition, e-commerce security, advantages of e-commerce, e-commerce disadvantages, e-commerce statistics, etc.

DIGITAL REFERENCE SERVICES AND LIBRARIES

A number of libraries have now begun to offer Web-based reference services and a number of recent studies report the current practice of reference services provided by libraries. Although this is not an exhaustive review of all the Web-based reference services provided by libraries, the following section provides a quick overview of some that are currently available.

DIGITAL REFERENCE SERVICES FOR THE GENERAL PUBLIC

Ask A Librarian is a Web-based reference service, primarily designed for UK residents, provided by a network of public libraries in the UK. The site says: "Mail us your factual question and we'll send you an answer within two working days, if not before". A user has to put the query through an enquiry page, which is automatically routed to one of the participating libraries, which receives it as an e-mail message. Within two days the library sends an e-mail message to the user with its response to the enquiry. The British Library provides special reference services for business, patent, scientific, technical, medical and environmental information. These services range from answering simple questions to finding answers to complex questions involving online database searching, etc. While some of these services are free, for others users need to pay. For example, users can ask simple business questions using a form, and can expect an answer within ten working days. Similarly, users can send e-mails with simple environmental queries.

A typical answer in such a case may include:

- A list of bibliographies from a British Library catalogue literature search; and/or;
- A list of organisations to contact for more detailed information, and/or
- Information retrieved from Internet sources.

Users are not charged for this kind of service. However, for complex queries users need to pay.

For example, the British Library provides a Science Technology Medicine (STM) search service for which users need to pay at the following rate:

- J 82.00 per hour of staff time divided into 15-minute periods;
- Plus costs of online searching;
- Plus Value Added Tax (VAT).

As stated in the Web site most searches take at least 30 minutes and therefore cost J 41.00 for staff time + costs for online searching + VAT. The site also mentions that the average list of references costs J 80.00 for medical subjects, and between J 100.00 and J 150.00 for other subjects.

Users are also charged a fee if the results are to be faxed. In order to obtain an STM search service, the user has to fill in a form that has three parts. In the first part users need to fill in their personal details, etc., in the second part, users need to enter the query, and in the third part they need to specify the modes of delivery, payment, etc. In the second part of the form, users can enter the detail specification of the query using Boolean operators and specifying date, language, etc., as limiting factors.

USING DIGITAL LIBRARIES TO DISSEMINATE HUMANITARIAN INFORMATION

Digital libraries provide perhaps the first really compelling *raison d'être* for computing technology in the developing world. Priorities in these countries include health, agriculture, nutrition, hygiene, sanitation, and safe drinking water. Though computers *per se* are not a priority, simple, reliable access to practical information relevant to these basic needs certainly is.

In an article entitled "*The promise of digital libraries in developing countries*" Witten mention ten information collections, available on the Web and CD-ROM, from organizations ranging from UN agencies to small NGOs, in which Greenstone is being used to deliver humanitarian and related information in developing countries.

For example, the Humanity Development Library described is a compendium of practical information aimed at helping reduce poverty, increasing human potential, and giving a practical and useful education. We describe four new ones that have been created recently, and distributed in the same way.

Fig. A Selection of Recent Humanitarian Digital Library Collections on CD-ROM.

The Researching Education Development library is a project of the *Department for International Development* (DFID), a British government department responsible for promoting develop-ment. Its central focus is a commitment to an internationally agreed target of halving the proportion of people living in extreme poverty by 2015.Associated targets include ensuring universal primary education, gender equality in schooling, and skills development. It works in partnership with other governments and multilateral institutions, with business and the private sector, with civil society and the research community. It has created a CD-ROM library containing many education research papers and other documents.

Each one represents a study or piece of commissioned research on some aspect of education and training in developing countries. The Energy for Sustainable Development library was initiated as part of the outreach phase of the World Energy Assessment, which was initiated jointly by the *United Nations Development Programme* (UNDP), the *United Nations Department of Economic and Social Affairs* (UNDESA), and the *World Energy Council* (WEC), along with funding from the United Nations Foundation. This library contains a broad and valuable collection of 350 documents from UNDP, UNDESA, WEC and many other organizations.

It includes titles that all these organizations have published on the subjects of energy for sustainable development—technical guidelines, journals and newsletters, case studies, manuals, reports, and other training material. The documents are in English, Spanish and French, and one document has Arabic, Russian and Chinese translations as well.

The UNAIDS Library contains publications in the "Best Practice" collection which form a unique resource for those working in planning and practice. It is produced by the Joint United Nations Programme on HIV/AIDS, whose global mission is to lead, strengthen and support a response to the AIDS epidemic that will prevent the spread of HIV, provide care and support for those infected by the disease, reduce the vulnerability of individuals and communities to HIV/AIDS, and alleviate the socioeconomic and human impact of the epidemic.

The Health Library for Disasters is the result of a collaboration between the emergency and disaster programmes of the *World Health Organization* (WHO) and the *Pan American Health Organization* (PAHO), with the participation of many other organizations: the *United Nations High Commissioner for Refugees* (UNHCR), the *United Nations Children's Fund* (UNICEF), the International Strategy for Disaster Reduction (EIRD); the Red Cross Movement (ICRC and IFRC); the SPHERE Project; Non--governmental organizations such as OXFAM; and national organizations such as the National Emergency Commission of Costa Rica.

It contains more that 300 technical and scientific documents on disaster reduction and public health issues related to emergencies and humanitarian assistance. A follow-up to the Spanish-language Biblioteca Virtual de Desastres discussed by Witten *et al.*, it includes technical guidelines, field guidelines, case studies, emergency kits, manuals, disaster reports, and other training materials.

UNIVERSAL ACCESS

Universal access to digital libraries presents huge challenges to software engineers and HCI practitioners. The Greenstone digital library software allows us to glimpse some of the issues, although it certainly does not yet effectively address them all.

Platforms and Distribution

Most digital libraries are accessed over the web, using any web browser. However, in many environments, particularly in developing countries, web access is insufficient and the system must run locally. And if people are to build and control their own libraries, a centralized solution is inadequate: the software must run on their own computers.

Thus digital library systems intended for broad access should run on a wide variety of computer systems, particularly low-end ones. Developed under Linux, the Greenstone server runs on any Windows, Unix, or MacOS/X system. All versions of Windows are supported, from 3.1 up.

Supporting primitive platforms poses substantial challenges of a rather mundane nature: for example, Microsoft compilers no longer support Windows 3.1 and it is necessary to acquire obsolete versions. Under Windows, pre-built collections can be viewed on any system with at least 8 Mb RAM, but collections cannot be built under Windows 3.1/3.11—for this at least a Pentium processor is generally required, except for very small collections.

The fact that Greenstone does not run on early Macintosh systems is a serious drawback in certain environments. In an international cooperative effort established in August 2000 with UNESCO and the Belgium-based Human Info NGO, Greenstone is being distributed widely in developing countries with the aim of empowering users, particularly in universities, libraries, and other public service institutions, to build their own digital libraries.

UNESCO recognizes that digital libraries are radically reforming how information is acquired and disseminated in its partner communities and institutions in the fields of education, science and culture around the world, and particularly in developing countries. Their hope is that this software will encourage the effective deployment of digital libraries to share information and place it in the public domain.

The UNESCO distribution of Greenstone is a CD-ROM that contains the full source code and executable binaries for Windows and Linux, along with all necessary associated software. Full documentation and five demonstration collections are included.

The current CD-ROM is trilingual, with complete interfaces, instructions, and documentation in English, French and Spanish. For those with Web access, the same package is also available for download from the Greenstone Web site, often in a form that is slightly ahead of the CD-ROM version—for example, many other language interfaces are included and full documentation is available in Russian and Kazakh too.

Providing accessibility in different languages is more difficult than one might at first realise. As well as the manuals, installation instructions and installation prompts, the licensing agreement, and the readme files have to be translated too.

Access for Readers

Greenstone collections like the Humanity Development Library can be published as standalone collections on removable media such as CD-ROM, or presented on the Web. CD-ROM is a very practical format in developing countries.

Any Greenstone collection can be converted into a self-contained Windows CD-ROM that includes the Greenstone server software itself and an integrated installation package. The installation procedure has been thoroughly honed to ensure that only the most basic of computer skills are needed to install and run a collection under Windows.

Even standalone Greenstone users interact through a Web browser: Netscape is supplied on each CD-ROM for those who do not already have a browser. In standalone mode the software runs locally but incorporates a Web server so that if the system happens to be connected to a network—say a hospital or school intranet—information is available to other machines that may not possess CD drives.

This happens automatically: no special configuration is necessary. Another difficult engineering challenge is checking for the existence of a network. While installed network software is easily detected, it is hard to determine Non--intrusively whether it is operational. Incorrectly installed or configured software is endemic in developing countries, because computers there are often cast-offs whose software is inappropriate to their present environment, yet system support to rectify the problems is unavailable.

It is essential for universal access that such problems are addressed properly and solved satisfactorily without involving the user, even though they are mundane and timeconsuming. Greenstone provides some support for the visually impaired by incorporating a "textual" mode of access that replaces all images by textual prompts. This output is suitable for users with speech synthesizers or other specialized access devices. However, the facility is not well advanced: in particular, we have not yet refined it through usability testing and interface improvement.

Building New Collections

Effective human development blossoms from empowerment rather than gifting. As the Chinese proverb says, "Give a man a fish and he will eat for a day; teach him to fish and he will eat for the rest of his days." Disseminating information originating in the developed world, like the Humanity Development Library, is a useful activity for developing countries.

But a more effective strategy for sustained long-term human development is to disseminate the capability of creating information collections, rather than the collections themselves. This will allow developing countries to participate actively in our information society, rather than observing it from outside. It will stimulate the creation of new industry. And it will help ensure that intellectual property remains where it belongs, in the hands of those who produce it. Users whose skills resemble those of librarians rather than computer specialists should be able to build and distribute their own digital library collections. As an initial step in this direction, Greenstone includes an interface called the "Collector" that is intended to help people build their own library collections.

Collections may be built and served locally from the user's own web server, or remotely on a shared digital library host. End users can build new collections styled after existing ones from material on the Web or from their local files—or both, and collections can be updated and new ones brought on-line at any time.

The interface, which is intended for Non--professional end users, is modeled after widely used commercial software installation packages, frequently called software "wizards"—a term we deprecate because of its appeal to mysticism and connotations of utter inexplicability. We chose this interaction style because it simplifies the choices and presents them very clearly.

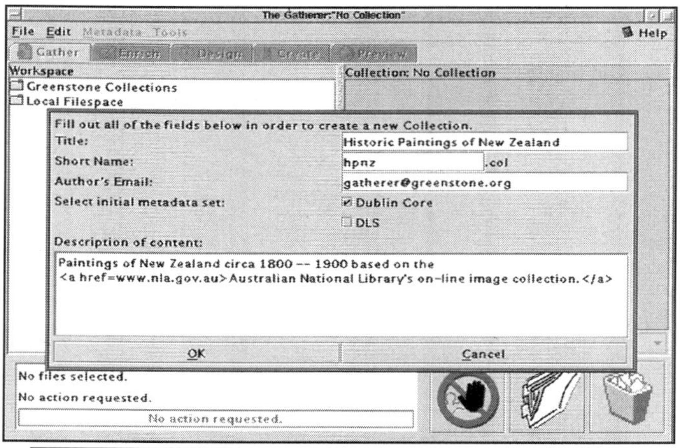

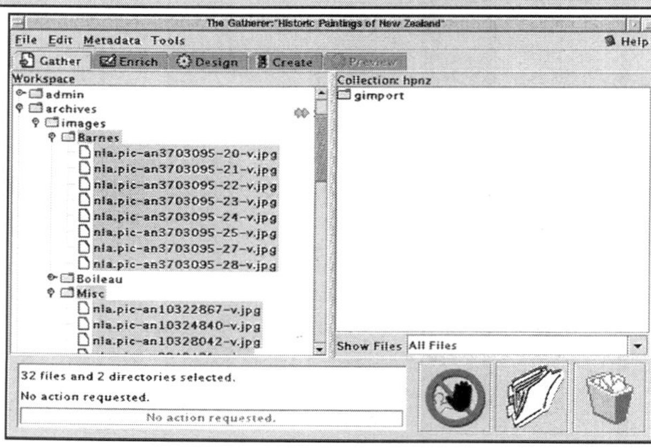

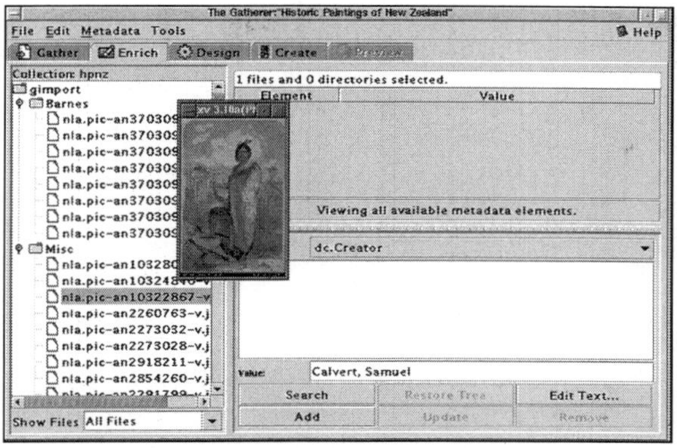

Fig. (Contd.)

Fig. Building a Collection with the Gatherer.

Figure shows a new Greenstone librarian interface, currently undergoing beta testing by UNESCO at sites in Argentina, India, Kazakhstan, Mexico, and South Africa, which builds on lessons learned from the Collector. It incorporates a great deal of additional functionality, particularly the ability for users to associate metadata with any item or group of items, and to reuse metadata elements without retyping them.

In figure, it is being used to collate a selection of images for a digital library collection, augment these source documents with textual metadata and then build and view the collection. From here, it is a matter of a few further clicks to produce a self-installing CD-ROM version of the collection.

In this illustration the user is developing a digital library collection of historic paintings of New Zealand. The user creates a new collection using the file menu, and a resulting popup window prompts for some general information about the collection. Once the user has filled out this form the main window becomes active. A series of panels guide the user through the processes required to build the collection.

The left-hand pane of the *Gather* panel shows the file system and the right-hand one represents the contents of the collection, initially empty, which the user populates by dragging and dropping files. In figure, the user has moved to the *Enrich* panel and is adding textual metadata to the selected documents. The next two panels, *Design*, *Create*, help the user structure the collection, control its appearance, and build it.

On completion the result is viewed in the *Preview* panel. Figure shows a page from the newly built collection, in which source documents are alphabetically listed by artist. Shown alongside each thumbnail are the artist's name, its catalog number, image dimensions, and its download size.

The full-size image is shown by clicking on the thumbnail. The user may skip backwards and forwards through the panels using them to augment and enhance the collection, perhaps adding further source documents, editing metadata values, and altering the collection's appearance.

Customization

An important component of access is allowing people to control the appearance of the collections they create. Many who build digital libraries want to brand them to ensure that they with an appropriate personal, institutional, or corporate image, and some can only contemplate software solutions that allow them to do so.

Although Greenstone comes with the standard appearance shown in figure—a distinctive bar down the side of all pages except those that show documents in the library, a green access bar with yellow buttons, etc.—the interface is highly configurable. Greenstone creates all pages that appear on the screen on the fly: none are stored in advance. They are generated using macros, written in a simple language specially designed for the job, that perform textual replacement.

One reason is that Greenstone accommodates a large number of different interface languages and macros help cope with this. All text fragments are couched as macro definitions. To add a new language, just the macro contents need to be translated—no web pages need be reworked.

Every page displayed by the system is passed through a macro interpreter that expands all the macros on the page. The interpreter checks a language variable and uses the macro definitions pertaining to it, which loads the page in the appropriate language.

Macros can have parameters. In this case, the parameter is the language variable: it causes the appropriate text fragment to be used for the macro's expansion. If there is no Arabic version for a particular macro, the interpreter will automatically substitute the default version.

This lets system developers experiment with the interface without having to worry about translating every little bit of new text immediately. Defaulting to English is not ideal—it reflects an Anglo-centric mindset—but it seems better than displaying nothing. Macros are also used to deal with display variables. Whenever a web page contains information that is not known in advance—like the number of documents returned by a search, or the value of a particular metadata item, or the content of a document page—a macro name is used in the page description.

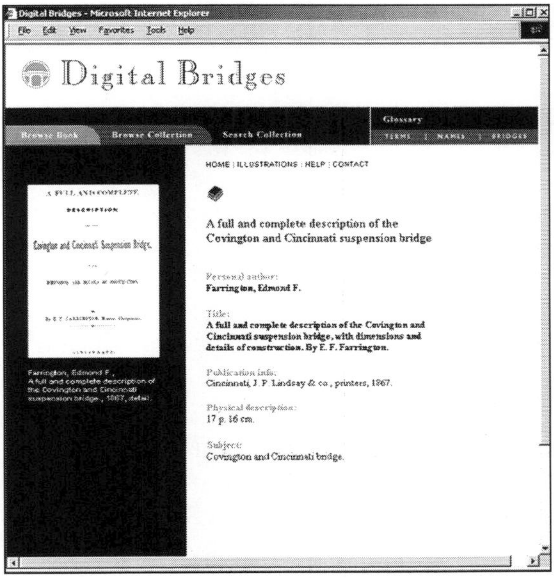

Fig. A Customised Interface to Greenstone.

Unlike language macros, these macros are *dynamic*: their content is not stored in advance but generated by the system in accordance with the value of the variable in question. Users can completely alter the form of the user interface by rewriting the macro files—or even by writing their own web pages which embed the dynamic macros that generate bits of Greenstone output.

Figure shows a Greenstone interface that has been heavily customised by Lehigh University Library, Pennsylvania. The standard Greenstone appearance has been completely obliterated in favour of an in-house style, yet all the Greenstone functionality is available. Figure shows a thumbnail of a book cover on the left, and full bibliographic information on the right. Entering a book displays facsimile images of its pages.

Internationalization

The international Unicode character set is used throughout Greenstone, and documents in any Unicode-supported language and character encoding can be imported. Collections of documents in Arabic, Chinese, Cyrillic, English, French, Spanish, German, Hindi, and Maori are publicly available.

The New Zealand Digital Library Web site hosts many of these, and the Greenstone Web site links to sites that contain further examples. It makes little sense to have a collection whose content is in Chinese or Russian, but whose supporting text—instructions, navigation buttons, labels, images, help text, and so on—are in English. Consequently, the entire Greenstone interface has been translated into a range of languages, and the interface language can be changed by the user as they browse from the *Preferences* page. All the language fragments in the interface are stored in macro files. These have been translated by Greenstone users in other parts of the world and contributed back to the project.

Figure shows an example: a Russian collection. Currently, interfaces are available in Arabic, Czech, Chinese, Dutch, French, Galician, German, Hebrew, Indonesian, Italian, Kazakh, Maori, Portuguese, Russian, Spanish, Turkish, and English. Managing the organizational and software complexity of any comprehensive and evolving open source software system presents a significant challenge.

Fig. A Russian Digital Library Collection.

However, the challenge is greatly magnified when the interface is available in different languages, for enhancements to the software and changes to the interface must be faithfully reflected in each language version. No single person knows all interface languages; no single person knows about all modifications to the software—indeed there is likely no overlap at all between those who translate the interface and those who build the software.

Currently, Greenstone has about twenty interface languages and there are around 600 linguistic fragments in each interface, ranging from single words like *search*, through short phrases like *search for*, *which contain*, *of the words*, to sentences like *More than... documents matched the query*, to complete paragraphs like those in the on-line help text. Maintaining the interface in many different languages is a logistic nightmare. The solution adopted by Greenstone is to incorporate a language translation facility, which allows authorized people to update the interface in specified languages. A standard version control system is used to manage software change, and from this the system automatically determines which language fragments need updating and presents them to the human translator.

DEFINITION OF DIGITAL LIBRARIES AND PERSONALISED SERVICES

While reviewing the definitions of digital libraries, Borgman noted that "in general, researchers (who primarily come from computer science and/or engineering backgrounds) focus on digital libraries as content collected on behalf of user communities, while librarians focus on digital libraries as institutions or services'". She further stressed that the current state of digital library research and development, especially in the USA, is influenced by the research definition of digital libraries.

The emphasis on the "enabling technologies" for access to digital resources rather than on the services traditionally provided by libraries becomes quite evident when one looks at the two special issues of the *Journal of the American Society for Information Science*, The two issues contain excellent articles reflecting the state of digital library research but none focus on digital library services *per se*. Even the editor of the two special issues did not discuss reference and information services. He mentioned that "digital libraries have the ability to provide a previously unattainable level of service". He emphasised access to information and suggested the various methods, tools and techniques that facilitate improved access to information in digital libraries. However, this is in sharp contrast to the views of the two editors of the special issue of *Information Processing and Management* on digital libraries. Marchionini and Fox in their editorial stated that "digital library work occurs in the context of a complex design space shaped by four dimensions: community, technology, services and content".

The fact that digital libraries should not be regarded only as point of access to digital information was emphasised by a definition of digital libraries given by Borgman as early as in 1992 whereby she contended that a digital library are:

- A service;
- an architecture;
- A set of information resources, databases of text, numbers, graphics, sound, video, etc. and
- A set of tools and capabilities to locate, retrieve and utilise the information resources available.

The definition of a digital library that came up in the March 1994 Digital Library Workshop emphasised that a full service digital library must accomplish all the essential services of traditional libraries and also exploit the well-known advantages of digital storage, searching and communication. There are many other definitions of digital libraries that mention the services aspect, either explicitly or implicitly. Pointing out the lack of emphasis on reference and information services, Sloan lamented that "human interaction in the digital library is discussed far less frequently.

One would almost get the impression that the service tradition of the physical library will be unnecessary and redundant in the digital library environment". He emphasised the point that "technology and information resources, on their own, cannot make up an effective digital library". Emphasising the need for personalised services in digital libraries, Lombardi mentioned that, "helping clients find resources in a digitally chaotic world is the first priority". In a Delphi study of digital libraries it was revealed that "the primary roles librarians play in digital libraries include organisation, selection and acquisition and acting as gateways to the provision of services involving information". This study also revealed that "the best reasons for developing a digital library include: increasing access to information, serving end users' needs and bringing organisation to the unstructured universe of electronically available information".

Thus, this study shows the importance of "serving end users' needs", and the need for the librarians to act as "gateways to the provision of services involving information" in a digital library. Another study conducted by Downs and Friedman indicated that "in the absence of human intermediaries, there is a need for end-user instruction on the use of digital libraries". Covi pointed out that "digital libraries will be used only when workers can readily integrate into social legimitated and legitimatable ways of working". She further suggested that subject specialists, as digital library service providers, help users formulate disciplinary search strategies and provide assistance in developing new resources. Arms, while trying to answer the question "whether or not we need reference librarians in a digital library", pointed out that automatic tools are steadily reducing the need for reference librarians in fields like medicine that required a significant amount of intermediation in information searching. The essence of Arms' paper is that while computers can do a lot in performing most of the traditional jobs of reference librarians, their skills may be required in case of complex information searches. Arms, however, believes that there have been significant improvements in the end-user search facilities, provided by electronic database search services and Web search engines, and hence, the need for human intermediaries in information searching has reduced significantly. Perhaps the most comprehensive view of the need for and the nature of personalised services in a digital library has been delineated by researchers.

They maintained that:

- Services reflect the functionality afforded by systems serving the community of users. Access services that facilitate search and browsing have been central to digital library research thus far, but there is great need for attention to reference and question-answering, on-demand help, and fostering of citisenship and literacy and mechanisms to simplify participatory involvement of user communities.

LIBRARY SERVICES: CHALLENGES AND OPPORTUNITIES

REFERENCE

E-learners require more than access to e-resources. Traditionally, a reference librarian acts as an additional type of resource, one who can be counted upon to provide expertise in making sense of library systems and research tools, and to offer a helping hand along that often slippery path known as the research process. Virtual library users face additional challenges in mining relevant information out of a computer system that "obstinately" returns zero hits in response to a query that does not match the character strings in its database files. The most common means of providing electronic reference services to remote users has been e-mail, the advantages and disadvantages of which have been well documented in the literature.

The around-the-clock and around-the-world accessibility of e-mail allows users to connect with librarians beyond the walls of library buildings and outside the usual hours of operation. E-mail provides a written record of requests and responses, permits the electronic transmission of search results, and allows librarians time to reflect on requests. One of the most serious concerns about e-mail reference services is their impact on the traditional face-to-face reference interview, particularly the absence of the verbal and Non--verbal cues that typically assist a librarian in effectively responding to a question. Hulshof identifies three issues related to the use of electronic communication in serving virtual patrons: immediacy, intricacy, and interaction. Because it is so easy for a learner to send a request electronically and have it arrive at the library instantly, there is a perception that the librarian's response will be as immediate.

The learner may become frustrated, not realising that the process of locating information and developing a response takes the librarian just as long when the request is made electronically as when it is made in person or in any other way. The more intricate or complex the request, the longer it will take for the librarian to clarify it and respond appropriately: a series of e-mail messages may be required, which will further reduce the immediacy of the e-mail request.

Immediacy and intricacy relate to the lack of interaction: the opportunity to discuss and clarify enquiries that occurs in person or over the telephone is not so easily accommodated by e-mail. There are ways to deal with some of these issues. A welldesigned reference Web form, such as that provided on the Ask AU Library: Ask about a Research Topic Web page, which encourages elearners to include full identifying and course information, to describe clearly their research problem and search terminology, and to state the parameters of the assignment, can clarify requests for librarians and reduce the need to e-mail back and forth.

Automated replies, which are sent out by the e-mail programme in response to the receipt of a message, can be used to reassure e-learners that their messages are being received, and can let them know what to expect in terms of service. E-mail reference service can be enhanced and supplemented with additional technologies that raise the level of interaction with realtime or live communication.Chat technology allows e-learners and librarians to send text messages back and forth instantly, using a form of communication that is familiar to most Internet users. There have been a number of library experiments with Web contact center software, which is modeled on the private sector's online solution to providing customer support. Web contact center software provides a higher level of interaction than does basic chat software, allowing for queuing and routing of messages, as well as enabling librarians to "push" Web pages to users. Providing e-learners with a toll-free telephone number remains an effective and convenient reference services strategy, particularly for intricate enquiries. The telephone reference interview works best when both librarian and e-learner are working in front of computers connected to the Internet.

INSTRUCTION

E-learners are frequently silent and invisible as they search and explore a library's online resources, and they do not have the same access that on-campus learners have to formal library instruction sessions. With the array of digital resources available to them, the multiplicity of interfaces and search tools, and the need for evaluation and critical thinking when using the Internet for research, "information literacy" skills are a must-have for e-learners. Information literacy refers to competencies with information sources in a variety of formats. According to the Association of College and Research Libraries, an information literate individual is able to:

- Determine the extent of information needed
- Access the needed information effectively and efficiently
- Evaluate information and its sources critically
- Incorporate selected information into one's knowledge base
- Use information effectively to accomplish a specific purpose
- Understand the economic, legal, and social issues surrounding the use of information, and access and use information ethically and legally

Supporting the integration of information literacy skills training into the core curriculum has become an important issue for libraries. As an extension of their traditional role of providing library instruction sessions and developing instructional materials, librarians are designing online tutorials and courses that promote information literacy and encourage active learning.

Particularly fine examples are the University of Texas System Digital Library's *TILT—Texas Information Literacy Tutorial*; and Utah Academic Library Consortium's *Internet Navigator*, a multi-institutional online course developed by a team of librarians and Web developers. The British Open University Library has developed *SAFARI*, a freely available interactive tutorial, as well as an information literacy course called *MOSAIC (Making Sense of Information in the Connected Age)*.

Many libraries provide instruction to e-learners by making information available on their Web pages, including frequently asked questions, library glossaries, research guides, and "how-to" pages. Athabasca University Library's Digital Reference Centre integrates resources with contextual instruction and provides links to instructional resources, including a detailed guide to Internet searching that encourages e-learners to think critically about Internet resources, and library research guides such as the *AU Library Guide to Researching Topics in Women's Studies*. Online tutorials usually operate on a model in which the e-learner interacts in isolation with a computer.

Their effectiveness can be enhanced by the addition of more interactive forms of instruction. The librarians at the Florida Distance Learning Reference and Referral Center, for example, have experimented with chat software to simulate a virtual classroom and open up "live" group instruction to e-learners. Librarians can also work with faculty to develop a library thread in a course discussion area, or to open a discussion forum on the library Web pages.

DIGITAL REFERENCE SERVICE: LIBRARIES ONLINE 24/7

The integration of the Internet Technology is affecting all functions of academic libraries. The mission of library professionals, providing excellent information service to users, has not changed, but technology has added several new dimensions and opened new avenues to their tasks. Librarians are moving into dramatically different roles as new services are implemented and the rate of change is breathtaking, especially for libraries that have been accustomed to stability in organization and in funding.

The utilization of new tools and methods for providing and collecting a variety of information to library users for diverse information needs of instructional, research, learning and entertainment activities has become common. While continuing to provide many traditional information services, librarians are developing new skills and accepting the new roles that are necessary to support technology-based services. Acquisitions librarians still selecting and purchasing books and traditional journals, but now they are also dealing with providing user access to leased electronic databases, full-text journal articles, Internet resources etc without "owning" the resources that are acquired only virtually. Catalogers are also moving into new roles as they attempt to provide enhanced access to the new resources like CD-ROMs, computer discs, multi-format items, and Cataloging the Internet itself is a task that has fallen to librarians. They are making these new resources accessible and applying Metadata standards. Reference librarians, while assisting users in the library, now have an additional set of remote users, who access the reference service online, who are more demanding, less patient users who have greater expectations.

LIBRARY REFERENCE SERVICE

Reference librarians assist users in finding, selecting and using various information sources and materials. They rely on a variety of printed and electronic sources to provide relevant and accurate information to their users. Internet is becoming more and more popular source among reference librarians and users. It enables them to search, retrieve, request, receive, and download information from sources scattered all over the world on the web. The traditional work of reference librarians has been greatly impacted by access to electronic publications on the World Wide Web. Now Reference librarians are also using the Web to create electronic publications for in-library users and Web surfers. By creating HTML documents that provide access to Web and other electronic resources, reference service is extended beyond the physical library and designated reference desk hours, opening the building for 24-hour access.

VIRTUAL/ DIGITAL/ LIVE/ ONLINE REFERENCE

The terms "virtual reference," "digital reference," "e-reference," "Internet information services," "live reference" and "real-time reference" are used interchangeably to describe reference services that utilize computer technology in some way. Whether it is e-mail reference, chat reference or an automated routing system, virtual reference is significantly influencing the delivery of high-quality library services. Digital reference techniques have been around, in one form or another, for almost a decade now. *VRS or DRS are simply defined as the provision of real-time personal assistance to users via web-based interactive software*. To satisfy the information need, the librarian can "chat" as a component of the software to answer a fairly specific or simple question, or deliver digital materials, or suggest relevant web resources to the user, and provide online bibliographic instruction. This service may happen when the library is closed, or when the user is unable to get to the library.

This way, users can still be in contact with experienced reference librarians. Questions submitted via e-mail and linked web pages require attention from reference staff, and the virtual reference transaction can be more complex and time-consuming than traditional in-library service. The Web medium that poses a new challenge for librarians offers major new tools to give us the power to control our own situation. With the expansion of reference modes to digital communication, namely e-mail and chat, there has been a delay in applying instruction to digital reference. Academic libraries started first offering e-mail reference where users could submit their questions via an e-mail address.

Recently the adoption of Web forms not only changed the quality of the e-mail reference engagement for the better, but also challenged librarians to develop effective means for managing questions and responses. A digital reference transaction will usually include the following elements: the user, the interface, electronic resources, as well as print resources and the information professional.

PLANNING FOR DIGITAL REFERENCE SERVICE

Detailed guidelines for a Digital Reference Service is drafted by IFLA with a purpose to promote digital reference best practices on an international basis. Planning should include consideration of the following:

- Physical service location
- Virtual service location
- Training in advanced web skills, reference interview and procedure
- Programming and web expertise
- Management and co-ordination of the service
- Completion time for transactions
- Quality control
- Service population
- Data collection for evaluation
- Promotion of the service
- Hardware and software
- Additional equipment
- Furniture

The staff necessary to run such a service includes:

- Researchers to gather the information to answer questions
- A co-ordinator to assign questions and to monitor answers; to schedule staff
- IT support for running networks, maintaining web pages and scripts
- Data entry staff to input and send responses.

Social Inclusion

E-mail-based and especially chat-based reference extends library services to those users with physical challenges. Not only can those users access information, but can receive real-time guidance from librarians, thus facilitating the 'human interaction' so important in reference transactions

E-government/Modernizing Government

The use of real-time technology increases accessibility to all types of government services. Libraries, experts in information delivery technologies, can provide the model in local authorities for reaching out to diverse user groups

NOF Training Expected Outcomes 2-8

Services, such as Ask A Librarian and chat reference, provide excellent training for staff in simple Internet searching to more complex user interaction with state-of-the art technologies.

All staff, from professional to clerical, have the opportunity to become conversant in different types of technologies while delivering real-time service.

DELIVERY METHODS OF DIGITAL REFERENCE

Digital reference services can be made through e-mail or chat. Libraries are also using a couple of different means of running an e-mail reference service: using basic e-mail or web forms. There are also a few different ways of operating a chat reference service: using simple chat software, web-based chat rooms, and web contact center software.

E-mail

User sends the library an e-mail with a reference query, supplying whatever information he or she feels is necessary. The library may reply by e-mail, phone, fax, letter, etc. Now days the Web Pages of Libraries are coming with "Ask a Librarian" option.

Web Forms

Here usually the user fills out an online form on the library's web site. The form asks the user to answer clarifying questions that will help the reference librarian responding to the query. The user sends the completed form to the library and the library may reply by e-mail, phone, fax, letter, etc. While e-mail reference allows the user to write down the query in his or her own words, a web form structures the user's request somewhat, prodding the user to supply additional information that will specify the request.

Chat Reference using Simple Technologies

In this method, user exchanges short, text messages back and forth with the librarian, in a chatting environment. This way doesn't allow for all the fancy interactivity that web contact center software allows, but it does allow for rapid, basic communication. There are three ways of running this kind of a service: with free, instant messaging software with a webbased chat room, or with chat software purchased by the library. With most of these services, the user types in an opening query or greeting to get the attention of the librarian staffing the chat reference service. The user and librarian may exchange a series of short messages to get to the heart of the user's request. This exchange of messages is live and allows for negotiation of the user's query.

Chat Reference Using Web Based Contact Software

Borrowing technology from online customer service, software for web contact centers not allow for instant messaging, but they also offer give the librarian power to control the user's browser. A librarian can actually make the user's browser display a recommended web page, such as a search engine or the main page for the library's online catalogue. As the librarian pushes pages onto the user's browser, the chat window can also appear on both user and librarian's screen, allowing them to have a typed conversation about the web pages being sent to the user.

Collaborative Networks for Reference

In this model, two or more libraries team up to offer reference service using any of the above online formats. The user would send to a member library his or her request, which would be forwarded to the library best able to answer the question. A library may get a question routed to it because it has particular strengths in its collection that match the needs of the user.Or a member library might get a question routed to it because it happens to be open when the user makes his or her request. For example, a user in New York who tries logging on at 3 a.m. Eastern time to the chat reference service of a member library in Boston could be automatically routed to a member library in Hawaii or Australia that, thanks to a time zone difference, is open.

Knowledgebase

Knowledge bases are used to retain questions and answers for reuse, in searchable database or archive. The use of previous answers to respond to new questions, knowledge bases reduce question response time and duplicated effort. If users search for and find prospective answers to their questions, knowledge bases allow libraries to meet users at their point of need. Knowledge base records will have high quality of information that users may not find on the Web. An effective knowledge base amounts to a peer-reviewed institutional memory, if only we add authoritative and reliable questions and answers to it. This is a typical way of the traditional reference service to keep all the reference questions and answers in files, through which the a "long range reference" becomes a "ready reference".

FACETS OF QUALITY FOR DIGITAL REFERENCE SERVICES

The 1997 Virtual Reference Desk Expert Panel has identified eleven characteristics and features for building a digital reference service for the educational community and its fifth version is published in June 2003. The facets are divided into two main categories: *user transaction* and *service development/ management*. The user transaction category includes those components that occur during the question-answering process; these features are generally visible to the user. The service development/management category involves decisions made in creating and maintaining the service that affect overall quality and user satisfaction.

User Transaction

- Accessible: Digital reference services should be easily reachable and navigable by any Internet user regardless of equipment sophistication, physical disability or language barrier.

- Prompt Turnaround: Questions should be addressed as quickly as possible. Actual turnaround time depends on a service's question-answer policy and available resources.
- Clear Response Policy: Clear communication should occur either before or at the start of every digital reference transaction in order to reduce opportunities for user confusion and inappropriate enquiries.
- Interactive: Digital reference services should provide opportunities for an effective reference interview, so that users can communicate necessary information to experts and to clarify vague user questions.
- Instructive: Digital reference services provide access to current information and expertise. Quality digital reference services offer more to users than straight, factual answers; they guide them in how to formulate questions, subject knowledge, and information literacy.

Service Development and Management

- Authoritative: Experts of a digital reference service should have the necessary knowledge and educational background in the service's given subject area or skill in order to qualify as an expert. Specific levels of knowledge, skill and experience are determined by each service and its related discipline or field.
- Trained Experts: Services should offer effective orientation or training processes to prepare experts to respond to enquiries using clear and effective language and following service response policies and procedures. Training of information specialists is one of the most important aspects of planning and operating a digital reference service.
- Private: All communications between users and experts should be held in complete privacy.
- Reviewed: Digital reference services should regularly evaluate their processes and services. Ongoing review and assessment help ensure quality, efficiency, and reliability of transactions as well as overall user satisfaction.
- Provides access to related information: Besides offering direct response to user questions, digital reference services should offer access to supporting resources and information. Services can reuse results from question-answer exchanges in resources such as archives and *frequently asked questions* (FAQs).
- Publicize: Services should inform potential users of the value that can be gained from use of the service. A well-defined public relations plan can ensure that services are well-publicized and promoted on a regular basis. Publicity should not create more demand than the service has capacity to handle.

6

Digital Library: Construction and Organization

The recent advances in computer, storage and communication technologies are so stunning that it prompted one of the authors of this paper (Raj Reddy) to envision and explore the possibility of storing in digital form all the knowledge ever produced by the human race and making this content available free of charge to be browsed and searched by anyone, anywhere and at anytime. This vision is the goal of the Universal Digital Library Project (UDL). In addition, Reddy envisions a future where almost all information will be readable by humans as well as machines.

The trend would be such that any information that is not on-line and accessible to search engines may become unusable. In a thousand years, only a few of the paper documents we have today will survive the ravages of deterioration, loss, and outright destruction. Hence there is an urgent need to preserve our knowledge and heritage in digital form.

As a part of Raj Reddy's grand vision, a mission to digitize one million books was embarked upon as a collaborative project involving many countries, especially India, the United States and China. In this paper, we present the approach taken and the technological challenges associated with the Million Books to the Web Project (MBP).

An interesting offshoot of our efforts to make knowledge available free of charge to everyone is the opening up of research opportunities in language technologies – particularly for Indian languages – in order to make sure the language in which that knowledge exists does not become a barrier to information access.

Language technologies research in Indian languages has so far been impaired by the lack of resources pertaining to Indian languages in the form of text or speech corpora. Compared to the corpora in English and other European languages, or in Chinese, the resources available for Indian languages have been very limited. This situation is being changed by the Digital Library of India (DLI) initiative, which is the Indian part of the UDL and MBP.

DLI today has scanned over 289,000 books composed of approximately 105 million pages in the Indian and English languages. Digital representation and storage mechanisms have been developed for Indian languages, and a large number of applications are being built to store, process, retrieve and present the Indian language content.

The Digital Library of India fosters a large number of research activities pertaining to language technologies for Indian languages, and acts as a testbed for developments made in areas such as text summarization, information retrieval, machine translation and transliteration, optical character recognition, handwriting recognition, and natural language parsing and morphological analyses. We present here an overview of the activities of DLI in these areas and show how DLI is acting as a multilingual resource, even without the availability of manually curated data.

VISION: DIGITIZATION OF ALL HUMAN KNOWLEDGE

For the first time in history, technology seems to favour the possibility of digital preservation of all the significant literary, artistic, and scientific works of mankind, as well as the potential of free access to them from every corner of the world. A Universal Digital Library (UDL) has the potential of improving the global society in ways beyond measurement. The Internet can house a Universal Library that is freely accessible to everyone. This would revolutionize education for all our future generations. There were about 10 million unique book and document editions before the year 1900, and about 100 million since the beginning of recorded history. An average-sized book is around 250 pages and would require about 50 MB of disk storage if the book were stored as compressed images.

Thus, all the books and documents ever produced by the human race would require 5 peta byte of storage. Even if we multiply this by a factor of 200 for all other forms of knowledge, such as music, images, audio and video, the total of that information could be stored in a zeta byte server.

With the storage capacity of digital disks increasing by a factor of 1,000 in ten years, it looks technically feasible and financially affordable to articulate the vision to store on the computer all forms of knowledge ever produced by the human race. With new digital technology, though, this task is within the reach of a single concerted effort for the public good, and this effort can be distributed to libraries, museums, and other groups in every country. This formed the motivation for the grand vision of the Universal Digital Library Project.

MISSION: A MILLION BOOKS ON THE WEB BY 2008

It is believed by some that the goal of creating a Universal Digital Library is impossible and that attempting to create it could take hundreds of years and still may never be completed. Nevertheless, as a first step Towards realizing this grand vision, a project was proposed that would create a Universal Library starting with a free-to-read, searchable collection of one million books available to everyone over the Internet by the year 2008. This first major project Towards building a Universal Library is named the Million Book Digital Library Project (MBP). Within 10 years, it is expected that the collection will grow to 10 Million books.

The result will be a unique resource accessible to anyone in the world, 24x7, without regard to nationality or socioeconomic background. Typical large high school libraries house fewer than 30,000 volumes. Most libraries in the world have fewer than a million volumes. The total number of different titles indexed in OCLC's WorldCat is about 55 million. A library of one million books, therefore, contains more than the holdings of most high schools, and is equivalent in number of volumes to the number in the libraries at many universities, representing a useful fraction of all available books.

The MBP is a multi-country project, and that part of the project being performed in India is called the Digital Library of India (DLI). A secondary objective of the MBP project, and hence the country-specific Digital Library exercises such as DLI, will be to provide a testbed that will support other researchers who are working on improving the technology required for scanning and indexing. The corpus the MBP project creates will be one to three orders of magnitude larger than any existing free resource. It is expected that when DLI matures, more than 10,000 books will be available in each of the major Indian Languages. Such an immense and unequaled volume of data would also provide an excellent resource for language processing research in areas such as optical character recognition (OCR), machine translation, summarization, intelligent indexing, and information retrieval.

COLLABORATION

Accessing, scanning and web hosting a million books is a major logistical challenge. A million books can be expected to comprise approximately 250 million pages. Throughput of a scanner used in the project (Minolta PS7000) is about 6,000 to 10,000 pages per day, based on three-shift operation. Using 100 scanners, and a 1,000-person workforce, the task of scanning a million books could be completed in about 420 working days, or roughly two years of three-shift operation. However, given the uncertainties of having skilled workers available at all times, and experiencing equipment failures and power outages, it is more reasonable to expect that the scanning would be completed in around four years.

The United States of America, India and China are currently the major collaborators in the MBP project with regard to technology development, operations and management. Collaboration among these countries has been a factor in the project's success so far, because these three countries provide access to a number of large academic libraries, of which over 700 are OCLC members from India and China. Also, since the scanning centres can be established anywhere, UDL has chosen to establish them close to these academic libraries so that the books can be transported with minimal difficulty.

The collaboration so far has been quite fruitful, with more than a few thousand books digitized every month from all the various scanning points established in India and the US. Currently, we have more than 200,000 books scanned and ready for use.

THE APPROACH: DIGITAL LIBRARY OF INDIA

The Indian Institute of Science (IISc), Carnegie Mellon University (CMU), the International Institute of Information Technology, Hyderabad (IIITH) and many other academic, religious and government organizations, totaling about 21 "Content Creation Centres", have become partners in the Digital Library of India (DLI) initiative for the digitization and preservation of Indian heritage present in the form of books, manuscripts, art and music. Each centre brings its own unique collection of literature into the digital library.

Many authors have cooperated by contributing their books to the digital library and making them available free of charge to anyone. This digital library is also intended to be a testbed for Indian language Research. DLI is intended to be a leading and contributing partner in worldwide efforts Towards making knowledge free. A pilot project to scan around 10,000 books was initiated at CMU and then followed up at IISc, IIITH and other organizations; all the processes involved have been perfected.

The vision is to use the disruptive technologies like the ICT to preserve all the knowledge of the human race in digital form and make that content searchable, independent of language and location, and to ensure that the rich cultural heritage of countries like India is not lost during the transition from paper to bits and bytes, as they were lost during a former transition of cultural content from palm leaves to paper.

Today, most of the works created by humans – be they in the form of books or music or movies – are "born digital". Hence if we build the digital library with a proper framework and architecture, it should become possible to bring the library up to date more easily than it was to digitize physical formats. But for the time being, we are concentrating on digitizing these physical formats.

For the digitization of old books, we have developed a complete process comprised of scanning with planetary scanners, cropping, cleaning up images, and using software for the OCR conversion of English documents, format conversions and search engines. With available technologies, a 500-page paper book can be digitized and made available on the web in about two hours without having to unbind the book. So far, more than 289,000 books have been scanned, of which nearly 170,000 are in Indian languages. More than 84,000 books (25 million pages) are available on the DLI web site hosted by the Indian Institute of Science (http://www.new.dli.ernet.in), and more than 149,000 books (43 million pages) are available on the DLI web site, which is hosted by the International Institute of Information Technology (http://dli.iiit.ac.in).

The link to other partner sites are also provided through (http://www.new.dli.ernet.in). Contents between the two sites overlap in order to ensure fail safe availability. The books can be accessed from either of these web sites. With the success of the joint efforts of the IISc-CMU collaboration, many other nations including China and Egypt have shown interest in participating in this effort, making it truly a global effort in knowledge sharing. China has made significant progress and has taken the Million Books to the Web as a National Initiative.

AIMS OF THE DIGITAL LIBRARY

The main aim, considering our hugely rich heritage, is and remains an eminently cultural one. The cultural aim is and remains in any case the main one also in all the other countries in the world, both where the Digital Library is used to create a support to academic studies and where the intention of documentation of historical memory prevails.

Actually, as is clearly seen from the international account which is widely summarised below, the two aims are complementary and the problem shifts to the choice to be made at the start, so that the Digital Library can be developed in a coherent and uniform way in both directions.

In the case of Italy, the attention to local memory and the support for research might be the two ideal boundaries within which Digital Library initiatives should be directed and maintained.

It should also be pointed out that this cultural aim is seen as the cog-wheel for the creation of new work, professional growth and recognition of national culture at an international level.

The Technical/librarianship Framework

Both from the definition and from indications deriving from the models analysed, the Digital Library undoubtedly presents itself as an extraordinarily complex structure. This complexity is analysed from various points of view, both the purely technical and the specifically librarianship ones.

Given the implications that the latter more than any other has in our view on the success of any project, we will focus on these themes in the summary and omit others for which we will simply refer to the main study.

Organisational Aspects

On the basis of the proposed analysis, the Digital Library is seen to be a "complex Library" and as a new information system in terms of:

- Objects to be handled
- Format of data

- Means of description (metadata)
- Organisation of research (search engines)
- Interfaces (informatics and/or human)
- Production activities (Workflow, Budgeting)
- Integration of different types of applications and systems
- Complex and distributed system

The Digital Library which organises production activities needs to define the methodologies for the treatment of the various materials in the context of a project (Workflow) and consequently the investment policies (Budgeting) both for the moment of production and for the subsequent conservational maintenance. A functional profile of the Digital Library is outlined with indication of the following functions:

Net infrastructures	Pac/web opac
Database bibliographic/metadata	Ocument management system
Digital repository	Maging
Storage	Raphics
Interface	Tatistics
Safety	

For each of these the functional requirements to be fulfilled in the Digital Library are specified. In particular it is stressed that in a Digital Library the objects to be handled are very different in nature:

- They can integrate metadata for description and management
- They can be local and remote
- They can concern other information data (online courses, Web pages)
- They can be multi-format (text, audio, video, images,....)
- They can be original digital objects: electronic publications

Evolution of Services and the Profession

The evolution of the potentialities of the services generated by the Digital Library and the parallel evolution of the profession are among the most significant and complex aspects of the Digital Library.

With the greater availability of information, the Digital Library still presents itself as a service structure.

Some of the many statements and definitions indicated and analysed strongly stress the function of service-provider in relation to other similar institutions. For example:

- The appeal for cooperation ("the Digital Library is not a separate entity")
- The appeal to the particular use of technologies ("the Digital Library needs technologies for connecting the resources of different libraries with information services")
- The appeal relative to access ("the aim of the Digital Library is universal access to its collections and services").

The characteristics of the service also change because of the changed attitude of the user and the different interaction between user and intermediary. This leads to a careful consideration of the qualitative evolution of the reference services, in which this mediation will be a strategic element in the development of the Digital Library.

Undoubtedly the problem of professionalism is one of the most significant of those related to the Digital Library, both because of how this professionalism is defined and how it is changing with the new services and the new skills which are required.

It is agreed that we are in the face of a true revolution, mostly brought about by facts which are outside the librarianship field in the strictest sense, but have evident repercussions on the functions and the very nature of the library, hence of the librarian. The librarian's work is the fruit of different, complementary kinds of know-how which mean that he/she operates as a:

- Professional handigital libraryer of digital information
- Producer of digital information
- Communicator of digital knowledge to provide this type of service the librarian of the digital library
- To know the users with whom he/she is in contact better in order to adapt adequate tools and products to specific demands
- To adapt the procedures for presenting data- interface and not to propose them according to a single standard procedure
- To give access also to Non--bibliographical inform-ation available on the Web From the analysis it emerges that there will be an affirmation of professional figures who are able to unite the more classic principles of librarianship with the prospects offered to the profession by digital technologies and telematic connections. The most substantial changes will be seen in the most classic areas of the librarian's profession, *i.e.,*:
- *In the description of resources*: With the advent of metadata and the implications dictated by the reflections deriving from the debate on Functional Requirements for Bibliographic Records;
- *In the services*: With particular regard to the sector of Reference and Document Delivery;
- *In conservation*: Where simple conservation is united with production and extended access to resources which were once inaccessible.

These changes are inevitably translated into practice by the emergence of new qualifications and new professional figures. At the basis we can identify a strong demand for entrepreneurship on the part of the managerial class, as has already been noted in the illustration of the model proposed by EFQM.

In this regard it appears that the prevailing librarian will be a professional with the ability to combine different solutions, different public and private operators within and outside the structure: a sort of professional who moves between the classic principles of the profession and the new technological possibilities and suggestions, a professional who is able to unite opportunities and risks in a productive way. The Italian scene does not favour great optimism in this sense. In many libraries we perceive a widespread situation of unawareness of the change in progress and a growing gap between those who know and those who do not, with the growing risk of a sort of "returning illiteracy".

This phenomenon seems particularly present in the large Italian libraries which are mainly government-run, and which are seriously behind as regards basic training, continuous updating and the retraining of the managerial class. Attending to basic and continuous training, also taking advantage of the possibilities offered nowadays by distance learning technologies, is becoming more and more a priority goal.

Thorough study of digital themes reveals that, though technology is important, it is more than ever an instrumental fact and hence secondary to that of giving staff the means for dominating the change.

Technologies and Standards

Undoubtedly the technological component is the factor through which a Digital Library is set up. The same can be said of the attention necessary for the application of descriptive standards (metadata) for access to the resources and their sharing, as well as for their fruition.

However, although the study reserves a significant part for these themes, it seems to us correct to emphasise here that technology presents itself above all as an instrumental and not a priority fact, due to its continual evolution.

In fact within a precise cultural and organisational reference framework, and with the availability of adequate skills, we should be careful to adopt market standards and move towards solutions which are technologically open to continual evolution. The study deals with the following themes under a series of sections:

- Digital supports (Text, Audio, Images, onwards: a comprehensive survey of the "objects" of the Digital Library.
- Telematic infrastructures and Internet onwards: an analysis of web demands and of the current range of offers in our country. The services offered by Infostrada, Albacom, I-net, Telecom, Garr and Rupa are examined.
- Automated management systems: a survey of to what extent and how the present library automation systems are being adapted to the advent of the digital. With a brief examination also of the Italian scene and of the features of SBN (servizio bibliotecario nazionale), which at the present time does not seem to be prepared for any kind of digital function.

Among the most innovative services is the ASP: "A further evolution, which may significantly influence the market in the years to come, is the starting-up of the so-called ASP (Application Service Provider). In practice, ASP is a service for library management which is completely entrusted to the outside. The only thing which the library has to manage locally is the connection to Internet. All the functions, from research to data input to the management of all the other functions are the concern of the system provider." It seems to us useful to recall this particular solution since it is proposed as one of the services that could be offered by the Digital Library., although with a different significance.

- Data Storage on the function of storage. It should be pointed out that in the face of a continually changing situation from both the technological viewpoint and that of competitiveness of the offer, a continual updating on each of these themes is crucial.

Digitisation

One of the most important technical aspects is that of acquiring a mastery of the materials and modes of treatment for digitisation. "The project of setting up a digital library needs thoroughly to evaluate the different types of document which are involved in the scanning process, whether it be a question of books, archive documents or more specifically museum documents, since also the latter are involved in the process of technological transformation of conservation and of fruition through informatics and telematic instruments".The theme of hybridism is dealt with. "(...) a theme which is closely related to the conservation of the library document at the moment when we are planning the setting-up of digital library. The demands of a conservation system are, in fact, better fulfilled by a combination of technologies".

"The practice of hybridism thus consists of combining the two technologies: converting into digital and producing microfilms from the digital or viceversa producing microfilms and converting them into digital". For each type of material, technical and methodological indications are provided in the second part. Indications are given in particular for the following materials:

- Supports of vegetable origin (papyri)
- Cloth supports
- Wooden supports
- Paper supports (with particular regard to manu-scripts [illuminated, illuminated with close binding, loose binding or loose-leaf, monochromatic], printed books, postcards and prints in general, tissue paper)
- Supports of animal origin (parchments)
- Supports of mineral origin
- Supports of chemical origin (microfilms, slides) Indications are given regarding the general criteria to apply for photographic and digital resolution.

The Organisation of a Project

Granted that each project has a separate story, a general reference scheme for the typical operations of a digitisation project is however proposed on the basis of what is offered by the professional literature.

Description of the Resources

In the Digital Library the problems of description take on more and more importance and a large part of the study is dedicated to these. What determines special attention to the problem is the need to understand all the different features of the digital object.

The various categories of Metadata necessary for identifying the object for its conservation and transmissability in time are analysed.

A survey of the standards of description and their evolution, directly influenced by the nature of the objects to which they will be applied, is proposed. Mention is made of ISBD (ER), of bibliographical formats such as MARC and Unimarc, of the problem of resource identifiers URN, DOI, URL, PURL, and finally a part is dedicated to the most significant standard so far developed for the purpose, *i.e.,* Dublin Core.

The debate on description also regards environments other than the library, in particular archives and museums; the EAD and CRM developed standards take this debate into account. Some international projects dedicated to this theme are of great importance. Some of these also include Italian participants.

The problems of the standards and Metadata return in the second part within a series of operational proposals and recommendations.

"The importance is underlined that some specific applications of projects for a digital library should start up the experimentation of the model IFLA FRBR because of its potential for analysing and documenting in a precise way the work, the expression, the manifestation, the copy, connections among them and respectively to the intellectual responsibility and the concepts treated.

This model is suitable for the treatment of electronic resources in their multiple versions, allowing documentation of critical editions, versions, new editions, translations, transpositions and revisions on similar or different supports.

This could be adequately applied in the treatment of prestigious collections which boast a rich literary history, thus furnishing a precious, rich access to which the function of digital conservation can be associated". And " metadata are necessary for the management of transactions which require the precise identification of the users of the objects treated, of the use that is to be made of them".

The initiatives of the digital library cannot ignore this function; they must define the parties involved and their role, the object of the transactions, the action to be carried out on the requested objects (*e.g.,* read, listen, see, save, transfer), the parameters which limit it (in terms of place, time, amount, repeatability, hence the number of times in which the action may be repeated), and also the action of whoever uses the service in exchange for acquired rights".

For conservation: "Regardless of the technique used to guarantee conservation and the future use of the digital resources, it is necessary to document clearly how to put these functions into practice and hence to define the features of the format of the software and of the instruments in order to use a certain resource over time".

"Besides the previously-expressed recommendations relative to the features of the metadata for the functions of identification and access, management of rights and conservation of the digital resources, some proposals are put forwards which cover on the one hand the activity of support to the description and management of the digital resources, on the other the actions of coordination which are necessary at an institutional and interinstitutional level, on both a national and an international scale".

Legal Problems (Copyright) in Italy

In this as in other cases, uncertainty prevails as to the behaviour to be adopted in the face of laws which are still mainly orientated towards traditional documentation. "The reference norms for copyright in a digital environment derive from the interpretation of the existing norms, from analogical application and from the appeal to the general principles of the law. In general there is even a lack of a consolidated jurisprudential doctrine and practice.

In view of the particular nature of the new technologies and the many different possibilities that they offer in comparison with traditional supports (paper, videocassettes, photographs etc.), the recourse to analogy and to interpretation of the existing norms is sometimes difficult.

Thus for a more complete protection, contractual solutions are often used to clarify the conditions of use of digital material, either through contracts (or licenses) or through regulations of access (or general conditions)."

Regarding services:

"In offering services to the users of a databank we must necessarily follow the legislation established for that type of support or negotiate with copyright-holders. If we wish to offer certain paid services on material which is still protected by copyright, we must necessarily negotiate the procedure to be adopted with the author, since he/she has all rights over the work".

Concerning the protection of the rights of a database: "In this case we can establish services, conditions of access to the database, limitations of liability, guarantees, applicable legislation and so on.

The contractual solution has undoubted advantages since the creator of the database defines his own liabilities and the conditions of access within a legislative picture which is not always clear and complete".

Even in the case of copyright we are faced with a situation which is continuously changing. "the legislation on this matter is still evolving, and there is very little jurisprudential doctrine and practice; despite this some guidelines can be already identified in current legislation or in analogical application. There are numerous problems regarding the possibility of offering paid services, in that obligations deriving from legislation on copyright, as well as some regulations about electronic trading, would emerge.

While the offering of "traditional" Non--profit-making services on material not protected by copyright (public property) in any case seems to be easier, even if a clear legal framework is lacking ". In this as in other cases, the need for constant observation of the evolution of the law remains open.

There is a similarly strong need to acquire the necessary skills in the case of negotiation for the acquisition of original digital resources. This is possible both by means of an internal process (special training as required), and thanks to the activation of external references (outsourcing) which are specifically dedicated to negotiation.

Examination of the Existing Situation

One of the fundamental elements in the setting-up of Digital Library in the world (but also in Italy for few but significant examples) is cooperation in terms of sharing of experience, knowledge and programmes. This assumption can clearly be drawn from the observation of what has actually happened and is in progress, above all outside our country.

A significant part of the study is that dedicated to an inventory of what has been created in Italy and abroad from all the previously-mentioned points of view. It is from this survey that the most significant part of the proposals arise; they are outlined concretely in the second section of the study.

General Summary

The Digital Library took off abroad much earlier than in Italy and this allows us to learn from a series of experiences, analyses, mistakes which have been identified and corrected, and thus to start from this point, exploiting the experiences metabolised by the library system thanks to forms of extended cooperation.

Features Chosen for the Study

The study has chosen from all the experiences analysed and has focused on the organisational aspects and the results which, thanks to these experiences, are being obtained in various, differentiated situations.

Situation Abroad

The study examines more or less in detail both the American and the European experiences.

To sum up, the elements that we feel it opportune to recall in this report are:

- The financial investment
- The political investment (understood as the politics of information)
- The training and professional investment
- The technological investment
- The constant investment of study and analysis

Let us examine the various points briefly:

- *The financial aspect is fundamental*: Not only in the sense that to set up any Digital Library project large funds have been invested, but also in the sense that in all countries the allocation of funds has been effected with extreme care and submitted to constant verification. Setting up a digital project not only costs a lot at the moment of its setting-up, but it costs as much again for its maintenance, digital resources not being static objects like traditional documents, but extremely dynamic ones.
- They are in fact subject to continual technological updating and, because of their possibilities of diffusion, produce expectations of service with consequences which must be continually foreseen, examined and dealt with opportunely.
- *The political investment*: This investment is clearly meant at an international level as the need to determine beforehand the "rules of the game", *i.e.*, guidelines of development of the digital within which to direct and coordinate the various initiatives, to avoid dispersion of resources of all kinds. In almost all the countries examined a sort of "Charter of Constitution of the digital" has been made out: this is wide and flexible but able to provide an indispensable reference point for any future initiative.

These declarations of intent, destined to constitute the "mission" of the various Digital Librarys, also have generic elements and in any case have the characteristic of being comprehensive of all the facets that local cultures inevitably carry with them. They are such as to fulfil all the requirements that the various countries regard as priority. As an example we cite (there are in fact others) the principles emanated by the National Library of Australia "*Digitisation Policy*" for the years 2000-2004.

The Training and Professional Investment

The advent of the Digital Library has overturned or, let us say, has better clarified, the idea of what the lines of investment for retraining and basic training should be.

In other countries where those working in libraries have a background of basic studies in librarianship, the greatest investment is being made in several directions: staff retraining in the sense of planning skill, management according to quality requirements, providing of new services and technological ability.

Particular attention is placed on what is nowadays offered by the possibilities of continuous distance training.There are numerous initiatives at various basic and higher levels, to guarantee a homogenous level of knowledge.

- *The technological investment*: The Digital Library obvio-usly has a strong technological component. Not only in the sense of the greater possibilities of application given by greater and more powerful means of production, storage and communication, but above all in the sense of using the technologies in the direction of all the categories of possible users.

From this derive the diffusion of studies and applications in the field of interfaces, in the qualification of services so as to cover all possible user groups from the scientific to the purely entertainment ones.

Another sector in which there is a large investment is that relative to the conservation of digital products, thanks to means of reconverting existing materials at the highest current technological level and according to the new market standards. Finally, the infrastructural aspect, which in many of the countries examined does not constitute a problem but which however is rightly pointed out as a precondition for the correct use of digital products. Some examples (continuously growing in number) are indicated both in the Bibliography and in the Bookmarks.

- The constant investment in study and analysis. The Digital Library is not static and this involves the presence in many countries of *ad hoc* structures for continuous study and extended sharing of studies and researches. International cooperation is no longer seen only as the sharing of information resources (also that), but above all as a sharing of experiences of research and technological results.

Many of the examples examined have within them structures suitable for scientific research in the digital field. T

Situation in Italy

A large section is dedicated to the Italian situation, whose main characteristics are the extremely fragmentary nature of the initiatives and poor coordination.

Features and Limitations

In our country a considerable number of initiatives have been undertaken or are in progress in the digital field. Most of these are aimed at the exploitation of single parts of collections (music, geographical maps, Galileo estate, etc.), rather than subscribing to wider projects with precise goals directed towards study or the systematic re-evaluation of areas of national culture.

In some universities and in the CNR (Consiglio Nazionale delle Ricerche), advanced projects are also created (three-dimensional digitisation, advanced workstations), but always in a way which is absolutely independent from other universities and, it sometimes seems, even in competition with them.

The same can be said of libraries, both government-run ones and those belonging to local government, in the absence of an overall plan. Almost all the initiatives also seem to obey the rule of incompleteness, in the sense that maintenance costs and the relative services are not planned ahead; the importance of elements like the implementation of metadata and conservation are not considered beforehand. That cooperation in the Italian libraries (apart from SBN (servizio bibliotecario nazionale)) is a sort of "optional", is clear also to those bodies which observe them in relation to international initiatives. This is, and it should be emphatically underlined, an element of great weakness in the case of the digital, where the complementary interaction of individual efforts acts to the advantage of better use of the financial resources, and not only of these.

A case apart, to which we will return in the proposals part, is SBN (servizio bibliotecario nazionale), whose main legacy is the very fact of having introduced a cooperative mentality into the Italian library environment. Organisations which differ in size and geographical location have learnt, thanks to the SBN (Servizio Bibliotecario Nazionale) principles, to discuss, take joint decisions and work for common objectives of resource sharing.

Despite the confusion which still prevails in the Italian digital situation, there are however initiatives which should be observed very carefully, these by no coincidence being those which show a joint effort on the part of different organisations towards a single goal (*e.g.,*: the CeBIT – Biblioteca Italiana Telematica, cited and described in the section on the Italian situation).

Introduction to Proposals

The proposal to which a large part of this summary as well as the study itself is dedicated, is fundamentally to:

- Fix precise criteria within which to carry out the activity of digitisation in our country.
- Opt for a strong series of initiatives of retraining and basic training.
- Set up a constant study.
- For the application of standards specific to the digital.
- For the definition of methodologies.
- For the definition of productive models directed at quality.

All this is to be done starting from the group of 46 libraries belonging to the government which, besides having the advantage of being under a single administration also have that (by no means secondary) of being part of one of the largest and most prestigious cultural heritages in the world.

Proposals

The proposals which are developed in the second part of the study are the fruit of a reflection on all the needs which have emerged in the light of the problems of all kinds highlighted in the inventory. The first part of the study ends with a mention of some aspects which are judged important and with a sort of summary of the problems.

"Two necessary levels of coordination are identified: local and central. By local coordination is meant everything pertaining to the single library structure. (...) It is thus a question of analysing the nature and extension of the new services and of the new professional figures required to handle these. The library also becomes a production centre, in that part of its collections will be destined to digital transposition; in this case we need

- A choice of the materials according to the ends which are proposed (conservation or service)
- Identification of the most appropriate methodologies for their treatment
- Creation of special operational task-forces or at least
- Coordination of outside forces in total or partial support of the digitization

From the central point of view, this coordination activity must have the function of supporting the initiatives of the single institutes, and they must be conceived as follows:

- According to general principles of coherence with the programmes of other institutions
- In compliance with consolidated standards which are updated each time
- Contributing to the financial support of the initiatives on the basis of the analysis of actual needs
- Providing where necessary the technical/logistic support for the setting-up and carrying out of digitisation initiatives
- Setting up the necessary training programmes for the acquisition of specific skills in the digital sector
- Creating the conditions for uncomplicated norms and regulations which fit the new tasks awaiting the single libraries".

The needs to be fulfilled should also be fixed, with particular regard to the features of the libraries belonging to the Ministry. The mixed features of these libraries requires a thorough knowledge of the users of the services provided.

"It does not appear that the government administration underst-ands these needs at a qualitative level but, from what emerges from the use made of statistical data, only at a quantitative one, even though data are collected which could help to define the characteristics of the users and their demands, on the basis of services provided. In the same way it does not seem that procedures of investigation specific to the users and their satisfaction (customer satisfaction) are ever undertaken.

This is an essential step in our opinion, one that should precede any project for the setting-up of Digital Librarys, as well as being coherent with the initiatives already underway relative to the quality of services. It is also coherent with debates at professional level on the so-called "Service Cards" in the library.

This would lead us to identify within the administration deficits related to regulations, organisation and the professional training of the staff, which may constitute a restriction to be overcome in order to achieve the effective working of a Digital Library project.

The analysis suggests the need for particular identification of:

- Which professional figures are today contemplated by the administration
- Which of these figures are coherent with the new professions which have become available with the advent of the digital
- How regulations and job descriptions fulfil the needs of the digital And from the point of view of regulations
- What the obstacles are which prevent the setting-up of value-added services (pricing of services etc.)
- What restrictions dictated by the budget items prevent the acquisition and activating of electronic sources (databases, electronic magazines as an alternative to printed ones, etc.)

"The proposal is moreover developed from a series of considerations which are the object of the "Analysis and Diagnosis" which we report herewith. ".

- In Italy, as in the rest of the world, digital projects are being developed but we have the sensation that "despite the technological and cultural validity of many of these projects each of them has taken off on a separate impulse, without any thought of inserting the initiative into a wider picture of coordinated and shared planning".
- "The majority of projects has a single structure as its promotor and main participant, thus generating the legitimate doubt that no attention has been paid to similar initiatives in a national field nor even to those at the international level."
- "It is very difficult to know the measure [and] the duration of investments".
- The destined use of the projects underway does not seem clear and hence also their practical application seems to lack consideration, above all regarding certain librarianship aspects (*e.g.*, use of metadata etc.)
- The large majority of library structures does not seem to be ready from the point of view of professional skills either for the starting up and running of the projects or for the offering of new services or of traditional services through new methods.
- More generally we note a lack of linkage among the *structures*

belonging to the various administrations, but also among offices belonging to the same administration".

Operational Proposals

These are a series of options which are compared regarding feasibility and times. We might call this series "transitory" and actually it is proposed as the necessary initial application of the more complex proposal, to be considered as the point of arrival of a wide process of reorganisation as a function of the setting-up of the Italian Digital Library.

Proposed Model

From the analysis it emerges that the proposed model can be seen as a centre which must interact with the existing systems. These existing systems are understood as hybrid bodies, hence libraries which extend their activities and services to the digital environment.The solution which emerges is thus not a purely technical one which quite simply stores in a single large "warehouse" the digital which is produced in Italy, but is instead orientated towards the coordination, support and management of the digital; in the Italian situation it will be above all new initiatives which will take on such service functions. In this way the single initiatives which will have to be constructed according to standard and quality criteria, will be able to flow together into that single entity which we can call the Italian Digital Library (IDL).

The Strategic Value of Cooperation and the Tradition of SBN (Servizio Bibliotecario Nazionale)

As already said several times during both the study and the present summary, cooperation, understood not in a formal but in a substantial way as sharing of intellectual, organis-ational and economic efforts orientated towards the digital, is the winning factor all over the world. It is in any case the factor which blocks impractical initiatives or those without any great prospects, as well as those which simply waste public resources.As already mentioned before, SBN (Servizio Bibliotecario Nazionale) is a positive "anomaly" on the Italian scene which has been nurturing the element of cooperation in the Italian library mentality and working habits for almost thirty years. It seems to us important to emphasise the following results:

- SBN (Servizio Bibliotecario Nazionale) is a distri-buted system.
- It is already in itself a "federation" of libraries.
- It has a wide, consolidated national extension.
- It has developed programmes and initiatives in a context of inter-institutional negotiation.
- It has developed a way of working and a transverse decisional model at both geographical and institutional levels (Government/Regions; relations among different Ministries)

- It has contributed to establishing operational relations among different sectors within the Ministry of Culture and Heritage itself.
- It has worked extensively with the private world.

These are elements which must in our opinion all be included without exception in the future Italian Digital Library, since they have furnished important political, technical and librarianship experiences.

Setting up of the Italian Digital Library

Despite the fragmentary nature of Digital Library experiences in Italy, we cannot ignore the presence of episodes which are valid from every point of view. These experiences have generated within the structures where they have been carried out a series of specific skills which must constitute the starting-point for any future development in the field.

We have also said that the group of libraries pertaining to the Ministry, to which can be added those active in the web thanks to SBN (Servizio Bibliotecario Nazionale), make up a potential Italian *"Digital Library Federation"*. It goes without saying that in the case of our proposal for setting up the Italian Digital Library we must consider the role and experiences of at least three of these libraries:The Biblioteca Nazionale Centrale of Florence, the Biblioteca Nazionale Marciana of Venice, the Biblioteca Nazionale Braidense of Milan. Next to these must also be put the ICCU with all the weight of its skills in the field of applications of bibliographical standards, and the Discoteca di Stato (National Sound Archive), for its specific skills in the field of sound resources.

The areas of responsibility of these structures are thus: ICCU bibliographical standards and metadata Government Record Library sound resources BNCF Conservation of digital resources; methodologies of digitisation BNMV- special materials (music, geographical maps) BNBM Periodicals The definitions of the themes to be treated with continuity must be fixed from the start by representatives from these institutes, who will gradually be joined by other institutes and other skills.

Coordination Structure (CS)

It is however felt that a series of duties must be entrusted to a coordination structure. "The need to have an organised structure which deals with coordinating and monitoring the various initiatives in the digital field arises from the complexity inherent in the Digital Library from the technical, organisational and economic points of view. The survey conducted both in Italy (few but significant examples) and above all abroad gives us a series of strong indications about the characteristics that the Digital Library must have in our country to give those guarantees of success and good return of investments.

The creation and running of a Digital Library is only partly comparable to the creation and running of a library automation system. In general, in our opinion, only in those parts regarding the technological choices (hw/sw solutions) and the activation of maintenance for the system.

All the rest is instead part of a production process which lies outside normal library functions. The complexity of these initiatives is obviously proportionate to the dimensions of the "production object". Hence the need at a national level of a CS which has the task of observing, directing and monitoring the various projects".

"This CS would have strong powers of directing and monitoring compliance of the fixed standard requirements. The tasks and limitations of the CS will also be defined in relation to other ministerial bodies, particularly all those directly dealing with matters in the library, archive and museum environment. It must in fact be remembered that the Digital Library goes beyond the mere library sphere and indeed, as has been amply demonstrated by numerous examples, has its maximum significance in the interaction among different institutions such as libraries, archives and museums".The tasks which must be undertaken at a central level are such because they cannot be delegated to peripheral structures, whose roles must concentrate more on operations and applications.

The "Mission" of the Italian Digital Library: its Definition and Creation

For the creation of the Italian Digital Library it is indispensable, as has already happened and is happening in other countries, to define the guidelines of the new Italian Digital Library.

We are talking about a sort of "Charter of Principles" of the digital, in which the fundamental principles and the cultural and scientific reference frameworks within which the existing initiatives will be placed and new initiatives will be set up, must be fixed.

We must define " a series of reference points which can be modified in time and adapted to the changing conditions and developments of the world of information.The CS will have as its prime task that of monitoring compliance with the principles which have been fixed, in the sense of encouraging and sustaining all the initiatives which are coherent with these principles and discouraging those which diverge from them.

Study and Research

The setting-up of the Digital Library involves a huge interaction of knowledge and experience from both the technological and the librarianship points of view. The primary task of the CS of the Italian Digital Library will thus be to act as a real "clearing-house" for the various problems that are encountered in the projects, in their creation and in their running in time.

For the various subjects of interest it may divide up into permanent working groups with specialists in the sector and "temporary guests" who are able to contribute with their concrete experience to the acquisition of information. We see four main paths along which to develop this type of organisation:

- Methodologies (planning, quality processes etc.)
- Technologies (hw/sw solutions, compression systems, new digital formats, etc.)
- Legal aspects (copyright, internal regulations, professional figures, deregulation directed to the service, etc.)
- The services (interfaces, pricing, joint ventures directed to resource sharing, etc.)

A National Directory of the Italian Digital Library

The starting point for any planning or goal definition is awareness of the existing situation. Also in Italy there are already numerous initiatives on the digital and some (very few) also of a certain significance; many are interesting as regards goals and less so as regards results.

In any case a Directory of the Digital must be set up, which is coordinated with other similar initiatives (for example the new one of the ICCU, more directed towards the use of metadata.

It can contain data both on the projects carried out (providing the necessary access via URL) and on those still in the planning stage, identified through inventories, papers, conventions, mention in professional and Non--professional periodicals. It will cover both technical, organisational and content aspects. There will be a parallel compilation of a kind of "Who's Who?" of the digital in Italy. It will need a stable inventory and editing structure.

Planning Support

The CS of the Italian Digital Library must become the reference point for providing consultancy services to the regions or to the large library structures for the correct formulation of the projects.

To this end it will from the start have to identify all the standards towards which the various projects must be directed, guaranteeing a tendency to homogeneity in the results.It must succeed in imposing a workflow standard for production and provide support for the drawing-up of plans according to quality requirements (Pert, GANNT). It will identify, also on the basis of indications by experts, programmes for optimising the national culture, themes (anniversaries, historical subjects) and types of material (periodicals, posters, statutes, etc.) which should all move towards the setting up of a complete Italian Digital Library (on the lines for example of the American Memory promoted by the Library of Congress), focusing on the integration of single projects which are developed on a local basis. It will favour the growth of these local initiatives (always within the standard reference grid) incentivating them with ad hoc grants and funding, on the basis of tenders as happens in other countries.

It must in any case encourage projects which are the fruit of joint efforts (several bodies, complementary projects etc.). It must favour projects integrating national and international projects which have already been started and particularly which regard themes of interest for Italian culture. The task force responsible for this important task of project definition must necessarily include: librarians, pure technicians, project management experts, marketing experts.

Training

The identification of training needs for adapting basic and advanced skills is another vital task. "The setting up of the Digital Library involves a revolution of skills, duties and roles which is not comparable to what was involved in the advent of automation of the library system. The librarian, seen both as manager and as employee responsible for certain duties, must necessarily be submitted to updating and often to a new technological literacy process.

This is not so much in order to transform librarians into pure technicians but to offer him/her all the tools for the understanding of the various technological components introduced by the Digital Library. The profession of librarian is transforming itself more and more into a sort of "aggregator" of solutions, aimed at obtaining a certain "object" (in our case: digital products) or at the activation of a certain service (in the case in question: new services of access to information).

The CS of the Italian Digital Library will play an important role in:

- Identifying training needs
- Defining the level of training/updating
- Developing new training methods and contents or having them developed
- Activating monitoring tools for verification of results

A task force for training will set up training paths and can also have the most suitable contents developed by outside companies which specialise in training. Particular use must be made of distance learning.

It can also set up agreements with community and extra-community countries for periods of study and updating exclusively aimed at the acquisition of skills in the Digital Library sector.

A particularly important point will be that related to the relations with schools and universities. Primary schools can be stimulated to become vehicles of Internet literacy and some of the first and most extensive users of Digital Library initiatives. Secondary schools and universities can instead be the main users of services offered by the Digital Library in terms of creativity, planning, distance learning.

Communication, Promotion and Outside Relations

One of the weak points of the present structures of the libraries is the low ability to communicate. The Cs and Italian Digital Library must break this negative tradition, setting up a continuous communication with the potential users of the proposed services. Not only through publicity campaigns but also above all thanks to detailed, constant strictly digital information on the current or finished initiatives, on projects and the various related initiatives.

The CS portal of the Italian Digital Library will be the natural vehicle of this information flow. The promotion of initiatives in progress or those already available must pass through the portal.

The CS of the Italian Digital Library must have a stable active editorial board (even located remotely and not necessarily centralised) which is coordinated by experts in communication able to constantly update the Web with information pertaining to the Digital Library. An electronic newsletter can be published in the currently fashionable method of brief review with links to the news or resource.

The aim of proposing Italian partnership in the great international initiatives will be particularly important for this PR Office. Expanding public relations also means activating channels of constant relations with interlocutors such as the publishing world, firms interested in the digital, as well as of course all those traditional partners like the Regions, the Provinces and the Boroughs.

With the latter in particular permanent negotiations must be set up to launch and/or monitor initiatives directed towards the Digital Library. The prototype developed shows how such a structure could communicate and provide specific services on the digital.

A National Conference on a Regular Basis

An extremely important task due to its communication value is that of organising a "National conference on the Digital" on a regular basis (for example every two years).

This will be the national and international showcase of the results obtained, with sessions of presentation of the most significant projects in progress or completed, technical workshops in cooperation with similar international structures, exhibition of specific technological solutions for the digital.

Times, Costs and Quality Requirements

Not all these objectives can be achieved at the same time and the last part of the study compares times, methods and costs of the proposals. Emphasis is on the requirement of quality as an element to be focused on and in this sense a synoptic classification of the characteristics which a quality Digital Library should have is proposed.

These requirements are examined both in regard to the local Digital Library (which is transformed into a centre of production of digital products and of supply of value-added services) and in regard to the true object of the study and of our proposal, *i.e.,* the Digital Library and its various services orientated towards the various local structures belonging to the system as a whole.

One section is dedicated to the "planned interventions on Non--informative components" which are in particular training and organisation. "The setting up of the Digital Library faces the traditional library with some questions finding the answer to which is a necessary prelude to the setting up of any initiative.

In particular the answer to what the essential conditions are for the feasibility of a project from the point of view of the processes which will be activated and their organisational impact on the functioning of the library and its staff".

This involves the redefinition of services, job definitions and training schemes. The final part of the study shows a list in table form of the main steps in this process of construction and an estimate of the costs to be faced at least during a first two-year period.

Breakdown of the Project

The overall plan of the project for the setting-up of the Italian Digital Library is developed using the formalism of the Work Breakdown Structure, which provides a proposal for the segmentation of the project, defining the varies activities (Work packages) of which it is composed. "*The main stages of the project which have been identified are:*

- *Pre-set-up Stage:* One of the stages for the setting up of the Italian Digital Library where the founding principles of the Italian Digital Library are outlined
- *Set-up Stage:* Where concreteness is lent to the action through a planning stage. It is in this stage that the tender specifications and/or outsourcing contracts for the creation of the technical/editorial infrastructures will be defined.
- *Creation Of Infrastructures:* Stage of development and transfer online of the Italian Digital Library services
- *Implementation Of Advanced Services:* this stage refers to the conception of the evolutionary nature of services offered by the Italian Digital Library." Through GANTT and Pert the project is described in its time course and in terms of the milestones of verification and/or checking of the activities.

Risks

"By risks we must above all understand Non--exploitation of the resource potential in the processes and activities. But we can better judge this "Non--exploitation" on the basis of the distinction of risks formulated as: -wastage (of human resources, materials, potential of internal functioning; organisational processes and activities) -losses of quality (dissatisfaction about the relations with the local Digital Library; with the final user; creation of a product not wholly complying with expectations and needs).

Costs

The costs expressed in the table refer to two orders of greatness:

- External costs refer to the adoption of resources outside the ministry such as: consultancies, telematic infrastructures, projects, outsourcing etc., to be found through contracts or tenders.
- Internal costs refer to the use of resources inside the organisational structure of the UCBL; in this case man-days were used as the unit of measurement to quantify the estimated expense.

A scheme is also provided for the calculation of the variable costs of a digitisation project, remembering that no universal scheme of budgeting so far exists for digitisation projects and that the orientation is rather that of working out a model on the basis of a prototype which is then extended to the whole project.

Benefits

In some final tables a methodology of evaluation is proposed without going into the attribution of the values expressed by the coefficients which will depend on the analysis of the various project situations. This illustration in table form is developed both for local Digital Librarys and for the Italian Digital Library. In the first case (Digital Library) it involves while in the second (Italian Digital Library) it instead involves

Conclusions

As explained in the introduction we have tried with this summary to provide a simpler and more direct key to the main concepts expressed in the study as a whole. We recommend however that this summary be used as an "entry key" to the complete study.

There are many subjects dealt with in it that are difficult to summarise without losing much of their value from the point of view of information or reflection on the complexity of the Digital Library.

CONSTRUCTION OF DYNAMIC DIGITAL LIBRARY

This chapter describes a digital library architecture and implementation that is configurable, extensible and dynamic in the way it presents content and in the services it provides. The design manifests itself as a network of modules that communicate in terms of XML messages.

All modules characterize the functionality they implement in response to a "describe yourself" message, and can transform messages using XSLT to support different levels of configurability.

Traditional library values such as backwards compatibility and multiplatform operation are combined with the ability to add new collections and services adaptively. The paper describes the new design and shows how it can be used to build four different digital library systems.

We conclude by showing how the design fits existing interoperability frameworks. This paper describes a digital library design that improves upon the Greenstone toolkit. First, it provides more flexible ways of dynamically configuring the run-time system and adding new services to it.

Second, it lowers the overhead incurred by collection developers when accessing this flexibility to organize and present their content. Third, it modularizes the internal structure and simplifies the addition of new modules.

The design is based on widely-accepted standards such as XML, current software practices such as simple protocols (like SOAP), cross-platform development strategies (Java), and contemporary schemes for software modularization and dynamic updates. Most important of all, it is informed by our experience with the current Greenstone system and the problems and challenges faced by real users, international collection developers, and practicing librarians.

The structure of the paper is as follows. First we give some background out of which the requirements for the digital library software arose. Next we describe the new design, called Greenstone, and discuss how it meets the identified needs. Fundamental to the approach is the use of XML throughout for data representation, combined with XSL Transforms to provide a flexible mechanism for adjusting the functionality of the runtime system without having to modify and recompile the source code.

To promote cross-platform independence (which has consumed inordinate human resources in the present Greenstone system) and facilitate the dynamic loading of services and other modules, the implementation uses Java. Following this we describe four very different examples built using the new design.

The first demonstrates backwards compatibility, and, in addition, operates within a distributed environment. The second augments text at display time, using an established software tool for text mining developed elsewhere, to show how functionality can be enriched through the introduction of a new service.

The third is a map-based digital library that introduces two new services to support geographic functionality and, while still accessed through a web-based interface, is highly tailored to the specific domain of its source documents.

The fourth is a radically different interface for the interactive viewing of search results as a hierarchically organized cluster of documents, and illustrates the versatility of the design in coping with fine-grained interaction. We conclude with a commentary on how the design fits existing interoperability frameworks, from which many valuable lessons have been learned.

Background

Over the years the Greenstone digital library software has been employed by many users internationally to develop a wide variety of digital libraries. In addition to operation over the Web, an early application, and still a major one, is collections of humanitarian information in the form of CD-ROMs that run on any Windows computer (including Windows 3.1).There are now over two dozen of these collections, and they have been distributed widely by the United Nations and other Non- government agencies. Many other styles of collection have been developed under Greenstone.They range from numerous personal collections based around common document formats such as E-mail, photographs, Word, and PDF documents through to largescale bibliographic catalogs such as the BBC radio and TV archives.

There are mixed media collections involving text, images and audio drawn from data such as historic newspapers and oral history. Several demonstration music collections support direct content-based retrieval through "query by humming." Many customized and branded user interfaces exist, such as the New York Botanical Gardens, and many international collections in local languages created by institutions in China, India, Croatia, Russia and Israel.

The software is distributed in source form, and for convenience binaries are available for Windows, Linux and MacOS X. The user interface is available in 30 languages. A recent addition is a graphical interface for collection design and construction which is also multilingual. A portfolio of demonstration collections is available at www.nzdl.org, and selected example collections built internationally can be found at www.greenstone.org.

Weaknesses

Many experimental interfaces have been built for Greenstone, some of which make use of a CORBA-based protocol to support distributed client-server interaction. These include a Venn diagram tool for formulating Boolean queries graphically, and a bibliographic visualization tool that plots matching citations on an x-y grid based on publication year and ranked relevance score to the query terms. However, while perfectly functional, some of these variants are implemented inelegantly, exposing limitations caused by certain aspects of the design.For instance, the immutable nature of the index files generated during the building process makes incremental adjustments to a collection expensive. Another hindrance is the low level of functional customization supported by the runtime system. Although minor presentation tweaks are easy, more extensive changes involve modifying and recompiling the source code. The strongly typed nature of the CORBA protocol was also found to be overly restrictive in many practical situations.

Requirements

From these and other considerations arose the following requirements for an improved design.

- *Backwards compatibility:* Naturally we wish to retain the existing system's strengths. This is accomplished by ensuring that the new design is backward compatible, which has the added benefit of providing existing developers and users with an easy migration path.

- *Levels of customization:* To match the different categories of people involved in constructing digital libraries, different levels of customization are required. For instance, a content developer may wish to include source documents in a new format; a collection editor may seek influence over diverse issues of presentation.
- *Software modularity:* To facilitate development and long-term management of the software, code modularization—a mantra of any software engineering approach—is essential. This is promoted by adopting off-the-shelf technology such as a database system, indexing tools, and page rendering software; and by the use of standards.
- *Service based:* Basing a digital library around a set of services is another way to accomplish modularity—in this case, modularity of function.
- *Distributed architecture:* A rich digital library infrastructure can only be supported by a distributed architecture, and the addition of an open protocol helps to foster interoperability.
- *Future compatibility*: Libraries are long-term institutions with a mandate for preservation, and it is essential that old collections can be presented by future versions of the system. This is a more ambitious requirement than mere extensibility which, although an admirable quality in any design, does not necessarily ensure that future versions can safely interact with current ones.
- *Dynamic:* Many aspects of the library should be dynamic, for example content, whereby documents and metadata can be added, revised and removed while a repository remains on-line, and configuration, where presentational issues can be adjusted and services added at runtime.
- *Integrated documentation:* Large-scale software systems such as digital libraries benefit immensely from the use of an integrated documentation system.
- *Self-describing modules:* This goes a stage further than the previous item: modules describe themselves in a machine-readable format so that other modules can interact with them without the need for explicit control. Computer environment integration. A digital library should mesh well into a user's existing computer environment. Full integration makes a digital library become a seamless component of each user's work environment.

SOFTWARE DESIGN

The new software design has evolved from the requirements articulated above, our own experience of developing digital library systems, and studies of other open source software and research projects.This section provides an overview of modularity and inter-module communication, and then works through a simple, stand-alone example. The next section describes four very different examples built using the new design, to illustrate the general applicability of the approach.

Modularity

We decided that the best way to meet the challenges posed by the list of requirements was to reimplement Greenstone using a modular topology. In the design, a digital library manifests itself as a network of modules, and communication between them is expressed through an instantiation of XML.

A mandatory requirement for a module—enforced through its base class definition—is that it handles "describe yourself" messages. What kinds of messages follow typically depend on the outcome of an initial "describe yourself".

Modules have the ability to transform messages by applying an XSL Transform. This is a particularly useful mechanism for dynamically controlling levels of configurability—one of our requirements. Within the network of modules comprising a digital library, a set of services are defined that prescribe the functionality supported by that particular digital library configuration.

Communication

Modules communicate using synchronous request-response pairs. Figure shows an example XML exchange, where the Text Query module in a collection called "demo" is asked to describe itself. It does this, providing information about the structure of the service as well as fragments of text to be used for display.

These are returned in the language specified in the request. While the language used is structured and typed, it has been crafted in such a way that the information it contains can be open-ended.

For example the paramList structure allows other items to be included, such as whether stemming is on or off. In addition to supporting optional parameters, extensions can be introduced without having to update the protocol's API, thereby avoiding the need to propagate code changes to the entire distributed network (which may require taking it off-line while the changes are made).

Programming for a sample XML exchange as a request/response pair.

```
<request to=’demo/TextQuery’ lang=’en’ type=’describe’ uid=’21’/>
<response from=’demo/TextQuery’ lang=’en’ type=’describe’>
<service name=’TextQuery’ type=’query’>
<displayItem name=’name’>Search</displayItem>
<displayItem name=’description’>Full text search</displayItem>
```

```
<displayItem name='submit'>Search</displayItem>
<paramList>
<param name='index' type='enum_single' default='stx'>
<displayItem name="name">Index to search in</displayItem>
<option name="dtx">
<displayItem name="name">entire documents</displayItem>
</option>
<option name="stx">
<displayItem name="name">chapters</displayItem>
</option>
</param>
<param name='maxDocs' type='integer' default='10'>
<displayItem name="name">Maximum hits to return</displayItem>
</param>
<param name="query" type="string">
<displayItem name="name">Query string</displayItem>
</param>
</paramList>
</service>
</response>
```

A Simple Stand-alone Example

The simple stand-alone example shown in Figure encapsulates many of the design's key features. It comprises a "back end" server, termed a digital library site in our design, coupled to a "front end" that provides the user interface. The modules' names were chosen to emphasize the roles they play.

The Receptionist's point of contact with the server is the Message Router (MR) module—all communication with the site occurs through this module. The configuration is designed to generalize to a distributed environment. The digital library back end in Figure contains two collections, demo and fao, and a cluster of collection-formation services.

Add Document is a service that adds a document to a collection. Import Collection imports into the system all documents associated with a collection, converting them wherpe necessary from their original form. Build Collection builds all indexes and browsing structures that are associated with a collection. Activate Collection makes a newly-built collection active, so that it can be seen by digital library users.

These services are all concerned with creating a digital library collection. Being related, they are grouped together into a "service cluster." In Figure the services just listed are accessed through the Collection Formation service cluster module.

As far as the digital library user is concerned, a "collection" is a focused group of documents with a uniform means of access. For the system, it is a service cluster that groups a set of services that are related by the data they work on. For example, the demo collection towards the lower left of Figure contains three modules providing four services to the user.

The modules are called "Search," which provides a Text Query service, "Retrieve," which provides a document retrieval service Resource Retrieve and a metadata retrieval service Metadata Retrieve, and "Browse," which provides a metadata browsing service Classifier Browse.

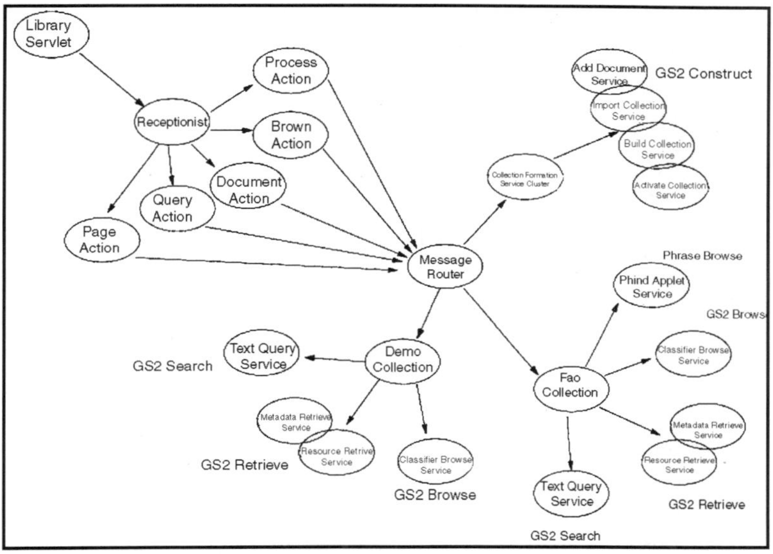

Fig. A Simple Stand-alone Site.

The Web-based front end at the upper left of Figure centers around the Receptionist, which is the point of contact for the interface generator. A servlet (labeled "Library Servlet") takes HTTP commands in the form of URLs and arguments and translates them into XML for the Receptionist.

The Receptionist is capable of executing various different actions, each of which involves (usually) many calls to the digital library's Message Router. The builtin ability for Receptionist modules to transform XML messages using XSLT is used—in conjunction with a style sheet—to generate the HTML that is finally presented to the user.

Examples

For pedagogical purposes, the example configuration in Figure is rudimentary. The front and back ends (receptionist and site server) are compiled together into a single executable process with a single Message Router handling all communication between them.

However, the design supports a far richer infrastructure than this. Message Routers have the capability to communicate across a distributed network with other Message Routers and with Receptionists.

Different implementations of the same service can be switched in and out to give a digital library site different algorithmic behaviour (such as incremental building); and new services can be introduced and brought on-line, dynamically if necessary. The library can also have many different user interfaces.We now describe four more interesting scenarios. The first emulates "classic" Greenstone

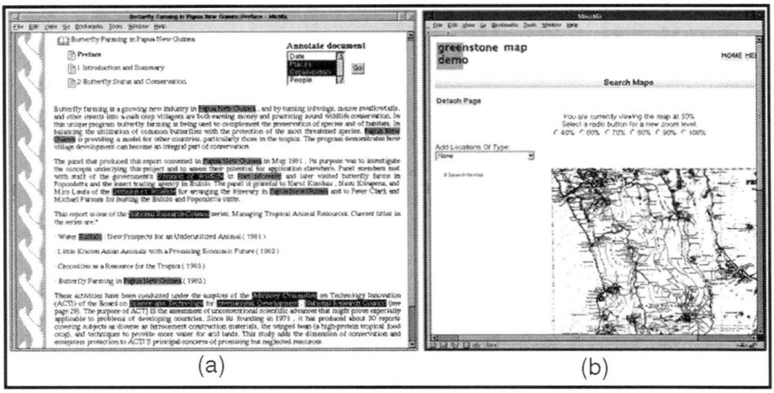

Fig. Additional Services to Augment run-time Functionally (a) text Augmentation of place names; (b) a novel map-based Interface.

to demonstrate backwards compatibility, with a distributed configuration a straightforward addition. The second augments text at display time, to show how functionality can be enriched through the introduction of a new service.

The third and fourth utilize novel interfaces to enrich the interaction: the former is specialized for geographic maps, and the latter for text based collections.

Classic Greenstone, with collections on remote sites

To provide backwards compatibility, a set of Greenstone services have been implemented that access index and database files generated by a Greenstone system. Indeed we have already seen these in Figure.

Moreover, using Cascading Style Sheets (CSS), the look and feel of the traditional interface has been matched one-for-one, so that the user's experience of the digital library remains the same. Of course with the more versatile design, more sophisticated internal structures can be built within the digital libary.

For instance, because of the design decision that all communication be XML based, it is straightforward to arrange for the XML messages sent between modules to be seamlessly streamed across remote machines.

For this we employ the Simple Object Access Protocol (SOAP), but any protocol that can process text can be used. To the user there is no disernable difference accessing collections this way. Backwards compatability is not the sole aim, however, and the structure allows increasingly interesting digital library designs—ones that do provide a distinctly different expierence for the user. We discuss three such examples next.

Dynamic Text Mining

The next example shows how a new Greenstone service can be provided that enhances documents for the reader, based upon the open source GATE system for text mining. The motivation is that highlighting selected items in documents can make it easier for users to scan them for particular pieces of information. In this implementation, digital library documents, once located, are mined on the fly marking up entities such as keywords and place names before presenting them to the user. Figure shows a section of a book on Butterfly Farming in Papua New Guinea (from the Humanity Development Library at www.nzdl.org) that the user is reading.

The Annotate document menu at the top right calls the display time text mining feature. When items on this menu are selected, text of the selected type is highlighted in the document displayed. In this case the user has selected Places and Organizations, and these are highlighted wherever they occur, in different colors (simulated by white-on-grey and black-on grey in the illustration).

The selectable items in Figure were identified and extracted by ANNIE, GATE's information extraction system. Whenever an annotation type is selected from the menu, Greenstone calls the information extraction module dynamically to identify items of that type.

This incurs a delay that depends on the document's size but is usually short: the system processes text at the average rate of 15 Kb/sec on a typical workstation. In order to achieve this the software is loaded when the Greenstone server is executed and remains resident in memory thereafter, to avoid a start-up delay (of about 10 seconds) in which all the text processors are initialized and prepared for use.

In Greenstone3, GATE is encapsulated in a module as just another service. It takes messages with two parameters, the type of annotation and a document, and returns the document with relevant items marked up with XML tags.

A style sheet in the server module chooses the colors in which the items are displayed. In order to generate the menu in the figure, a "describe yourself" message is sent to the GATE module, which returns a list of the annotations that are available.

Apart from this one module, the rest of the digital library system knows nothing of GATE.

However, it does know about a general class of services, Enrich, that take a document and return the same document with some elements marked up. To add this text-mining ability to an existing Greenstone site dynamically the Java class files for the new service need to added to the correct folder on the DL site's file system, the site's configuration file updated to name the new service, and a "reconfigure" signal sent (which can be initiated through a web browser) to the DL site server.

Geographical map based interface Figure is taken from a site configured to support map searching based on a small collection of New Zealand maps drawn between 1770 and 1953, part of our university library's special collections.

It shows the result of searching for "Rangiriri"—a township in the North Island of New Zealand and, on a hill nearby of the same name, the scene of a battle in 1863 between Maori and British soldiers. Two crosses (colored red when viewed online) have been overlaid on the map showing the position of the township and hill, and can be seen slightly above the centre of the map.

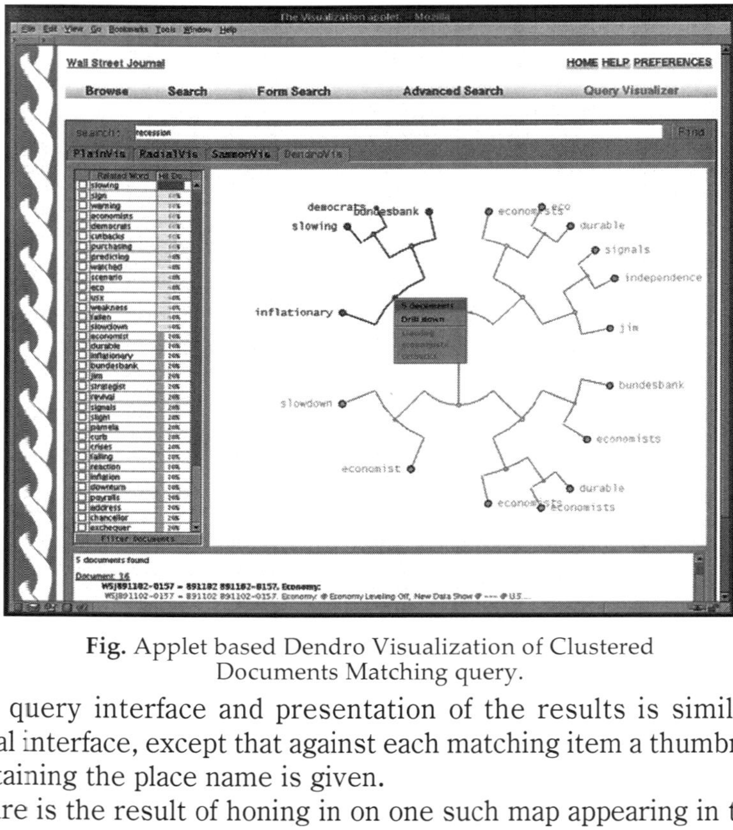

Fig. Applet based Dendro Visualization of Clustered Documents Matching query.

The query interface and presentation of the results is similar to the traditional interface, except that against each matching item a thumbnail of the map containing the place name is given.

Figure is the result of honing in on one such map appearing in the result set. Through the interface the user can change the level of magnification of the map and request that additional features such as cemeteries, bridges, and estuaries be marked.This new functionality is provided by adding two new services, including geographic metadata with the collection's source documents (the maps), and a gazetteer of over 40,000 entries from Land Information New Zealand (LINZ). Searching is handled by the Map Query service. For each place name query term that is located in the gazetteer, its longitude and latitude are checked against each map to see if it falls within its boundaries.Once all cross-referencing is complete, the list of maps with matching entries is sorted by the number of query terms on each map. Image manipulation and the results display are handled by the Map Retrieve service, which makes use of the open source Image Magick toolkit for copying, annotating (such as placing a cross at an x, y location) and resizing images.

Cluster Visualizations

Figure shows a web-based interface, but there may be other forms, ranging from standalone applications and applets that display documents in different ways to alert services that recognize when new information becomes available in one of the collections and formulate appropriate E-mail to users. Figure is one such instance: a Java applet that supports browsing result sets as document clusters through a multi-viewed, interactive interface.

To function it needs the addition of a new build-time service, Vis Construct, which is responsible for computing additional statistics about the collection necessary to perform subsequent document clustering operations, and a sub-classing of the Applet service, tailored for the HTML necessary to embed the visualization applet within a web page.

Besides this, the visualization can interact with any text-based Greenstone collection that defines keyword metadata. The distinctly different interface behaviour is achieved through fine-grained interaction with the existing Text Query and Metadata Retrieve services using SOAP. Derived from the query term entered, there are four views in the visualization.

The first is the standard result list format; the other three are based around a shared model of hierarchically clustered documents.

In Figure the user has entered the query term "recession" to a collection based on the Wall Street Journal and is viewing the result as a Dendro map—the circular arranged tree displayed in the main panel—which contains words like slowing, slowdown and inflationary around the circumference. The size of nodes in the tree represents the number of documents clustered at that point in the hierarchy, and for reasons of space only 5 levels of the tree are shown at a time. Clicking on a node shows a popup menu with the precise number of documents in the cluster and the option of "drilling down" as shown in the figure.

The consequence of choosing this option is for the tree to be redrawn with the selected node at the centre of the map, thereby exposing more of the detail in that part of the hierarchy.

While all this is going on, the left-panel displays the keywords relevant to the selected cluster, and the bottom panel lists the documents involved. Within the left panel, keywords can be activated or deactivated and the bottom panel dynamically filtered to reflect the changes.

TYPES OF DIGITAL LIBRARIES

The term digital library is diffuse enough to be applied to a wide range of collections and organizations, but, to be considered a digital library, an online collection of information must be managed by and made accessible to a community of users. Thus, some web sites can be considered digital libraries, but far from all. Many of the best known digital libraries are older than the web including Project Perseus, Project Gutenberg, and ibiblio. Nevertheless, as a result of the development of the internet and its search potential, digital libraries such as the European Library and the Library of Congress are now developing in a Web-based environment. Public, school and college libraries are also able to develop digital download websites, featuring eBooks, audiobooks, music and video. A distinction is often made between content that was created in a digital format, known as born-digital, and information that has been converted from a physical medium, *e.g.,*, paper, by digitizing. The term hybrid library is sometimes used for libraries that have both physical collections and digital collections. For example, American Memory is a digital library within the Library of Congress. Some important digital libraries also serve as long term archives, for example, the ePrint arXiv, and the Internet Archive.

Academic Repositories

Many academic libraries are actively involved in building institutional repositories of the institution's books, papers, theses, and other works which can be digitized or were 'born digital'. Many of these repositories are made available to the general public with few restrictions, in accordance with the goals of open access, in contrast to the publication of research in commercial journals, where the publishers often limit access rights. Institutional, truly free, and corporate repositories are sometimes referred to as digital libraries.

Digital Archives

Physical archives differ from physical libraries in several ways. Traditionally, archives were defined as:

- Containing primary sources of information (typically letters and papers directly produced by an individual or organization) rather than the secondary sources found in a library (books, periodicals, etc);
- Having their contents organized in groups rather than individual items;
- Having unique contents.

The technology used to create digital libraries has been even more revolutionary for archives since it breaks down the second and third of these general rules. In other words, "digital archives" or "online archives" will still generally contain primary sources, but they are likely to be described individually rather than (or in addition to) in groups or collections, and because they are digital their contents are easily reproducible and may indeed have been reproduced from elsewhere. The Oxford Text Archive is generally considered to be the oldest digital archive of academic physical primary source materials.

Leaders in the Field

Project Gutenberg, Google Book Search, Windows Live Search Books(shutdown), Internet Archive, Cornell University, The Library of Congress World Digital Library, The Digital Library at the University of Michigan, and Carnegie Mellon University's Million Book Project are considered leaders in the field of digital library creation and management.

The Future

Large scale digitization projects are underway at Google, the Million Book Project, and Internet Archive. With continued improvements in book handling and presentation technologies such as optical character recognition and ebooks, and development of alternative depositories and business models, digital libraries are rapidly growing in popularity as demonstrated by Google, Yahoo!, and MSN's efforts. Just as libraries have ventured into audio and video collections, so have digital libraries such as the Internet Archive.

Searching

Most digital libraries provide a search interface which allows resources to be found. These resources are typically deep web (or invisible web) resources since they frequently cannot be located by search engine crawlers. Some digital libraries create special pages or sitemaps to allow search engines to find all their resources.

Digital libraries frequently use the Open Archives Initiative Protocol for Metadata Harvesting (OAI-PMH) to expose their metadata to other digital libraries, and search engines like Google Scholar, Yahoo! and Scirus can also use OAI-PMH to find these deep web resources.

There are two general strategies for searching a federation of digital libraries:

- Distributed searching, and
- Searching previously harvested metadata.

Distributed searching typically involves a client sending multiple search requests in parallel to a number of servers in the federation. The results are gathered, duplicates are eliminated or clustered, and the remaining items are sorted and presented back to the client. Protocols like Z39.50 are frequently used in distributed searching. A benefit to this approach is that the resource-intensive tasks of indexing and storage are left to the respective servers in the federation. A drawback to this approach is that the search mechanism is limited by the different indexing and ranking capabilities of each database, making it difficult to assemble a combined result consisting of the most relevant found items.

Searching over previously harvested metadata involves searching a locally stored index of information that has previously been collected from the libraries in the federation. When a search is performed, the search mechanism does not need to make connections with the digital libraries it is searching - it already has a local representation of the information.This approach requires the creation of an indexing and harvesting mechanism which operates regularly, connecting to all the digital libraries and querying the whole collection in order to discover new and updated resources. OAI-PMH is frequently used by digital libraries for allowing metadata to be harvested. A benefit to this approach is that the search mechanism has full control over indexing and ranking algorithms, possibly allowing more consistent results. A drawback is that harvesting and indexing systems are more resource-intensive and therefore expensive.

DESIGN OF DIGITAL LIBRARY MEDIND WEB SITE

The medIND project is having its own domain name at the Internet (http://medind.nic.in). It has pneumonic value and stands for Medical Journals on Internet [from India]. Home page gives details of the project listing of the participating journals. This listing is hyperlinked to each participating journal home page at the medIND web site. The site provides two approaches to access the journal articles.

Browsing

Journals are hyperlinked and arranged in alphabetical order. Such hyperlinked list leads to pages giving details of selected journals such as editors, instructions to authors, contact address, parent body etc. Further, this leads to listing of issues of the journal by years/volume wise. The content page provides hyperlinks to the individual article.

Searching

The searching is being provided through the bibliographic database IndMED. Each record of the IndMED has been linked to the individual article in the MedIND site. The searching of the articles can be achieved through from http://indmed.nic.in as well as from http://mednic.nic.in web sites. The references will display icons indicating the availability of the full text. In developing digital collection, issues of intellectual property rights have been dealt to strengthen the cooperation between editors and content service provider to facilitate access to digital content through Internet to end users in the area of biomedicine on Non--commercial basis.

The design of digital collection should be usable, flexible and simple enough to accommodate future changes and also enables other applications to utilize data for development of future applications.

The naming convention of digital collection is acted as bridge between metadata base and full text of content. This project fulfills the demand of providing full text of documents to health professionals free of cost throughout the world. It serves as a model for the development of similar collections in others S&T areas, medIND is a step in the process of making it as an open archive source where Indian journals covered in Medline database as well in IndMED database will be stored and will be provided access free of cost to health professionals throughout the world. This will give enough visibility and exposure to Indian biomedical journals and demand for Indian literature would be met through the medIND project. In future, more visibility to articles included in medIND journals would be provided by adopting and exposing metadata in OAI-PMH and RSS protocols.

CONSTRUCTION AND ORGANIZATION

FRAMEWORKS

A digital library can be built around specific repository software. The best known examples of this are DSpace, Eprints, Fedora, dLibra(Poland), and Greenstone Digital Library Software. In 2009, Fedora Commons and the DSpace Foundation merged to create a new organization, DuraSpaceThe Reference Model for an Open Archival Information System (OAIS) provides a framework to address digital preservation.Other formal frameworks include the DELOS Reference Model(Agosti, et al., 2006) and the Streams, Structures, Spaces, Scenarios, Societies (5S) formal framework.

Digitization

In the past few years, procedures for digitizing books at high speed and comparatively low cost have improved considerably with the result that it is now possible to plan the digitization of millions of books per year for creating digital libraries.

ADVANTAGES

The advantages of digital libraries as a means of easily and rapidly accessing books, archives and images of various types are now widely recognized by commercial interests and public bodies alike.Traditional libraries are limited by storage space; digital libraries have the potential to store much more information, simply because digital information requires very little physical space to contain it. As such, the cost of maintaining a digital library is much lower than that of a traditional library.

A traditional library must spend large sums of money paying for staff, book maintenance, rent, and additional books. Digital libraries do away with these fees. Both types of library require cataloguing input to allow users to locate and retrieve material.Digital libraries may be more willing to adopt innovations in technology providing users with improvements in electronic and audio book technology as well as presenting new forms of communication such as wikis and blogs; conventional libraries may consider that providing online access to their OPAC catalogue is sufficient.

An important advantage to digital conversion is increased accessibility to users. There in also availability to individuals who may not be traditional patrons of a library, due to geographic location or organizational affiliation.

- *No physical boundary*: The user of a digital library need not to go to the library physically; people from all over the world can gain access to the same information, as long as an Internet connection is available.
- *Round the clock availability*: A major advantage of digital libraries is that people can gain access to the information at any time, night or day.
- *Multiple access*: The same resources can be used simultaneously by a number of institutions and patrons. This may not be the case for copyrighted material: a library may have a license for "lending out" only one copy at a time; this is achieved with a system of digital rights management where a resource can become inaccessible after expiration of the lending period or after the lender chooses to make it inaccessible (equivalent to returning the resource).
- *Information retrieval*: The user is able to use any search term (word, phrase, title, name, subject) to search the entire collection. Digital libraries can provide very user-friendly interfaces, giving clickable access to its resources.
- *Preservation and conservation*: Digitization is not a long-term preservation solution for physical collections, but does succeed in providing access copies for materials that would otherwise fall to degradation from repeated use. Digitized collections and born-digital objects pose many preservation and conservation concerns that analog materials do not.
- *Space*: Whereas traditional libraries are limited by storage space, digital libraries have the potential to store much more information, simply because digital information requires very little physical space to contain them and media storage technologies are more affordable than ever before.
- *Added value*: Certain characteristics of objects, primarily the quality of images, may be improved. Digitization can enhance legibility and remove visible flaws such as stains and discoloration.

PROBLEMS

Digital Preservation

The work needed to ensure that digital content is maintained and accessible into the future is beginning to be addressed.Technological standards change over time and forward migration must be a constant consideration of every library. Migration is a means of transferring an unstable digital object to another more stable format, operating system, or programming language. Migration allows the ability to retrieve and display digital objects that are in danger of becoming extinct. This is a rather successful short-term solution for the problem of aging and obsolete digital formats, but with the ever-changing nature of computer technologies, migration becomes this never-ending race to transfer digital objects to new and more stable formats. Migration is also flawed in the sense that when the digital files are being transferred, the new platform may not be able to capture the full integrity of the original object. There are countless artifacts sitting in libraries all over the world that are essentially useless because the technology required to access the source is obsolete. In addition to obsolescence, there are rising costs that result from continually replacing the older technologies. This issue can dominate preservation policy and may put more focus on instant user access in place of physical preservation.

Copyright and Licensing

Some people have criticized that digital libraries are hampered by copyright law, because works cannot be shared over different periods of time in the manner of a traditional library. The republication of material on the Web by libraries may require permission from rights holders, and there is a conflict of interest between them and publishers who may wish to create Web versions of their content for commercial purposes. There is a dilution of responsibility that occurs as a result of the spread-out nature of digital resources. Complex intellectual property matters may become involved since digital material isn't always owned by a library. The content is, in many cases, public domain or self-generated content only. Some digital libraries, such as Project Gutenberg, work to digitize out-of-copyright works and make them freely available to the public. An estimate of the number of distinct books still existent in library catalogues from 2000BC to 1960, has been made. The Fair Use Provisions (17 USC § 107) under copyright law provide specific guidelines under which circumstances libraries are allowed to copy digital resources. Four factors that constitute fair use are purpose of use, nature of the work, market impact, and amount or substantiality used. Some digital libraries acquire a license to "lend out" its resources. This may involve the restriction of lending out only one copy at a time for each license, and applying a system of digital rights management for this purpose.

Metadata Creation

The ability to find works of interest in large libraries is directly related to how well they are catalogued. While cataloguing electronic works digitised from a libraries' existing holding may be as simple as copying moving a record for the print to the electronic item, with complex and born-digital works require substantially more effort. While full text search can be used for some searches, there are many common catalog searches which can't be performed using full text, including:

- Finding texts which are the translation of other texts
- Linking texts published under pseudonyms to the real author (Samuel Clemens and Mark Twain, for example)
- Differentiating Non--fiction from parody (The Onion from The New York Times, for example)

7

Library Infrastructure for Digital Management

INTRODUCTION

We are living to-day in a world of change and the changes we see all around us due to availability of information quicker than before, faster communication through E-mail, voice mail and video conferencing and the great influence of the Internet and web pages. The use of computer-based system in the libraries and information units is now commonplace all over the world. Computers are used to assist in a variety of functions such as maintaining and providing access to the catalogue of items in the collection, managing the issuing and returning of items from the collection, the acquisition of new items for the collection, controlling the serial publications and allowing the retrieval of information from the databases relating to bibliographic data financial or numeric data or the full text of documents.

DIGITAL ASSETS

- Floppies: Certain Books are accompanying floppies; such floppies are assigned the concerned Book Accession Numbers. These floppies are arranged serially and kept in the floppy boxes. J.N.N. College of Engineering Library has 200 floppies. Users lend and read these floppies in OPAC systems.
- CDs: Some new books contain CDs also. Such CDs are assigned the Concerned accession Number and kept in CD container. There are about 1,400 CDs available in Library. Users refer these CDs through OPAC system.
- Software used in J.N.N. College of Engineering: There was one software, which was developed by one programmer of computer science Dept. It had some limitations. Now, 'LIBRIS SOFTWARE' has been purchased and installed. This software put into use.
- LAN: Local Area Network was established by connecting all 6 systems in Library with a Main Server. Each system was connected Ethernet and Win proxy Card through Co-Axial cables.

- UPS: An UPS was purchased and connected with all 6 terminals in the Library.
- Computers: There are 7 computers available in the Library. PC's Configuration: -
  - Pentium III/650 MHZ and above, 512 KB internal and external
  - Cache memory 815 E-Intel
  - Chipset motherboard 128 MB SD RAM.
  - Minimum 17.1 GB/HDD IDE Drive.
  - 1.44 MB FDD, 32 Bit Graphic Card 52*CD Drive, 17 inch Colour
  - Monitor with electronic turner and energy saving windows
  - Keyboard, Logitech Mouse, ATX Cabinet with preloaded and O.S.Windows 95/98.
- Printers: There are one Dot Matrix and one Laser Printer available in the Library.
- Bar-Code Printer: One Bar-Code Printer is also printing in barcode labels in Laser Printer was purchased along with 2,500 Book Barcode sheets and 5000 ID Barcode Label Sticker Sheets.
- Book Database: A book database was created with 53,500 records. Bibliographic information about each Access No. Title, Author, Call Number, Keywords, Publisher, Price, etc.
- Periodical Database: A periodical database was created entering all current journal's bibliographic information. The data entry for receipt of periodicals is being entered into computer. Reminders for Non--receipt of periodicals is taken as print out and sent to the periodical suppliers.

ADVANTAGES

Computerization of Library operations saves much time of the Library Staff and users. Students and Staff members feel happy to handle Bar-coded Membership Card. Bar-coding facilities stock verification of books and journals.

DRAWBACKS

Since we implement computerization, our library staff does dual job entering all operations manually and through computer. Staff finds this as a job. In the beginning it may be do their, jobs through computer only. During power failure time, staff face problems to operate computer. These problems can be solved using UPS. An UPS* was purchased and connected to all systems in the library. This UPS solves power problem up to some extent.

HOW TO IMPLEMENT IN FUTURE

Our library staff will prepare bar-coded identity cards for fresh students in future using the barcode equipments. Similarly barcode labels will be generated and pasted in three places of each new book purchased in future. Stock verification will be done online using the barcode scanner in future.

PURCHASING CD CABINET

To preserve CDs it is proposed to purchase a CD Cabinet. All CDs will be serially arranged and kept in proper order. Whenever a user requires particular CD, Library Staff can provide the same for reference purpose.

DIGITAL INITIATIVES AT J.N.N. COLLEGE OF ENGINEERING LIBRARY

It is experienced that Bar-coding has revolutioned the library activities globally. A Laser Barcode printer was purchased and Bar-coding software was also installed. The Bar-coding labels for each book were generated.

BAR-CODING OF BOOKS

Printing barcode labels and pasting in three places of each book, *viz.*, Title page, Secrete page and due date slip were entrusted with a contractor. This generating of Bar-coding labels and pasting the labels for all 53,500 volumes were completed within five months. Retrieving of information through barcode labels using barcode scanner was tested. The computer displayed the Accession Number and the relevant bibliographic information was retrieved from the book database. The bibliographic information includes Accession Number, Author, Title, Call Number, Publisher and Keywords.

BAR-CODED IDENTITY CARDS

The work of bar-coding of identity cards for all users J.N.N. College of Engineering. College was entrusted to the Frontier Information Technology, Secundarbad. The identity card contains the attributes: Class, Dept, Eligibility, Valid up to, Blood group, Residential address, residence phone number. A stamp size photo of each member was scanned and printed on each card. Both Librarian and Principal are signed on this ID card. The identity cards looked good rather than the old traditional plastic card. Each user used to carry this card and produce the same in the issue counter along with the books and get it issued. Now user feels happy in handling this bar-coded identity card. They also feel proud in producing the same card wherever he visits either inside the college or outside the campus.

NETWORKING AND MANPOWER TRAINING

J. N. N. College of Engineering, Library is a member of the DELNET. The users of the library access the resources listed in this network through the net connectivity. The library staff had their sufficient training at Frontier Information Technology, Secundarbad on various divisions of the library such as Acquisition, Cataloguing, Circulation and Periodicals control. They received special training with regard to preparation of Bar-coded identity card. Various processes include:

- Scanning of the User's Photo.

- Printing the photo in the special art paper using the colour printer.
- Composing various fields, *viz.*, name class, branch, valid up to, eligibility, blood group, residential address, residence phone.
- Laminating the above paper using laminating machine.
- Books issue through scanner.
- Books return through scanner.

Our Library staffs were sent to nearest libraries to have practical exposure towards developing of barcoded identity cards. J.N.N. College of Engineering Library staff underwent hands on training nearest libraries studied the system form all perspectives. The hands on training assisted the Library staff to develop the barcode identity cards. For this purpose the following equipments have been identified.

- Digital camera.
- Colour printer.
- Scanner.
- Laminating Machine.

J. N. N. College of Engineering Library staff has also studied various operations in DRTC Library, Bangalore.

CHALLENGES OF DISTRIBUTED SEARCH ACROSS DIGITAL LIBRARIES

The peer-to-peer (P2P) approach allows handling huge amounts of data of digital libraries in a distributed and self-organising way. These characteristics offer enormous potential benefit for search capabilities powerful in terms of scalability, efficiency, and resilience to failures and dynamics. Additionally, such a search engine can potentially benefit from the intellectual input of a large user community.

However, recent research on structured P2P architectures is typically limited to exact-match queries on keys. This is insufficient for text queries that consist of a variable number of keywords, and it is absolutely inappropriate for full-fledged Web search where keyword queries should return a ranked result list of the most relevant approximate matches. This stage builds upon the MINERVA system architecture presented in and brings current challenges to ultimatively making distributed search across digital libraries feasible. MINERVA provides ranked search on data and an efficient query mechanism that adheres to reasonable space and bandwidth limits. Unlike the approach criticised in, we do not spread inverted lists across the directory, but use only pointers to promising digital libraries as compact metadata and utilise these pointers to efficiently answer multiple-keyword queries. We leverage the extensive local indexes to incorporate features that are impossible in the approach studied in, such as phrase matching or proximity searches. Our bandwidth requirements are well within the postulation that a query should send no more data than the size of the documents ultimatively retrieved.

RELATED WORK

Recent research on structured P2P systems, such as Chord, CAN, Pastry, or P-Grid is typically based on various forms of distributed hash tables (DHTs) and supports mappings from keys to locations in a decentralised manner such that routing scales well with the number of peers in the system. We briefly discuss some prior and ongoing projects towards P2P Web search. Galanx is a P2P search engine implemented using the Apache HTTP server and Berkeley DB.

The Web site servers are the peers of this architecture; pages are stored only where they originate from. PlanetP is a publish subscribe service for P2P communities, supporting content ranking search. PlanetP distinguishes local indexes and a global index to describe all peers and their shared information. The global index is replicated using a gossiping algorithm. The system appears to be limited to a few thousand peers. Odissea assumes a two-layered search engine architecture with a global index structure distributed over the nodes in the system. A single node holds the complete, Web-scale, index for a given text term. Query execution uses a distributed version of Fagin's threshold algorithm.

The system appears to cause high network traffic when posting document metadata into the network, and the presented query execution method seems limited to queries with at most two keywords. The paper actually advocates using a limited number of nodes, in the spirit of a server farm. The system outlined in uses a fully distributed inverted text index, in which every participant is responsible for a specific subset of terms and manages the respective index structures. Particular emphasis is put on minimising the bandwidth used during multi-keyword searches. considers content-based retrieval in hybrid P2P networks.

The peer selection for forwarding queries is based on the Kullback- Leibler divergence between peer-specific statistical models of term distributions. In addition to this recent work on P2P search, prior research on distributed IR and metasearch engines is also potentially relevant; see for overviews. However, their work has assumed a relatively small number of digital libraries or databases and a fairly static configuration.

SYSTEM DESIGN

As a detailed description of the system design has already been given in, we only present a brief overview here and refer the interested reader to this prior work. We view every library as autonomous. A conceptually global but physically distributed directory, which is layered on top of a Chord-style dynamic hash table (DHT), holds only very compact, aggregated information about the peers' local indexes and only to the extent that the individual peers are willing to disclose. Every peer is responsible for a randomised subset of the global directory. The global directory consists of aggregated information (Posts) that contains contact information about the digital library who posted this summary together with statistics to calculate IR-style relevance measures that try to estimate the relevance of a particular digital library to a query. These measures are used to support the peer selection process, *i.e.*, determining the most promising libraries for a particular query. If, at query time, the local query result is considered unsatisfactory by the user, a library retrieves a list of potentially useful libraries. Using collection selection methods from distributed IR and metasearch, a number of promising libraries for the complete query is computed from these PeerLists. In we have studied promising and efficient techniques for this purpose. Subsequently, the query is forwarded to these libraries and executed based on their local indexes.

The results from the various libraries are combined at the querying peer into a single result list; this step is referred to as result merging. The goal of finding high-quality search results with respect to precision and recall cannot be easily reconciled with the design goal of unlimited scalability, as the best information retrieval techniques for query execution rely on large amounts of document metadata. Posting only compact, aggregated information about local indexes and using appropriate peer selection methods to limit the number of peers involved in a query keeps the global directory manageable and reduces network traffic. We expect this approach to scale very well as more and more peers jointly maintain the moderately growing global directory.

CHALLENGES

Our work is driven by the question of how a collaborative search across digital libraries can benefit from the unique nature of the P2P paradigm. We want to address the shortcomings of centralised search engines and further benefit from the intellectual input of a large user community.

Democratic Community Search

To overcome the danger of the infiltration of a centralised index by (commercial) interest groups we leverage the indexes from potentially thousands of digital libraries, making it harder to bias the final query results.

Implicit User Feedback

Additionally, we want to incorporate the fact that every library has its own local index, *e.g.*, by executing all queries first locally at the initiating library and using implicit-feedback techniques for automated query expansion.

User Recommendations

We want to incorporate local user bookmarks into our query execution. Bookmarks represent strong recommendations for specific documents. Also, user bookmarks can be considered as compact samples of peer indexes that describe their fields of interest. Queries could be exclusively forwarded to thematically related libraries with similarly interested users, to improve the chances of finding subjectively relevant pages.

Replication

In order to achieve service levels comparable to today's search engines and in order to actually benefit from the infrastructural advantage of a distributed system, we are going to introduce a certain degree of replication to the directory. Currently, as dictated by the DHT-style maintenance approach, a peer gracefully leaving the system forwards its share of the global directory to another peer. Analogously, a library entering the system asks for its appropriate share of the directory.

While one approach to ensure a valid, complete, and up-todate directory is to simply rely on the libraries to regularly re-send their Posts to the directory, it is also necessary to replicate parts of the directory to avoid data loss as libraries ungracefully leave the system. Also, replication can serve as a load-balancing measure, relieving the burden from peers that host popular parts of the directory, and increases data availability.

Adaptive, self-tuning strategies for choosing appropriate degrees of replication and placing replicas are an open issue in our ongoing work.

Caching and Proactive Dissemination

To further enhance query efficiency, statistical summaries and also the results of queries from across the network may be cached in a way that allows other peers not only to instantly benefit from the existing query results but also to benefit from click streamst that were recorded on the occasion of similar queries. Statistical summaries may also be disseminated proactively among thematically related peers. Finding good strategies to this end is a widely open issue.

Overlap-aware Query Routing

Peer selection has been a research issue for years. Most of the existing literature estimates the expected result quality of a collection, typically using pre-computed statistics, and ranks the collections accordingly. We believe that this is insufficient if the collections overlap, *e.g.*, in the scenario of digital libraries that share an arbitrarily large fraction of documents.

We argue for the extension of existing quality measures using estimators of mutual overlap among collections. Preliminary experiments show that such a combination can outperform popular approaches based on quality estimation only, such as CORI.

Taking overlap into account during collection selection in this scenario can drastically decrease the number of libraries that have to be contacted in order to reach a satisfactory level of recall, which is a great step towards the feasibility of distributed search across digital libraries.

Benefit/Cost Optimisation

Ultimatively, we want to introduce a sophisticated benefit/cost ratio when selecting remote libraries for query forwarding. For the benefit estimation, it is intuitive to consider such measures. Defining a meaningful cost measure, however, is an even more challenging issue. While there are techniques for observing and inferring network bandwidth or other infrastructural information, expected response times are changing over time. One approach is to create a distributed Quality-of-Service directory that, for all peers, holds moving averages of recent response times.

DEFINITION OF DIGITAL LIBRARIES

In this unit we ask two questions:

- What is a digital library?
- What are its characteristics?

In answering these questions we will learn about digital coherence, discuss the origins of digital libraries, and discover synonyms and metaphors for digital libraries. We will also touch on assumptions about a digital library, technologies of library collections, and the act of information seeking.

Digital Coherence

The term digital library has been applied to a wide variety of offerings from collections of electronic journals to software agents that support inquiry-based education to collections of e-mail to electronic versions of a public library, to personal information collections, and even to the entire Internet. The one property these various entities have in common is their digitization or digital coherence (Daniel Atkins).

Digital coherence means all the objects in a digital library, whether sounds, images, texts, or some other media, can be treated in essentially the same way.

Prior to digital coherence, libraries needed to treat various media, for example, books, journals, videos, and musical recordings, differently.

One could say that digital coherence is the mechanism which permits a form of equality among various information resources. This equality has importance for delivery and integration of information.

Envisioning a World Brain and The Memex

The concept of a digital library is not new. In fact, the concept of digital libraries pre-dates the development of the first computer. H. G. Wells was one of the first authors to write about idea of a world brain that could supplement, add functionality to, and even replace traditional libraries.

It is generally agreed that Vannevar Bush's 1945 article in the Atlantic Monthly, in which Bush conceives of a memex machine, inspired much of the early application of computers to information retrieval. The memex is a mechanical device based on microfilm technology. The concept of the memex included [a community of scholars indexing and creating] links between pieces of information in a [microfilm-based] research library combined with [microfilmed] personal notes (and classification system) and notes of colleagues, anticipating the ideas of both hypertext and personal information retrieval systems.

Lesk assures us that by 2015 (70 years after Vannevar Bush published his memex dream) "we will have the equivalent of a major research library on each desk. And it will have searching capabilities beyond those Bush imagined".

Synonyms for the Term Digital Library

In the early 1950s computers entered library services in the form of punched card applications in technical services operations and through the development of the MARC (MAchine-Readable Cataloging) standard for digitizing and communicating library catalog information.

The vision of a fully computer-based library began to emerge in terminology in the mid-60s with J. C. R. Licklider's the library of the future.

Over the years, other terms have been coined to refer to the concept of a digitized library, including electronic library, virtual library, library without walls, and bionic library. Library science professor Winfred Lancaster extended this concept beyond the functions of the library, using the term paperless society.

The use of the term digital library can be traced to the Digital Libraries Initiative, established through funding in 1994, by the National Science Foundation, the Advanced Research Projects Agency, and the National Aeronautics and Space Admini-stration in the United States. Under this funding, six U.S. universities were granted a total of $24.4 million for digital library research.

Two events motivated this funding: the sudden explosive growth of the Internet and the development of graphical Web browsers.

These two developments significantly increased the viability of extending library resources and services beyond their current walls and communities, facilitating the sharing of scarce resources and the reaching of under-served populations.

Metaphors for Digital Libraries

There is little discussion or agreement in the literature about what constitutes a digital library. Harter juxtaposes two extreme views: the most inclusive view, which takes a digital library to be essentially what the Internet is today, and the metaphor of the traditional library.

The essential differences between these two metaphors deal with their [presumed] properties of location, content, selection criteria, organization, authority control*, authorship, stability, access, and user groups, services and fees. The Internet has no physical or logical location; no quality control and no entry barriers; no organization scheme, authority control, or surrogates; no concept of author; and is fluid and transient.

Everyone has access to the Internet, but access may require payment and purchase of equipment by the individual user. The traditional library is perceived to have their properties and no entry fee for the individual.

*Names of authors, variants of works (editions), and subject headings or descriptors are all controlled and common variants are cross-listed to the designated official form.

TEACH ABOUT DIGITAL LIBRARIES

The answer depends, to a large extent, on having a relatively clear idea about what are digital libraries. As mentioned, no agreed upon definition exists, which is fine, because the same constructs can be viewed from a number of viewpoints or perspectives. Let us explore some of these perspectives through definitions offered. Of course, a choice of a given perspective dictates the choice of the content.

Different perspectives about digital libraries, together with competing visions and associated definitions, come from several communities that are involved in digital library work. We are concentrating here on two communities: research and practice.

While they work and proceed independently of each other, they can be considered on two ends of a spectrum, which as yet have not met in the middle. To use another metaphor: the research and practice communities are in the same planetary system, but one is on Mars, the other on Venus.

The research community grounded mostly in computer science, on one end of the spectrum, asks research questions directed Towards future vision or visions of digital libraries, or rather of their various technology oriented aspects and components, unrestricted by practice.

On the other end of the spectrum, the practice community, grounded mostly in librarianship and information science, asks developmental, operational, and use questions in real-life economic and institutional contexts, restrictions, and possibilities, concentrating on applications on the use end of the spectrum.

In research, DLIs did not define 'digital library.' In order to incorporate a wide range of possible approaches and domains, the concept is treated broadly and vaguely. Thus, the projects, particularly in DLI-2, cover a wide range of topics, stretching the possible meaning of digital library to and even beyond the limit of what can be considered as being digital and at the same time recognizable as any kind of a library or a part thereof.

This is perfectly acceptable for research frontiers need to be stretched. But at the same time, it makes choices for educational content diffuse and difficult. The closest to the definition applicable to the approaches taken by the research community is the one given by Lesk in the first textbook on the topic:

- "Digital libraries are *organized collections* of digital information. They combine the *structure and gathering of information*, which libraries and archives have always done, with the *digital representation* that computers have made possible." (Emphasis in this and following definitions is added to illustrate possible choices for educational content).

Arms in a newer text on digital libraries, also from a research community and technology applications perspective, provides what he calls an "informal definition:"

- "A digital library is a *managed collection* of inform-ation, with associated *services*, where the information is *stored in digital formats* and *accessible* over a *network*."

The practice community, whose majority is residing in operational libraries, concentrates on building operational digital libraries, their maintenance and operations, and providing services to users. The approach is developmental, operational, and eminently practical, with relatively little or no research involved.

As a result, hundreds, if not thousands of digital libraries have emerged worldwide, with more becoming operational every day. The efforts are diverse. Many approaches are being used. Many types of collections and media are included and processed in many different ways. Many are located in libraries, creating a hybrid library (combination of a traditional and digital library); others are not bound to brick and mortar libraries at all.

In the US, the Digital Libraries Federation (DLF) (formed in 1995) is an organization of research libraries and various national institutions. The stated goal of DLF is "to establish the conditions necessary for the creation, maintenance, expansion, and preservation of a distributed collection of digital materials accessible to scholars and the wider public." The organization represents libraries and practitioners.

After considerable deliberation, DFL agreed on a "working definition of digital library," representing the definition of the practice community:

- Digital libraries are organizations that provide the resources, including the specialized staff, to select, structure, offer intellectual access to, interpret, distribute, preserve the integrity of, and ensure the persistence over time of collections of digital works so that they are readily and economically available for use by a defined community or set of communities.

Borgman provides a more complex definition (including an extensive discussion) of digital libraries, a definition that may be considered as a bridge between the research community definition and practical community definitions:

- Digital libraries are a set of electronic resources and associated technical capabilities for creating, searching, and using information. They are an extension and enhancement of information storage and retrieval systems that manipulate digital data in any medium The content of digital libraries includes data, [and] metadata Digital libraries are constructed, collected, and organized, by (and for) a community of users, and their functional capabilities support the information needs and uses of that community.

Following these perspectives, the content choices fall into categories that are based on: systems, networks, and technology; collection and resources in various media; representation, organization, and operability; storage and searching; functionality, access and use; institutions and services; and user communities and related applications.

The educational choices are among technology, resources, organization, access, institutions, and use, or a mix thereof. A balanced and at the same time a comprehensive mix is difficult, if not impossible, to achieve.

SURVEY OF APPLICATIONS

In order to go beyond generalities and into observation of existing educational practices we conducted a survey. The survey consisted of two parts: a *Web survey* of curriculum and course information as posted on the sites of a number of schools and an *E-mail survey* of answers to invited questions posted on several listserves. We report the results of each survey separately.

Each of the survey methods has strengths and definite limitations. Deriving conclusions about the content of education of given institutions through an examination of information provided on their own Web sites is fraught with peril. It is similar to the well-known peril of examination of catalogs.

However, Web listings are more current and inclusive; they provide, by and large, much more information than catalog listings, up to inclusion of syllabi; and they are updated more often. As a rule, general e-mail surveys have a small rate of self-selected returns.

But the answers tend to be specific to the questions. Both surveys complement each other. The methodology was considered appropriate for a general (rather than detailed) assessment of the emerging approaches to what is taught and how these approaches are positioned in the existing teaching practice.

Web Survey

Method

In the first part we examined the Web sites of 56 accredited Programmes listed in the directory of the Association of Library and Information Science Education (ALISE) as found on their web site.

The schools housing these Programmes are generally known as schools of library and information science (LIS), but in reality a good number of them have changed from this designation to several classes of different names. For brevity, we will use the LIS label for the Programmes. The accreditation is by the American Library Association (ALA) and covers the professional degree programme on the master's level. It does *not* cover doctoral or undergraduate education, offered by a number of these schools. Geographically, it covers schools in North America the U.S. and Canada. Thus in this part no other countries were included.

We looked at course titles, course descriptions and syllabi when available. In line with the broad definition of digital libraries (or lack of definition) as discussed above, we cast the net widely. We concentrated on courses where *digital libraries* or *digital librarianship* were mentioned as a term, but we also included courses that used synonymous concepts, exemplified by terms such as *electronic library*, or *library of the future*; we also included *virtual museums*, as having a strong connection with digital libraries.

On a broader level, we included courses that mention processes that are closely related to digital libraries, such as management and preservation of electronic records, electronic text design, metadata for digital collections, production of network multimedia, designing accessible web based materials, and electronic text.

Finally, on the broadest level we included courses that are oriented Towards *information technology* and address the technological bases of digital libraries, such as *network architecture, managing networks, digital tool kits, Internet applications*, and the like. We used these gradations and distinctions as tools for classification as incorporated in tables below.

Inclusion

Of the 56 LIS Programmes, 47 (89%) include digital library in some form or another or to some degree in their curriculum; for 5 (9%) Programmes, this cannot be determined and 4 (7%) Programmes show no presence of digital library education. This analysis shows that digital library education is included in the curriculum of most LIS Programmes. However, the degree of inclusion varies widely. When considered closely, the inclusion ranges from a full course or courses on digital libraries to metadata standards being covered in organization of information courses to cases in which digital library focus is relegated to continuing education. Participation of the students in a local digital library project is another way of including the digital library topics within LIS education.

Integration

To what degree are digital library courses offered as independent or full-blown courses? To what degree are digital library topics integrated in other courses? Table addresses these questions.

Table. Course Integration in Digital Library Education in ALA-accredited Library and Information Science Programmes. (N=47 Programmes that Include Digital Library Educationfrom 56 Accredited Programmes).

Digital library content in relation to the curriculum	No. of LIS Programmes
1. Independent DL courses	15 (32%)
2. Combination of independent DL course and DL content integrated in other courses	8 (17%)
3. DL content integrated in other courses (without independent DL courses)	23 (49%)
4. Other (DL content integrated with continuing education)	1 (2%)

Note: Two major types of courses are

- Tndependent digital library courses (typically titled "Digital Libraries" or a similar version), and
- Digital library content integrated in other courses.

As shown in Table, half of the schools have significant digital library content in the curriculum. They include schools with specialized digital library courses on the books; we call these independent courses, although we cannot tell to what degree these are also segregated courses, with little or no connection to the rest of the curriculum.

Such an independent course is either an elective or special topics course offered either as the only course with digital library content in the school's programme or a course offered in addition to other digital library topics that appears elsewhere in the curriculum.

The other half of the schools have some level of digital library content integrated in their programme, but no course specifically focusing on digital libraries. The Programmes that integrate digital library topics in their courses vary in the level of inclusion and strategies for inclusion.

LIS Programmes

LIS Programmes at the masters level are *professional* Programmes; this defines the context for digital library education in such schools. An examination of digital library course descriptions from Web sites reflects that education for digital librarianship in many cases does not reflect a systematic view or programme of education.

Presumably, digital library content is simply an acknowledgment of an emerging field of practice and institutional realities. Even schools with a full course devoted to the problem area of digital libraries show variation in their approaches.

The courses offered under the umbrella term 'digital libraries' range from theoretical and survey courses to project-focused courses. Some are broader and some narrow in focus. A combination of theory (highlighting multiple facets of digital library research) and application (giving an overview of existing practices and providing hands-on experience) seem not to be practiced in such courses. Weighing one against the other, theory against hands-on experience, it seems that theoretical and survey courses provide a more flexible framework to be expanded with an on-the-job training and apprenticeship in the changing digital library practical environment. An ideal would be the integration of practice-based with survey and theory-based approach to digital library education.

As mentioned, we have been inclusive rather than exclusive in defining what constitutes integrated content. We have considered courses in networking, topics in telecommunications, metadata standards, courses integrating topics on the preservation of electronic-born information as integrating digital library content and digital libraries as developmental form in the history of knowledge records and therefore contributing to digital library education.

In many cases, from brief course descriptions and sparse online syllabi, the degree to which digital library problems were truly addressed is not always clear. In our conservative estimate, in more than half of the schools.

The degree of inclusion cannot be determined with certainty with the methodology used here. The question is whether information technology course addressing the *'library of the future,'* a course dealing with social roles of information organization that includes traditional and digital libraries, archives, network architecture, or the concern with 'structures, processes, dynamics and applications that determine the effective use of motion imagery in multimedia, on-line, and other digital media,' all relate to the problem area of digital libraries.

Together, the approaches represent a pandemonium typical of the general uncertainty Towards digital library education. The choices result from an undisciplined mix of the pressures of the libraries as market for graduates, ten years of research and development in the area of digital libraries, and varying degrees of faculty expertise and perceptions of what constitutes a meaningful approach. Multiple and often overlapping approaches in different schools are symptomatic of that general uncertainty. Because the schedule and frequency of offering is a determinant of impact of specific courses or a mix of courses on digital library education in specific LIS Programmes, clearly one cannot make sweeping statements. Several schools that integrate digital library content into other courses, or offer courses that do not have digital libraries in their title but focus on the creation of distributed electronic repositories of information, are taking an integrated rather than independent approach.

The "independent" (segregated) vs. "integrated" approach and the "combined independent with integrated" approaches reveal an underlying philosophy of digital library education. Integration is the ideal, but it may suffer from superficiality. Segregation is also fraught with peril of a different sort of offering a view of compartmentalized technology. A smaller fraction offers a combination of independent and integrated approach to digital library education (17 per cent). There may be a number of reasons for this, one of which may be a reflection of competing perspectives within a given programme. We did not detect that any school has a organized course of study in digital libraries, such as a specialization or track.

E-mail Survey

We also invited e-mail answers to a list of questions posted on several listserves oriented Towards audiences as individuals (rather then institutions) in different areas. They included: listserve JESSE in library science, the member list of the American Society for Information Science and Technology (ASIST), listserve of the Special Interest Group on Information Retrieval, Association for Computing Machinery (ACM SIGIR), listserve of the Humanist Discussion Group, and ETEXT-L.

We sought answers to the following questions:

- Does your institution offer course(s), seminars or institutes in digital libraries and/or related areas? If so, please provide as much information as possible, particularly including URLs.
- Does your institution teach digital library topics within (or as a part of) other courses, seminars, or institutes? If so, please provide as much information as possible, particularly including URLs.
- In what department or school are the digital library course(s) offered?
- On what level undergraduate, graduate, doctoral, professional development?

While the listserves reach great many recipients, we received only a total of 27 responses, of these 20 were relevant. The small number of responses was very disappointing, but then responses to general surveys are always low. We know that in reality there are many more Programmes and courses related to digital libraries, and that this is but a very small sample. We cannot tell how representative it is. Still it is worthwhile to analyse this sample. Given the nature of the sample and the size of the returns, about all that could safely be concluded is that there is an interesting and broadening array of disciplines other than LIS in which digital library courses are being taught and such courses are at a variety of levels, undergraduate and graduate.

Digital Libraries Taught

To answer the question on how were digital libraries taught we did not look at pedagogy. Instead, we have looked at broader issues: How did various Programmes address the basic and connecting areas for digital library education? What models have emerged? This illuminates the contexts of digital library education within the Programmes; more specifically it shows area clusters where digital library education has gravitated.

Method

Here we deal only with 47 ALA accredited LIS Programmes that have presence in digital library education to some degree or other. We undertook a detailed examination of presented curricula, course descriptions, syllabi, and other information as provided. The level of available information differs greatly from programme to programme, thus our conclusions are only as good as the information available on the programs' Web sites. The analysis is qualitative, with all the strengths and weaknesses of such methods.In a grounded theory approach, we derived classes from data, and then grouped the data in these classes. Subjective? Of course. But the derivative approach also enables to show clusters in the greater body of data, which are otherwise not visible. To provide consistency, we applied the same analysis criteria to all Programmes.

Results

We identified several dimensions or models of digital library education emerging in the Programmes examined. Various approaches that LIS Programmes are taking in conceptualizing the digital library education, with regard to areas of application. Of the 47 LIS Programmes that were identified as including digital library education in their Programmes, six have digital library content contained within a single course, one programme shows digital library content to be integrated across the curriculum; and for six Programmes we could not determine the area of application. The derived classification is divided in two classes. The first or general class identifies four broad areas of application, *i.e.,* the general domain of emphasis and orientation for digital library education that could be identified as predominant in a given programme.

These are:

- T-tools (technologies and technology based processes);
- Environments (the context in which digital libraries operate),
- Objects (representation, structure and life cycle of documents in various formats), and
- Combined (several areas of applications present without any one being distinctive).

The second, or specific class, identifies perspectives within the broad areas. It shows a more detailed or specific orientation of Programmes. In the perspectives the'basic' and'advanced' tools refer to the level of technological sophistication. The'compartm-entalized' approach is one in which digital library is conceived as a contained phenomenon.

These models show how digital library education is conceptualized and focused within a particular programme. The approaches are not exclusive and many schools combine several of these approaches. We presume that this is either as a result of competing discourses within the schools themselves or because of the uncertainty that the notion of digital library entails.

8

Digital Library Technology

INFLUENCE OF THE LIBRARY ON DIGITAL LIBRARY TECHNOLOGY

The previous part described the set of assumptions about libraries and networked information that led to the choice of the term "digital libraries." This part describes the manner in which that term and the presumptions underlying it have affected the nature of the technical artifacts produced by digital library research. This effect is reflected in both the overall architectural framework and on the individual architectural components of that framework.

Table. Comparison of Digital Library and Web Architectures.

	Digital Libraries	Web Architecture
Core Architecture	Repository-centric	Resource-centric
User Model	Portal Searching	Browsing
Content Model	Digital Objects	Resources
Indexing Model	Surrogates	Full-text and links
Identification	Persistent IDs	URIs
Federation Model	Federated Search, Metadata Harvesting	Centralized Indexing

CORE ARCHITECTURE: REPOSITORY-CENTRIC VERSUS RESOURCE-CENTRIC

Digital library systems are by and large based on the notion of the institutionallymanaged *repository* as the central architec-tural entity. The repository acts as the container for storage of and access to "digital objects", the content "within" the library. In this manner, the repository is a virtual boundary defining the locus of institutional management, curation, and preservation of the contained digital objects.This virtual boundary is the functional equivalent of the physical boundary in the "bricks and mortar" library in which the physical structure defines the limits of library curation and stewardship of the information resources within it. In contrast, the *resource* is the central entity in the web architecture.

Uniquely identified resources are the nodes in a virtual directed graph, in which the edges are the hyperlinks that connect resources. Notably absent from this graph model is the notion of containment or location. There is no first-class entity that corresponds to the repository in digital architecture. Although repositories are sometimes compared to websites, the comparison is incorrect due to the nature of the latter.

A Web site is an ambiguously defined, second-class technical artifact – it may be all the web pages served within the same DNS domain, or those accessible through a single server. Technically, it has no identity (URI) and therefore it cannot be the target of any protocol requests. Conceptually, it does not imply control or management in the same manner as a repository. The remainder of this part describes the major components of digital library systems that support this repository-centric architectural core.

PORTALS

The portal, or the "front door of the digital library", serves the same purpose as the physical entry to the traditional library. It provides the user with the clear notion of being "inside" the digital library. Services and content within the portal are thereby blessed with the imprimatur of the library, endowing them with a level of trust and integrity. This is commonly known as "branding".

Correspondingly, most digital library applications clearly indicate to the user when they are "leaving the library", for example by traversing a hyperlink to a page outside the boundary of the library. The focus of a portal is usually a search interface, that in most cases is field-based, providing more functionality than the single text box search paradigm employed by most web search engines.

This allows users to search on specific bibliographic fields such as title, author, or subject. This search paradigm reflects the influence of the library cataloguing tradition, which eschews simple keyword searching that is predominant in mainstream crawler-based search engines (*e.g.*, Google) in favour of more targeted search capabilities.

Metadata, which is the basis of this field-based searching. In contrast to this "front-door" paradigm, the web user metaphorically "surfs" among linked information resources without regard for their location on the network. The informal notion of a "homepage" for a Web site does exist, but there is no presumption or enforcement of this as the uniform entry point to the collection of pages of that site.

The notion of uniform, location-independent sources has proven to be quite powerful. In its simplest form it makes it possible to aggregate information from multiple sources in a single webpage, in the manner that a page may include an image that is stored in some other location on the net. As I will describe later, location independence is leveraged in Web 2.0 in a much more powerful manner in the form of "mash-ups."

METADATA–CATALOGUING IN THE DIGITAL CONTEXT

The shaping effect of the library tradition on digital libraries is perhaps most evident in the focus on descriptive metadata. This focus has its roots in cataloguing, one of the core functions of the modern library. The traditional catalogue developed for a number of reasons. At the simplest level, in a library of physical resources it gave users an easy and compact tool for finding information resources without having to traverse the shelves.

However, describing the catalogue as merely a compact shelf list trivializes its complexity and intellectual content. Underlying cataloguing is the concept of information entities having uniform attributes, such as author, title, or subject classification, and the utility of those attributes for logical organization of those entities. This organization presents multiple *access points* based on those uniform attributes, and allows users to search and browse within those access points.

For example, a user may search for information by author name and then traverse the resources associated with that author, or alternatively they may search for information by subject classification and traverse the resources associated within that class. As a result, the organization of the catalogue and the manner in which it is made available to the user (*e.g.*, cards in drawers or screens in an electronic catalogue) is independent of the manner in which the physical, or digital, resources are organized on shelves, or in repositories.

Furthermore, an individual information resource (*e.g.*, a book) may have multiple catalogue instances, each accessible through specific access points (*e.g.*, title, author, subject, etc.). Efforts to extend the practice of cataloguing into the context of online information reflects an ongoing belief that in a world where even the books that are part of library collections have been digitized and are available for full-text search, structured search over surrogates is more functional and ultimately preferred by users.

This is despite empirical evidence that users seem to prefer the "one text box" search paradigm of Google to the fielded-search paradigm employed in most digital library portals and online catalogs, and decades-old evidence of the frequent superiority in recall and precision of automated full-text search to human-assisted indexing and cataloguing.

Traditional library cataloguing is both complex and expensive, especially when applied to the rapidly expanding and diverse set of digital resources. The notion of metadata emerged as a simpler and less expensive alternative to traditional cataloguing records, perhaps making it possible for nonprofess-ionals to create structured bibliographic information.

The predominant digital library metadata effort is the Dublin Core Metadata Initiative. Ironically, the origins of Dublin Core lie in improving search and retrieval on the general web. However, this effort to develop easy-to-use bibliographic standards for networked information objects has been deemed irrelevant, ill-conceived, or even counterproductive by the mainstream web community and most notably the search engines that dominate it.

As I describe later, the attempts to translate the benefits of cataloguing to the online domain via metadata have been compromised by problems with ensuring the quality of the metadata records that are produced by Non--professionals and preventing so-called "metadata spamming" by unscrupulous agents trying to falsely lead information consumers to their sites.

DIGITAL OBJECTS — CONTAINERS FOR COMPLEX DATA AND METADATA

The content model of most digital library architectures is based on the notion of a *digital object*. an identified (first-class) information resource that is an aggregation of multiple information units consisting of multiple formats, multiple subsidiary units, versions, or document components (*e.g.*, the text, data, images, etc. of a scholarly paper).These are generally known as *compound objects*. These object models reflect an ongoing effort by the library community to account for the complexity of information in both its abstract form and the physical or digital manifestations of it.

These efforts have focused on mechanisms to represent the various relationships among information resources. and to describe those resources at multiple levels of granularity, for various purposes, and in various descriptive formats. Access to compound objects and their components is frequently mediated by protocols unique to the particular repository architecture.

These protocols are usually embedded in the URLs that carry user requests from the digital library portal to the repository. These protocols allow operations such as access a digital object in a specific form, access a portion of a digital object such as its descriptive metadata, and the like.The proliferation of these architecture-specific access protocols has spawned a virtual cottage industry of repository interoperability initiatives in the digital library community. In contrast, the web architecture includes a quite simple information model based on the atomic resource.

"Interoperability" is defined in the simple terms of the web architecture–resources, URIs, and HTTP. There is no architectural notion of a compound object, or aggregation of resources. Ad hoc and de facto aggregations exist, for example a logical document split into a set of interlinked web pages.However, these aggregations are not first-class objects. they do not have a unique identity and are essentially ephemeral. There is, in fact, an increased awareness in the web community that more complex information models are appropriate in a number of instances. for example, scholarly publishing.

FEDERATION

The issue of federation arises because digital library systems are conceived as discrete institutionally-managed entities with distinct boundaries accessible to the user through branded portals. Sometimes, a user might want to search across multiple digital libraries when a selected resource is not available in their "local" library. In the physical library domain, this problem is solved by union catalogs such as WorldCat and by interlibrary loan.

Digital library applications employ two mechanisms to allow users to search for and access information outside the confines of a single digital library. The first is federated searching or meta-searching, in which a single search query is multicast to several digital library search engines.

The query is then individually processed at those search engines. the individual result sets are then returned and integrated at the site from which the original query was multicast. Federated searching was the subject of substantial work in the early years of digital library research describes our own work in this area.

Although instances of federated search still exist, the technique has fallen into some disfavour because of problems with dependence on the reliability of multiple search sites and the problems with the ranking of search results from several sources. The second is metadata harvesting, in which bibliographic records from several distributed institutional sources are combined at a single indexing site, which provides a search interface across the resulting "union catalogue".

The most widely deployed mechanism for metadata harvesting is the Open Archives Protocol for Metadata Harvesting (OAI-PMH). That same chapter describes complica-tions with metadata harvesting. Neither of these techniques has achieved widespread deployment in the general web information space.

Boundaries and the repositories that implement them are not a part of the web architecture. Web search engines such as Google crawl the web via graph traversal, ignoring the notion of the location of a webpage, except as a tool for optimizing graph traversal strategies. In addition, ranking algorithms such as PageRank are designed to operate over a centralized index, and are difficult if not impossible in the context of distributed methods such as federated search,

PERSISTENT IDENTITY FOR NETWORK INFORMATION

A final example of the difference between digital library and web architecture is the notion of "persistent identity" for information stored in digital repositories. The attention to this issue in the digital library contexts reflects concerns about both preservation and control of intellectual property. The Handle System is the best known of this class of technologies.Like many persistent naming systems, the Handle System depends on a hierarchy of identity resolvers, and therefore the notion of a central *root* name server. These efforts have gained little traction in the mainstream web community, which has historically resisted centralization and has comfortably adapted to the fragility of URLs, deeming identity persistence as a policy problem rather than a technical problem.

SECURITY AND DIGITAL LIBRARIES

Security is an important issue in digital library design. Security weaknesses in digital libraries, coupled with attacks or other types of failures, can lead to confidential information being inappropriately accessed, or loss of integrity of the data stored. These in turn can have a damaging effect on the trust of publishers or other content providers, can cause embarrassment or even economic loss to digital library owners, and can even lead to pain and suffering or other serious problems if urgently needed information is unavailable. There are many security requirements to consider because of the variety of different actors working with a digital library. Each of these actors has different security needs.Thus, a digital library content provider might be concerned with protecting intellectual property rights and the terms of use of content, while a digital library user might be concerned with reliable access to content stored in the digital library. Requirements based on these needs sometimes are in conflict, which can make the security architecture of a digital library even more complex. The design of the security architecture of a digital library must go beyond simply adding one or a few modules to a previously designed system. This is because there may be security holes in pre-existing modules, and because difficulties can arise when attempting to integrate the modules.

The security architecture of a digital library must be designed so that security concerns are handled holistically. A security system designer must view the whole architecture and consider all of the applicable security factors when designing a secure digital library. The nature of a security attack may differ according to the architecture of the digital library; a distributed digital library has more security weaknesses than a centralized digital library. Security attacks can be categorised as physical attacks and logical attacks. A physical attack involves hardware security where keys, locks, cards, and visitor monitoring is used. A logical attack involves an attack on the content or digital library system. We focus on the logical attacks and software security of digital libraries.

SECURITY ISSUES WITH DIGITAL LIBRARIES

According to the DELOS Reference Model there are 6 main concepts in a digital library universe: content, user, functionality, architecture, quality, and policy. Each of these concepts has security issues that affect it.

Content

The content of a digital library includes the information objects that a digital library provides to the users. Some of the security issues involved are integrity and access control. Integrity requires that each object/resource has not been altered or changed by an unauthorised person. Access control encompasses two security requirements. The first is authentication where the user must log into the system while the second is confidentiality, which means that the content of an object is inaccessible by a person unless they have authorisation. Not all digital libraries are free; often content is provided to digital library users for a certain fee, whereupon access control is needed to protect the content.

Further, some content is inappropriate for some users, or targeted to particular user groups; there are a whole host of such other reasons for access control. Logical attacks such as hacking and message tampering can affect the integrity and confidentiality of the content. Improved information access in digital libraries has raised many issues that affect the management of digital libraries. Content Management, or more specifically Digital Rights Management, refers to the protection of content from the different logical security attacks and issues relating to intellectual property rights and authenticity.

Digital Rights Management

DRM provides content protection by encrypting the content and associating it with a digital licence. The licence identifies the user allowed to view the content, lists the content of the product, and states the rights the user has to the resource in a computer readable format using a digital rights expression language (DREL) or extensible Rights Markup Language (XrML) that also describes constraints and conditions. There are 7 technologies used to provide DRM. Table summarises the DRM components and supporting technology.

Each of these components involves mechanisms used to provide DRM:

- *Encryption:* Encryption techniques such as symmetric and asymmetric ciphers can be used to provide access control; public-key encryption is used in payment systems that control how and by whom the content is used. Symmetric ciphers using DES, 3DES, AES, and RC4 algorithms require the use of a shared secret key to encrypt data before it is sent. At the receiver's end the cipher text is decrypted using the same secret key. Symmetric ciphers depend on both the sender and receiver knowing the shared key. Asymmetric ciphers use a pair of keys, public and private, for each of the sender and the receiver. The public keys of both the sender and the receiver are known but the private key is kept secret. If encryption is performed using the public key then only the private key can be used for decryption and vice versa.
- *Passwords:* Stored strings must be matched by users desiring access.
- *Watermarking:* Characters or images are added to reflect ownership. Steganography is used to conceal data inside audio, video, or images. Different watermarking techniques have different aims; some watermarks might be visible while others invisible. Some watermarks are reversible; it depends on the desired use of the watermark and what is being protected.

- *Digital Signature:* Asymmetric encryption can be used. Likewise, hash algorithms such as MD5 and SHA can be used to create a signature.
- *Digital Fingerprint:* Digital fingerprints are a more powerful technique involving digital signatures and watermarking. The creator of the content creates a unique copy of the content marked for each user; the marks are user-specific hence, called fingerprints. Should a user illegally distribute the content, the creator can use search robots to find those copies.
- *Copy Detection Systems:* Search engines also can help locate such copied objects. Copydetecting browsers can protect digital content too.
- *Payment Systems:* Users must divulge personal information to pay for content. Installing payment systems can help protect digital content.

There is no standard mechanism for providing DRM, mainly due to the lack of regulations, however there are various systems and protocols introduced to provide content management and support fair usage policies. There is a tradeoff between security and performance. Nadeem and Javed use a Pentium-4, 2.4 GHz machine running Microsoft Windows XP operating system, encrypt 20527 bytes to 2323398 bytes of data using DES, 3DES, and AES. For 20527 bytes of data it took 2 seconds to encrypt using the DES algorithm and 4 seconds to encrypt using the AES algorithm. It can be seen that the more complex the encryption algorithm the longer it takes to encrypt the data. In another study, encrypting data with the RSA algorithm using a key size of 1024 took 0.08 milliseconds/operation on an Intel Core 2 1.83 GHz processor under Windows Vista in 32-bit mode, while using a key size of 2048 took 0.16 milliseconds/operation.

User

The User in a digital library refers to 'the various actors entitled to interact with digital libraries'. Digital libraries connect the different actors with the information they have and allow the users to consume old or generate new information. Security issues relating to the users of a digital library intersect with content issues. A main logical security issue relating to users and content is access control. Different access control requirements arise for distributed systems to ensure both confidentiality and authentication:

- Access control must be applied and enforced at a distributed platform level, so should be scalable and available at various levels of granularity.
- Access control models should allow a varied definition of access rights depending on different information and must be dynamic where changes to policies are easily made and easy to manage.
- 'Access control models must allow high-level specification of access rights.'

Digital library users may need to be authenticated before they can access content. Global/universal identification may not suffice. A service provider that provides content based on a Non--identity based criteria like age will not benefit from global identification because there is no way to verify the authenticated user's personal information. Usernames and passwords are not efficient ways to provide authentication. One of the most widely used authentication protocols is Kerberos.It is a client–server model, which secures communication with servers on a local network. Developed at MIT in the 1980s to provide security across a large campus network, it is based on the Needham-Schroeder protocol and has now been standardised and included in many operating systems such as UNIX, Linux, Windows 2000, NT, XP, etc. Kerberos is used as an authentication protocol in cases where attackers monitor network traffic to intercept passwords. It secures communication, provides single sign on and mutual authentication, and does not send a user's password in the clear on an insecure network.

An alternative solution suitable for digital libraries is to represent information about an individual using credentials. Credentials are "abstract objects which contain statements expressing knowledge or information from a definite context." Credentials do not specify direct information about a client and their attributes, they describe the local environment and context in which the requests originate. Digital credentials can be used as a means of authentication in providing DL access control. Two agents can be used to assist in the management: a personal security assistant and a server security assistant, to manage digital credentials using a client/server model. The server must notify the client of the credentials required for the current request. The client then sends its credentials for authentication.The client must have some trust of the server to give its credentials, which raises privacy issues. The personal security assistant is used to obtain credentials on behalf of the client, store the credentials, parse and interpret the required credentials, and manage the acceptance policies. A server security assistant is available to specify the credential acceptance policies and their usage. There is a tradeoff between flexibility and security that must be considered when choosing an access control model.

Access Matrix Model

This conceptual model specifies the rights that each subject possesses for each object. Actions on objects are allowed or denied based on the access rights specified.

There are 2 implementations of the AMM:

- An Access Control List provides a direct mapping of each object the subjects are allowed to access, and their usage right; and
- A Capability List defines the objects each subject is allowed to access and the usage rights.

Access control lists and capability lists are not suitable for distributed systems. Their limitations lead to multiple problems. ACL provides limited expressibility of policies. Any change in the policies will propagate in the system/ application. Authentication in a system that uses ACL solely is a problem because using username and password in a distributed system is not practical.

In a distributed system, administration of the system should be decentralised by delegation to reduce the overhead. The owner of the object specifies a policy in ACL. If an overall policy is specified by an entity higher than the object owner, then conflicts may occur in the access rights. The number of administrative entities in a distributed system can be very large. Not all the administrators may have trust amongst themselves, resulting in incorrectly defined policies. For example, admin A may trust B but not C, however B may trust C. If A were to define policy for B then it would be implicitly applicable to C, causing problems.

Role-based Access Control

Role-based access control involves policies that regulate information access based on the activities the users perform. Such policies require the definition of roles in the system: "a set of actions and responsibilities associated with a particular working activity". Permissions are assigned to roles instead of individual users. Specifying user authorisation involves 2 steps: first assigning the user to a role, second defining the access control that the role has over certain objects. RBAC is easier to manage and is more extensible than ACL. However RBAC doesn't flexibly handle constraints, where a user with a specific role may need specific permission on an object. An example of RBAC architecture addressing key limitations is OASIS, for use in distributed systems. Role management in OASIS is decentralised and service specific. OASIS is integrated with an event-based middleware that notifies applications of any environmental changes. Roles are parameterised by applications and services to define their client roles, and to enforce policies for role activation and service invocation within each session. Role membership certificates (RMC) are returned to each user on successful login, to be used as a credential to activate other roles. RBAC is suitable for use with digital libraries because it supports decentralised architectures and varying roles, however RBAC doesn't allow for the definition of different roles in a collaborative group.

Task-based Access Control

The Task-based access control model extends subject/object access control by allowing the definition of domains by task-based contextual information. Steps required to perform the task are used to define access control; the steps are associated with a protection state containing a set of permissions for each state, which change according to the task. TBAC uses dynamic management of permissions. TBAC systems are limited to defining contexts in relation to activities, tasks, or workflow progress. Since, it is implemented by recording usage and validity of permissions, therefore, TBAC requires a central access control module to manage permissions activation and deactivation in a just-in-time fashion.

Team-based Access Control

RBAC doesn't address cases where group members of different roles want to collaborate in a single group. The TMAC model defines collaboration by user context and object context. "User context provides a way of identifying specific users playing a role on a team at any given moment" while object context defines the objects required. TMAC offers the advantages of RBAC along with ability to specify fine-grained control on users and on object instances.A scalable access control data structure can be used with large collections, applying concepts of team based access control, focusing mainly on the access control data structure, and employing an access control framework called Document Access Control Method (DACM) with a Document Storage System (DocSS). DACM allows the decentralised administration of privileges, the definition of different rule sets to control a single collection, and different delegation patterns as models. Current object access control policies use an array of rules to record the privileges each subject is allowed to each object.This is impractical to manage in the large data collections found in digital libraries. DACM solves this problem by finding symmetries in a permission function to allow a brief expression without losing important distinctions.

Content-based Access Control

Another approach to access control models involves defining models according to content. This approach is applicable in digital libraries and distributed systems, where the access rights to the user are dynamic and may change with each login. Content-based access control policies are very well suited for digital libraries and distributed systems. Recent research has proposed different models; most use digital credentials for authentication, but vary in the definition/storage of the policy.An important content-based access control model introduces a contentbased access control system, Digital Library Authorisation System, that utilises the Digital Library Authorisation Model (DLAM). Subject, object, and privilege sets can't be used to define policies in digital libraries mainly because DLs are dynamic with large collections of data and subjects. It defines access control policies based on subject qualifications and characteristics. DLAM provides a means to specify the qualifications and characteristics of subjects. It uses content dependant and independent access control and allows the definition of policies with varied granularity.

Functionality

The concept of functionality encompasses the services that a Digital Library offers to its users. The minimum functions of a Digital Library include adding new objects to the library or searching and browsing the library and other functions relating to DL management. A security attack that can affect the functionality of the Digital Library is a Denial of Service attack, which can affect the performance of the system and prevent users from accessing the system.

Architecture

Digital libraries are complex forms of information systems, interoperable across different libraries and so require an architectural framework mapping content and functionality onto software and hardware components. There are various models for architecture, *e.g.*, client-server, peer-to-peer, and distributed. All these require the protection of the communication channels between 2 parties, where sensitive data might be transferred. Securing the connections involves different layers—Internet, transport, or application layer-depending on the architecture of the system

. The distributed model is scalable and flexible. It is useful when building a digital library with changing content from different sources and offers potential for increased reliability.

The security requirements for a distributed digital library are challenging, since, the content and operations are decentralised. Fault tolerance and error recovery are issues that affect a distributed system. Replication is used to increase the availability of the system. While this approach solves problems with denial of service attacks, it complicates the protection of the content because a replica of the content exists.

The client-server model doesn't have the same security problems as a general distributed model, however, it presents a major security weakness, the server being a single point of failure. Attacks are concentrated on one server rather than on the multiple replicas of a distributed model.

Quality

The content and behaviour of a Digital Library is characterised and evaluated by quality parameters. Quality is a concept not only used to classify functionality and content, but also used with objects and services. Some of the parameters are automatically measured and are objective while others are considered subjective; some are measured through user evaluations.

Policy

Policy is the concept that represents the different regulations and conditions that govern the interaction between the Digital Library and users. Policy supports both extrinsic and intrinsic interactions and their definition and modification. Examples of security issues relating to policies include providing digital rights management, privacy, and confidentiality of the content and users, defining user behaviour, and collection delivery.

THE DIGITAL LIBRARIES UNIVERSE: A THREE-TIER FRAMEWORK

A Digital Library is a live organization that comes to existence through a series of development steps that bring together all necessary constituents. Figure presents this process pictorially and indicates three distinct notions of "systems" that are developed along the way: Digital Library, Digital Library System, and Digital Library Management System. These also correspond to three different levels of conceptualization of the universe of Digital Libraries.

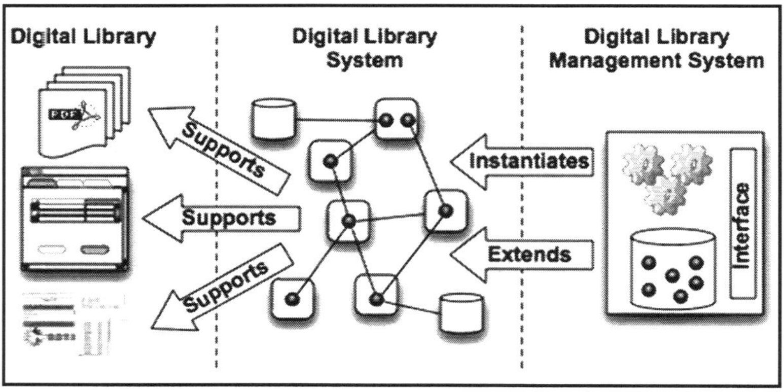

Fig. DL, DLS, and DLMS: A Three-Tier Framework

Unfortunately, these three system notions are often confused and used interchangeably in the literature. Nevertheless, as shown in Figure, they play a central and distinct role in the Digital Library development process.

To clarify their differences and their individual characteristics, they are explicitly defined here as follows:

- *Digital Library (DL): A (potentially virtual) organization that comprehensively collects, manages, and preserves for the long term rich digital content and offers to its user communities specialized functionality on that content, of measurable quality, and according to prescribed policies.*
- *Digital Library System (DLS): A software system that is based on a (potentially distributed) architecture and provides all functionality that is required by a particular Digital Library.*
  Users interact with a Digital Library through the corresponding Digital Library System.
- *Digital Library Management System (DLMS): A generic software system that provides the appropriate software infrastructure to both:*
  - Produce and administer a Digital Library System that incorporates all functionality that is considered foundational for Digital Libraries and
  - Integrate additional software offering more refined, specialized, or advanced functionality.

A Digital Library Management System is what one may call "system software". As in several other domains (*e.g.,*, operating systems, databases, user interfaces), such kernel software may be used as a foundation to produce Digital Library Systems. Depending on the philosophy it follows, a DLMS belongs to one of the following three categories:

- *Extensible Digital Library System:* A complete Digital Library System that is fully operational with respect to basic/foundational functionality required. It is based on an open software architecture, so that further software components can be incorporated on top of the ones already there with ease. DelosDLMS is a prototypical example of a system that is based on this philosophy.
- *Digital Library System Warehouse:* A collection of software components that cover all basic/foundational functionality required and a set of tools that can be used to combine these components in arbitrary ways (in Lego-like fashion) to create Digital Library Systems offering diverse sets of functionality. New software components can easily be incorporated into the Warehouse for subsequent combination with those already there. BRICKS and DILIGENT are two prototypical examples of systems that are based on this philosophy.
- *Digital Library System Generator:* A highly parameterized software system that encapsulates templates for a broad range of functionality, which includes all basic/foundational as well as any advanced functionality that has been deemed appropriate. Through an initialization session, the appropriate parameters are set and tuned; at the end of that session, software is automatically generated that constitutes essentially a Digital Library System ready to be installed and deployed.

Note that, while the concept of Digital Library is intended to capture an abstract system that consists of both physical and virtual components, the remaining two capture concrete software systems. For every Digital Library, there is a unique Digital Library System in operation (possibly consisting of many interconnected smaller DLSs in the most general case), whereas all Digital Library Systems are based on a handful of Digital Library Management Systems.It is also important to note that until now, most Digital Libraries have been created by developing DLSs from scratch without any basis on a DLMS. The notion of DLMS has been recently introduced by the DL community in order to overcome the many drawbacks arising from the current DL development process. When the digital library field reaches maturity, one should expect that only a small number of industrial-strength Digital Library Management Systems will be available on the market.

THE DIGITAL LIBRARIES UNIVERSE: MAIN CONCEPTS

Despite the great richness and diversity one finds among existing digital libraries, there are still a rather small number of concepts that are considered fundamental and essentially characterize all relevant systems and, in fact, the entire field. These concepts are identifiable in every digital library and should be the starting point for any researcher who wants to study and understand the field, for any system designer and developer who is about to embark in an effort to build a Digital Library, and for any content owner who wants to offer it externally. In this section, we identify these concepts and briefly discuss their roles.

Given that there are three kinds of "systems" in the digital library world, in principle each one may have, in addition to the common fundamental concepts, a number of other related concepts associated with it.Nevertheless, from the definitions of these systems in the previous section, one may easily derive that there is a natural inclusion relationship on the concepts that refer to these systems: the set of concepts used to define the Digital Library is completely included in that used for Digital Library System, which is in turn completely included in that characterising the Digital Library Management System. This inclusion relationship is depicted in Figure.

As a consequence of the above, we introduce below each of these concepts in reference to the highest level of a system (in the three-tier framework) for which it makes sense. All concepts, however, could also be described in reference to lower-level systems, focusing on the characteristics that are of primary concern there. More details can be found elsewhere.The main concepts that are foundational in the Digital Library world are six. Five of them have been alluded to in the definition of Digital Libraries and are introduced in reference to them: *Content*, *User*, *Functionality*, *Quality*, and *Policy*; one of them has been alluded to in the definition of a Digital Library Systems and is introduced in reference to them: *Architecture*. All six concepts are shown together, influencing the Digital Library framework, in Figure and are defined immediately after that.

Content

The Content concept represents the data and information that Digital Libraries handle and make available to their users. It is composed of a set of information objects organised in collections. Content is an umbrella concept that is used to aggregate all forms of information that a Digital Library may require to offer its services. For example, metadata play an important role in the information domain because they describe the contents of other information objects and express their structure.

User

The User concept represents the actors (whether human or not) entitled to interact with Digital Libraries. The aim of Digital Libraries is to connect such actors with information and to support them in consuming already available information and produce new information. As in the case of the previous concept, User is an umbrella concept that covers all notions related to the representation and management of actor entities within a Digital Library, *i.e.,*, the digital entities representing the actors, the rights that they have within the system, the profiles of the actors with characteristics that personalize the system's behaviour or represent these actors in collaborations, and others.

Functionality

The Functionality concept represents the services that Digital Libraries offer to their users. In the most general case, the functionality expected from Digital Libraries is extremely rich.

One may not expect, however, that all Digital Libraries must support the complete spectrum. Some core functionality represents the bare minimum that is required by all Digital Libraries, *e.g.,*, new information object registration, search, and browse.

Beyond that, depending on the particular needs of its community of users and/or the information it is aimed to manage, each Digital Library may offer diverse additional functionality to serve those needs.

Quality

The Quality concept represents the parameters that can be used to characterize and evaluate the content and behaviour of Digital Libraries. It potentially includes several diverse parameters associated with each class of content or functionality, possibly even with each distinct information object or service. Some of these parameters are objective in nature and can be automatically measured, whereas others are subjective in nature and can only be measured through human experiments.

Policy

The Policy concept represents a set of rules that govern the interaction between users and Digital Libraries. Several mechanisms should be available to enable such interaction and the Digital Library should activate those mechanisms in the form prescribed by its policies. The policy concept includes all aspects of system security, digital rights management, system load control, and other similar issues.

ARCHITECTURE

The Architecture concept (which refers to a Digital Library System) represents a mapping of the functionality and content offered by a DL onto hardware and software components6. Having this as a main concept is important due to the following considerations:

- Digital Libraries are often assumed to be among the most complex and advanced forms of information systems ;

- Interoperability of Digital Libraries is one of the greatest challenges of the research community. Having a clear architectural understanding of Digital Library Systems offers ammunition in addressing both the above issues effectively.

In addition to the above primary Digital Library concepts, there is one more that is a derivative of them and is also very useful. That is the concept of Resource, which aggregates the concepts of Content, User, Functionality, and Policy, *i.e.*, , all concepts that refer to internal entities of a Digital Library and can be sensed by the external world. There are several aspects of all these concepts that are very similar or identical.

Approached as instances of the more general concept of Resource, the Digital Library should treat them in the same fashion. Having described the main concepts characterising the foundation of the digital library universe, we proceed in introducing four main roles of actors that interact with digital libraries at different levels and for different purposes.

THE DIGITAL LIBRARY UNIVERSE: THE MAIN ROLES OF ACTORS

We envisage four different and complementary roles of actors interacting with digital libraries: *DL End-Users*, *DL Designers*, *DL System Administrators*, and *DL Application Developers*.

As depicted in Figure, each role is primarily associated with one of the three "systems" in the three-tier framework and, therefore, has the view that corresponds to that system. These roles are defined below.

DL End-Users

These exploit the DL functionality for providing, consuming, and managing the DL Content as well as some of its other constituents. They perceive the DL as a stateful entity that serves their functional needs. The behaviour and output of the DL depend on its state at the time a particular part of its functionality is activated.

The state of the DL corresponds to the state of its resources, *i.e.*,, it consists of the collections of information objects managed by the DL, its set of authorized users, its functionality, and its set of policies. This state changes during the Digital Library lifetime according to the functionality activated by the users and their inputs. DL end-users may be further partitioned into *Content Creator*, *Content Consumer*, and *Librarian*.

DL Designers

These exploit their knowledge of the application semantic domain to define, customise, and maintain the Digital Library so that it is aligned with the information and functional needs of its end-users.

To perform this task, they interact with the DLMS providing functional and content configuration parameters. The former capture aspects of the DL functionality perceived by the end-users, *e.g.*,, the result set format, the query language, the user profile formats, and the document model.

The latter capture third-party resources that are exploited by the specific DL, *e.g.*,, repositories of content, ontologies, classification schemas, authority files, and gazetteers. The values of these parameters, which can be modified during the DL lifetime, configure the specific DL perceived by the end-users because they determine the particular Digital Library System instance serving the Digital Library.

DL SYSTEM ADMINISTRATORS

These select the software components necessary to create the Digital Library System needed to serve the required DL and decide where and how to deploy them. They interact with the DLMS by providing architectural configuration parameters, such as the selected software components, the hosting nodes, and the components allocation.

Their task is to identify the architectural configuration that better fits the DLS in target ensuring the appropriate level of quality. The value of the architectural configuration parameters can be changed over the DL lifetime. Any change of these parameters may result in the provision of different DL functionality and/or different quality.

DL APPLICATION DEVELOPERS

These develop the software components of DLMSs and DLSs, realizing the necessary functionality.

These four roles cover the whole spectrum of actors interacting with digital libraries. Their models of the digital library universe are linked together in a hierarchical fashion as depicted in Figure. This is a direct consequence of the above definitions since DL end-users act on the Digital Library, whereas the remaining three roles operate on the DLMS and consequently on the DLS and DL as well.

This relationship ensures that roles designed to directly co-operate share a common vocabulary/knowledge. For instance, the DL end-user expresses its requirements in terms of the DL model and, subsequently, the DL designer understands these requirements and defines the DL accordingly.

REFERENCE FRAMEWORKS

The Digital Library Universe is quite complex and comprises multiple elements. The representation of the details of these elements requires the introduction of several frameworks at different levels of abstraction:

Reference Model

it is a set of inter-related concepts that collectively circumscribe and capture the essence of a distinct part of human knowledge, be it a whole scientific field or an individual idea or anything in between. It is a framework that helps in understanding of the basic elements of its concept(s) of concern.

As stated in, "A Reference Model consists of a minimal set of unifying concepts, axioms and relationships within a particular problem domain, and is independent of specific standards, technologies, implementations, or other concrete details".

It can be established at various levels of abstraction, from very high-level and flexible to very concrete and precise. Although independent of them, it often leads to standards that have to be followed by all systems dealing with the particular parts of knowledge corresponding to it.

Digital libraries need to obtain a corresponding reference model in order to consolidate the diversity of existing approaches into a cohesive and consistent whole and provide a common basis for further advancement.

Reference Architecture

it is an architectural design pattern indicating an abstract solution in implementing the concepts and relationships identified in the Reference Model. Essentially, the reference architecture acts as a blueprint for the implementation of a DLS. There may be more than one reference architecture that addresses how to design digital libraries systems.

Each of them proposes an optimal architectural pattern for a particular class of DLSs serving the needs of DLs characterised by similar goals, motivations and requirements. For example, we might have a reference architecture for DLSs supporting federated DLs, *i.e.,* DLs built by federating local resources of multiple organizations, and another one for personal DLs, or for specialised applications.

Concrete Architecture

it introduces additional elements making the reference architecture more concrete, *e.g.,* replaces the mechanisms envisaged in the Reference Architecture with concrete standards and specifications. For example, it may specify that the run-time environment deployed on the hosting nodes is CORBA or the Web Services Application Framework, and that the Search functional component is implemented by four specific communicating Web Services.

The three frameworks above are shown in Figure in relationship to the general digital library environment. At the top is the most abstract Reference Model, which guides the more specific Reference Architecture and Concrete Architecture further down. In turn, these should constrain the development of any actual Implementation of a system.

The three reference frameworks are the outcome of an abstraction process that has taken into account all the natural Inputs, shown to the left, *e.g.,*, the systems already existing on the market, and has taken into consideration all existing Related Work, shown to the right, *e.g.,*, best practices and relevant research. When these frameworks are adopted and followed by the community, the resulting systems will be largely compatible with each other; the interoperability thus afforded will open up significant new horizons for the field.

The goal of '*The Digital Library Manifesto*' has been to set the foundations and identify the entities of discourse within the universe of digital libraries. It has introduced the relationships among three kinds of relevant "systems" in this area: Digital Library, Digital Library System, and Digital Library Management System.

It has presented the main concepts characterising the above, *i.e.,*, content, user, functionality, quality, policy, and architecture, and has identified the main roles that actors may play within a digital library, *i.e.,*, end-user, designer, administrator, and application developer. Finally, it has described the reference frameworks that are needed to clarify the digital library universe at different detailed levels of abstraction, *i.e.,*, the Reference Model and the Reference and Concrete Architectures.

'*The Digital Library Manifesto*' is accompanied currently by two other documents, which correspond precisely to the aforementioned reference frameworks. These documents come as a first attempt to fulfil the needs of the field in these areas.

Clearly, diversity of needs among different digital libraries will continue to introduce new concepts that will require incorporation into the Reference Model and the Reference and Concrete Architectures. Hence, these documents should be considered as first versions of otherwise dynamic documents that will keep evolving, having the Manifesto as a firm foundation.

9

The Role of LIS Professionals to Manage E-resources

Traditional integrated library-management systems were designed for managing print resources and are not well suited to managing electronic resources. For example, library systems typically lack the ability to describe the hierarchical nature of electronic resources: that an e-journal is part of a package, and the package is supplied by an interface provider. Nor do traditional library systems have the means to describe attributes such as license and access information; to handle the various workflows required specifically for eresource management, such as a trial workflow; and to deal with archival rights and the restriction of access to specific locations and specific communities.

Lacking such capabilities, many libraries have been looking for solutions to help them manage this new form of resource. An ERM system should not only deal with the daily tasks related to e-resources but also provide comprehensive analyses related to a library's expenditure on electronic materials. Furthermore, an ERM system can open up new horizons related to collection management, in which information about the global marketplace and also about the institution's collection and expenditures can serve as decision-making tools for library staff. Today's consumers are accustomed to meeting information, business, and entertainment needs instantly. Library patrons are accessing electronic holdings from their home, office, or anywhere they need information and expect an efficient user experience. These expectations inform the changing roles and services provided by librarians. Librarians often have direct influence in the development and implementation of their WebPages, an autonomy that allows for quicker progression of change. An area where we have less power to drive changes involves our data providers. In the next few years the electronic resources librarian will need to take an active role working with vendors to provide mobile access to their electronic resources.

USAGE PATTERN OF INFORMATION RESOURCES AT CSIR

The aim and objective of any Information Centre is to provide pinpoint, exhaustive, and nascent information to readers who use information for a variety of purposes. A library, therefore, is always adjudged good or bad on by its usage. This goal makes the collection development evaluation imminent. Considering the importance of such usage, an attempt has been made in this study to evaluate the current usage of literature at CSIR-National Metallurgical Laboratory, Jamshedpur, Jharkhand (Erstwhile Bihar). The worth of a library collection can be judged through various methods like, circulation of documents, user survey, download analysis of literature, Citation/Reference analysis, etc. The present study, however, evaluates the library usage through reference analysis. Today, citation and ranking information are becoming key aspects of knowledge management in R&D Knowledge Resource Centers.

It helps to examine the changing user needs and products so as to understand and manage the information resources besides responding the user needs better. Effective collection analysis and assessment provides quantitative and qualitative data for evaluating the usefulness and utility of a library's holdings. It assists with determining budget requirements by focusing attention on how well the library's collections in specific areas support the needs of the users and the institution as well. It also points out whether the institution's investment in the collection is being managed responsibly. The aim of such assessment is, therefore, to determine as to how well the collection supports the goals, needs, and mission of the library or parent organisation. The collection (both locally held and remotely accessed materials) is assessed in the local context. Evaluation seeks to examine or describe collections either in their own terms or in relation to other collections and checking mechanisms, such as lists. Both evaluation and assessment provide a better understanding of the collection and the user community. The major problem of research libraries all over the world today is deciding as to which serials should be subscribed to meet the needs of their specialised users without subscribing to any unnecessary journals.

The problem has been further aggravated recently by shortages of funds and subsequent cuts in library book budgets. In order to operate effectively, libraries must identify literature of high utility to their clients, and must acquire and organise the literature in such a way to ensure their optimal use. One of the generally accepted methods of scientific investigation is, indeed, to follow the scientific literature by the simplest means. Various sources are used by scientists to gather information, for example, through regular reading of all available texts, recommendations of colleagues and superiors, and references or citations in other related publications.

LITERATURE SURVEYED

The citation analysis technique can be traced by using references found in scholarly works. In the early 1970s, Coale evaluated the Latin American colonial history collection at Chicago's Newberry library using bibliographies of a group of scholarly monographs. These bibliographies were also checked against the holdings of other libraries for comparison. In addition to scholarly works as the source for compiling checklists as noted in studies by Olaosun, Bland and Stelk and Lancaster, recommended readings and textbooks were also used. Citations drawn from student's dissertations or term papers was another source of checklist used in numerous studies, the earliest being that of Emerson's analysis of 23 engineering doctoral dissertations at the Columbia University between 1950 and 1954 to determine the percentage of references held or not held by the other campus libraries in the university. Sylvia analyses the serial titles cited by the psychology students in their research bibliographies to evaluate the use of a journals collection for the purpose of journal selection or de-selection. In another study using doctoral dissertations, Buzzard and New investigated library collections used by doctoral students in the humanities, sciences, and social sciences.

However, the use of this method is determining the percentage held; collection usage, because of the possible links between physical accessibility and use or citation of an item, is questionable. Moreover, materials consulted for background knowledge may be under represented while the patrons may not necessarily use sources that were cited. Nevertheless, it is a valid method of evaluation as shown by Nisonger's test of the Lopez method conducted at the University of Manitoba and his test of two citations checking techniques in which citations were drawn from journal articles. Being inspired by earlier studies, an attempt has been made to determine the usage pattern of the information resource of CSIR-NML by way of case study.

RESEARCH METHOD AND DATA

A total of 187 Research papers published in various formats like, SCI, Non--SCI, National proceedings, Internatioal proceedings and book chapters were identified by institutional affiliation.Fig.1 depicts the status of R&D publications, a maximum of 120 papers appeared in SCI was downloaded from Web of Science with complete reference data and the remaining 54 papers were scanned form Non--SCI journals, proceedings and book chapters. Thus, the total number of references cited in the 187 research papers was 3,825. The average number of references per paper was 20. The availability of references was coded under the following four categories:

- Available in electronic form;
- Vailable in print form;
- Available in the open network; and
- Not available.

The bibliographic references in each article in the sample were first examined by classifying each citation into one of the following nine source categories by format of publications: books/monographs (includes chapters in a book, monograph series, sourcebook), journals (*i.e.* scholarly and academic serials in the form of print or online, articles 'in press' with journal title cited), periodicals (*i.e.* magazines, newspapers, working papers, Newsletters), conferences proceedings (proceedings, seminars meetings, workshops, forums), unpublished (*i.e.* unpublished manuscripts, thesis/dissertation, documents, reports/documents, unpublished test and short communications), reference sources (*i.e.* government documents, dictionaries, handbooks, encyclopaedias) reports (*i.e.* published reports by institutions or corporations), web documents (documents retrieved from the internet via the worldwide web with Uniform Resource Locator (URL) provided, and others. 'Conference proceedings' was designated for compilations of papers presented at conferences or symposia that were not published as a regular issue of a journal.

CONSORTIA MODELS FOR NETWORKING SOME ISSUES ON CSIR CONSORTIA

The word consortium has been derived from Latin, meaning association or partnership. In general a Consortium could be described as a group of organisations who come together to fulfil a common objective that usefully requires co-operation and the sharing of resources, and need to have a clear mutual goal in order to ensure their success. Various definitions are there in different dictionaries on consortium but almost the meaning is same in the context of library. An e-journal consortium means the collaborative acquisition of access rights to electronic databases and journals and the aim of is to achieve what the members of the group cannot achieve individually. Journals play a major role in the R&D but unfortunately the number and cost of journals are increasing at very high speed. Number of journals and their costs has increased by threefolds every 15 years and 226 per cent, respectively.

During the last 20 years in terms of dollars, this may be further compounded by currency conversion whereas the increase in library 1 budget was only 110 per cent during the same period. In another study by the Association of Research Libraries in USA, it was found that average CPI (Consumer Price Index) for US increased by 73 per cent during 1986-2004, but the research libraries expenditure for journals 2 increased by 273 per cent during the same period due to the increase in number of research scholars, institutions and global competition.

The estimated number of STM (Science, Technology and Medicine) journals is about 25,000. Out of this 15,000 journals are peer- 3 reviewed and 12,000 are in e-form. All types of libraries/information centres are not in a position to subscribe all the information resources required by their users. Not even a single library can meet the thrust of knowledge required by all the readers from its stock of information to the full extent.To solve this, libraries have started library cooperation, *i.e.* inter-library loan (ILL), resource sharing, and library consortium, etc. For the past four centuries, dissemination of information was done through print media alone, but now the electronic media has taken over this mean of communication. Basic purpose of the consortia is sharing of resources, money, and manpower. In the digital context, it is the access to information rather than holding information. 'Collection building' concept has changed to 'Connection building' with the help of Information and Communication technologies (ICT).

Access to the e-resources and the subscription amount is shared among the participating libraries. Significant price reduction can be achieved through consortium and individual libraries in the consortium will have collaborative acquisition of access rights to databases and e-journals.

Library consortia's have become powerful negotiating parties and incorporating their own clauses in the contracts with the publishers and just no longer signing the standard contract texts provided by the 4 publishers.

TYPES OF CONSORTIA

The types of consortia identified are generally based on various models evolved in India in Variety of forms depending upon participations' affiliation and funding sources.

- *Open Consortia*: This type of consortia is very flexible and it is the wish of members of consortia can join and leave any they please. INDEST Consortium is an example to this.
- *Closed Group Consortia*: This kind of consortia emerges either by affiliation and collaboration among them like CSIR, DAE, IIM Consortium. The formation and operation of the consortia guidelines and its administration are fairly simple and easy.
- *Centrally Funded Model*: In this model, consortium will solely depend on the parent body. A few examples are CSIR, INDEST, UGC-INFONET and ICMR Consortia, etc.
- *Shared-budget Model*: In this model the participating libraries take the lead and form the consortium. IIM and FORSA are examples of this model.
- *Publisher Initiatives*: The Emerald Full-Text Library published by the Emerald Publishing Group (formerly MCB University Press) is recent example. Here, the consortium members will get deep discount price to the participating libraries.
- *National Consortium*: This is a model perceived at national level which includes member libraries from one country.

BENEFITS OF CONSORTIUM

Some of the important advantages of the proposed library consortium are as follows:

- Main advantage of e-journal consortium is, it checks the space problem, shelving, binding, lending, and related aspects of member libraries.

- Instead of user coming to the library, the library is available at the user's desktop/laptop virtually all the time (24/7). Available 24 hours a day, 7 days a week.
- It saves the time of the user since instant access will be available after every updating unlike the shipping time, missing issues, and mutilations. etc., which prevail in respect of print media.
- Consortium builds communication among different libraries and avoids duplication of core journals.
- Consortium provides high quality literature and faster document delivery service, *i.e.*, it provides a wealth of relevant resources readily available and helps in facing the challenges to have a meaningful presence in this digital era to its users.
- It is easy to assess the areas of interest of users so that efficient services can be provided by the concerned librarians through usage statistics given by the publisher.
- The consortium have been offered better terms of licenses for use, archival access and preservation of subscribed electronic resources, which would not have been possible for any single institution and facilities to build up digital libraries.
- Helpful to provide better library services like CAS and SDI.

BOTTLENECKS OF CONSORTIUM

- Absence of a printed copy of Journals and lack of archiving and back files availability.
- Require training of staffs in handling electronic documents etc.
- A consortium requires high initial investments in licensees and infrastructure, internet connectivity, and other accessories.
- Copyright problems. Problems like copyright/ excess downloads from the publisher.
- Content provider/publisher combines both essential and Non--essential journals as a package. Whereas in print collection, the selection is done by subject expert(s) and only journals of core area are subscribed. Therefore, measures have to be taken to avoid unwanted items and recall the most relevant items.

GROWTH OF CONSORTIA IN INDIA

The new technology or the modern information technology has made the task of resource sharing very simple and convenient. The new technology brings forward to the information field many products and services which have changed the nature of fundamental library objectives and operations.

Over the last 2 decades, the libraries have witnessed the impact of information technology that has been affecting the structure of the services to a great extent. Library networks have grown mostly during the last 30 years in different geographical environment in order to cater the specific needs of the users. In the U.S., there has been a proliferation of them. In the developed countries, resource sharing networking was started long back, *e.g.* the growth of the network in the U.S., can be traced from mid 1960. USA is the birthplace of library networking and by now libraries in each state are networked to local, regional and national network.

On the other hand, the growth of library networks in India can be traced to the initiatives made by NISSAT in establishing 6 CALIBNET in 1986 and DELNET in 1988 and other networks like UGC/INFLIBNET has established UGC-INFONET Consortium, Digital Library in Engineering Science and Technology (INDEST) Consortium of all Indian institute of Technologies (IITs), Indian Institute of Science (IISc) and a few other institutions which include RECs, NITs, IIMs, etc., the Forum for Resource Sharing in Astronomy and Astrophysics (FORSA) is a consortium of Raman Research Institute (RRI), Indian Institute of Astrophysics (IIA), Tata Institute of Fundamental Research (TIFR), Inter-university Centre for Astronomy and Astrophysics (IUCAA), National Centre for Radio Astrophysics (NCRA), and Physical Research Laboratory (PRL) subsequently.

CSIR CONSORTIUM

The Council of Scientific and Industrial Research (CSIR), a public-funded organisation, is India's largest R&D organisation established in 1942 with a chain of 37 National laboratories and institutes. CSIR is carrying out the research work in various disciplines all over the country.

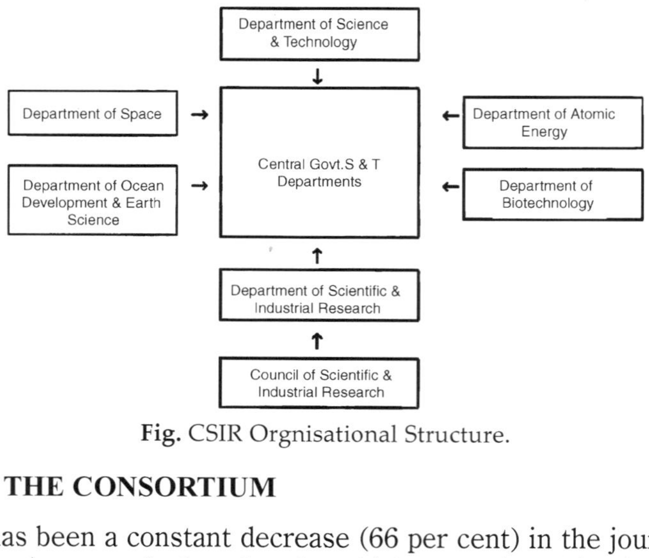

Fig. CSIR Orgnisational Structure.

NEED FOR THE CONSORTIUM

There has been a constant decrease (66 per cent) in the journals base of CSIR laboratories over the last decade, which necessitated its libraries to find out alternate solution to make available R&D information.While laboratory size, areas of work and number of researchers vary, it is desirable to have comparable and adequate information 7 resources irrespective of the size or strength of the laboratory.

OBJECTIVES OF THE CONSORTIUM

- The primary objective of the overall programme focuses on enhancing the visibility and impact of CSIR research output internationally in terms of papers and patents.
- This will be attempted by providing access to maximum possible e-resources to the researchers.
- To provide CSIR and S&T staff electronic access to global knowledge with continues to subscribe existing e-resources.
- To expand the information base of CSIR and provide divergent nature of contents of information to CSIR users subscribe to additional e-resources.

E-JOURNAL CONSORTIUM

The Director General set up a study group in April 2001 to collect/study and compile information to the journals subscribed by the CSIR labs. After several deliberations the eth journal Consortium project finally took shape as a Network Project of CSIR under 10 Five Year Plan with a budget layout of Rs11.79 crores for the plan period 2002-2007 targeting to access 4500 e-journals. E-Journal consortium is being coordinated centrally by CSIR's National Institute of Science Communication and Information Resources (NISCAIR) as nodal agency for implementing the Consortium, with a task force team established with senior scientists from CSIR laboratories and also negotiation committees to negotiate and finalise the agreements with the publishers in providing required e-journals, databases, etc., for CSIR's constituent laboratories.

The heads of the libraries of the participating labs are designated as 8 the nodal officers to implement the Consortium access to e-journals at their respective labs. CSIR e-Journal Consortium strengthens its library resources by pooling, sharing and providing electronic access services like e-journals and international databases to its scholars and scientists. On 10 June 2002, CSIR signed an agreement with M/s Elsevier Science to 9 access around 1500 world class e-journals.

NISCAIR has coordinated well by constituting different committees like Core Committee, Negotiating Committees, etc., for effective implementation of the consortium.

'Electronic plus' price model was chosen to maintain the print collection of the individual institution libraries irrespective of the duplicate and triplicate subscriptions from the same publisher and paying an extra amount of 9 per cent of the print to ScienceDirect at the beginning of the project.

This extra amount is varied subsequently in the following years based on effective negotiations by the concerned committees. Usage statistics is being provided by the publisher to the individual institutes for effective monitoring of the consortium. Archival issues pertaining to past five years are also being provided by the concerned publisher as per the agreement. E-Journals and other document requirements of the constituent laboratories have been put forth by the nodal officers to coordinating agencies. The coordinating agency prepares the financial document and gets the money from CSIR negotiation committees to allocate this money to different publishers based on the suggestions received from the nodal officers. In this way it receives 10 more than 4000 e-journals. CSIR Consortium has proved to be a great success and its impact can be measured in terms of revenue savings, usage of e-journals in terms of downloads and contribution of articles in international journals, etc. Substantial revenue has been saved, and significant growth in number of papers and IF (Impact Factor) have been achieved.

Quantitative as well as qualitative improvements have been achieved in the years following the access to e-journals through the Consortium. Continual and steep increase in the number of downloads has also been recorded. In this way CSIR became a leading institutions of the world and the contribution of CSIR researchers in international journals have raised. The 11 National savings on this account is around ₹~535 crores. Upgrading the CSIR information system is proving effective in meeting its researcher's divergent nature of information requirements.

ELSEVIER CONTEXT

To fill the lack of information in the CSIR laboratories, decided to subscribe e-journals of Elsevier by individual laboratories and sharing these resources among the CSIR laboratories. The coordinating agencies suggested subscribing only the unique journals and avoiding for the duplication for maximum possible so that sharing of e-journals shall be easier through the CSIR network. As scientific literature is exploding, publishing has become an increasingly profitable enterprise. The competition in the publishing world is very fast, with even old scientific societies turning to commercial publishers, to bring a degree of professionalism of producing and marketing their journals. As journals multiply and costs increase, libraries must worry about budgets and coverage. Problems are compounded by growing costs of maintaining both print and online subscriptions and issues related to continuing electronic access to back files. Large publishing houses like Elsevier Science and Springer-Verlag are beginning to monopolise the world of science journals, which arises a situation that 12 promotes a seller's market. CSIR Consortium did not agreed to the price hike proposed by publisher and termed it as unreasonable and gave a counter proposal for consideration of the publisher.

However, access to ScienceDirect was stopped in April 2008 as the agreement was not renewed between the CSIR Consortium and the publisher due to failure of negotiations with the regard to price hike by the publisher. In this way after 2008 CSIR laboratories were felt the necessity for a strong networking among their constituent laboratories.

SUBSCRIPTION TO JCCC@VIC: *J-GATE CUSTOM CONTENT FOR CONSORTIA*

After this CSIR entering into JCCC for exchange of holdings of individual CSIR laboratories on inter library loan basis but problems with JCCC are it is a platform which is common to all for accessing information which becomes a great problem to serve the users. As CSIR laboratories are scientific in nature so their members are also dealing with scientific field, but it is difficult to analyse the member of JCCC. It becomes a question mark in their authenticity in identification.

NAL CONTEXT

For possible solution NAL (National Aeronautics Limited) compile a union catalogue for CSIR laboratories and it has come forward flood the updated union catalogue with the cooperation from the member CSIR libraries, an alternatives mode to avoid JCCC.

EXPERIENCE NETWORK WITH DST

After seeing the experience of CSIR consortium with the publishers, DST (Department of Science and Technology) has also decided to join with CSIR consortium for their e-journal subscription.

NATIONAL KNOWLEDGE RESOURCE CONSORTIUM FINAL SOLUTION

Open Consortium- Consortium of S&T institutions, will help to expand the information base will strengthen the negotiating power, develop uniformity across different departments. NISCAIR should perform a leading role to bring other S&T organisations under Consortium.

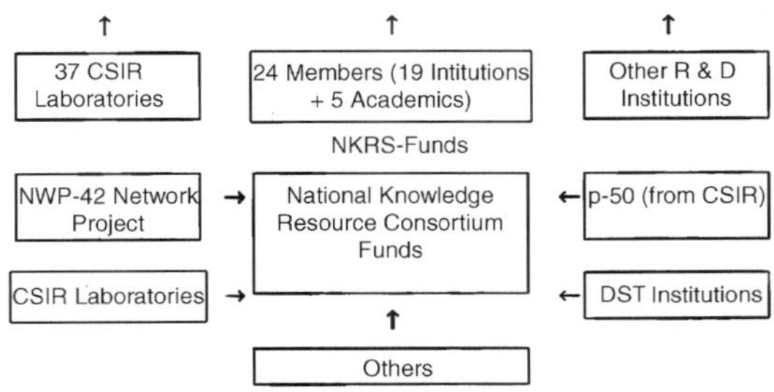

Fig. National Knowledge Resource Consortium.

CSIR going to interconnected all the scientific laboratories with powerful computer networks with one CSIR slogans and the solution is formation of

National Consortium of Scientific Departments and named as National Knowledge Resource Consortium (NKRC).

ELECTRONIC RESOURCE MANAGEMENT INITIATIVES

As institutions realised that effective communication about their common problem of managing electronic resources could lead to satisfying solutions they began to seek discussion outside their own academic institutions. The "Web hub for developing administrative metadata for electronic resource management" was constructed to facilitate the sharing of information about institutions developing their own electronic resource management systems. The Web hub was a Web site managed by Adam Chandler and Tim Jewell, which listed the names of the universities that were building systems or creating initiatives to address their own electronic resource management needs.

The site also listed descriptions of the systems and contact persons at each university. The site was built so that universities could read how other institutions were developing their tools, and could communicate with those universities if they had similar needs. The Web hub was a successful facilitator for those institutions that were considering building their own electronic resource management systems but needed more information or support before beginning their projects.

The creators of the Web hub started the Digital Library Federation's Electronic Resource Management Initiative steering group in 2001. The purpose of the Electronic Resource Management Initiative (ERMI) was to define an essential list of data elements that would construct a full and complete electronic resource management system. In addition to defining the data elements, the group sought to develop workflows and promote standards for the management of the data.The Web hub served as a fertile space from which the ERMI could pull information to begin their discussions.

In the final report of the Digital Library Federation's ERMI seven functional areas required to construct a comprehensive management system are identified: 'listing and descriptive;' 'license related;' 'financial and purchasing;' 'process and status;' 'systems and technical;' 'contact and support;' and 'usage'. By identifying these functional areas the ERMI hopes to convey accurately to vendors or others wishing to build management systems what elements are needed. As the Digital Library Federation's ERMI outlined its own goals it also included conversations with library vendors. By communicating with the vendors the ERMI created a successful ongoing rapport about what was needed to develop a complete electronic resource management system. By including vendors in this discussion the ERMI could provide the data backbone of a system that could then be developed by the vendors; in this way libraries could depend on vendors for development support and collaboration rather than acting as independent system creators.

FEATURES OF SYSTEMS

Features of some ERM systems include:

- Supporting acquisition and management of licensed e-resources
- May be integrated into other library system modules or may be a standalone system
- May have a public interface, either separate or integrated into the OPAC
- Providing descriptions of resources at the package (database) level and relate package contents (*e.g.* e-journals) to the package record
- Encoding and perhaps publicly displaying licensed rights such as e-reserves, course packs, and interlibrary loan
- Tracking electronic resources from point of order through licensing and final access
- Providing information about the data providers, consortia arrangements, access platform
- Providing contact information for all content providers
- Logging problems with resources and providers
- Providing customisable e-mail alerting systems
- Linking license documents to resource records

ACQUISITION OF ELECTRONIC RESOURCES DEALING WITH LICENSING ISSUES

The electronic publishing has a very short history, compared to traditional form of publishing. The first known form of e-publishing is in the early 1980s when plain text e-mails were sent to the subscriber via a mailing list.

But, the subsequent technological advancements made a tremendous impact on the information cycle process of creation, gathering/production and dissemination of information, which in turn hugely influenced the electronic publishing itself. In 1994-95 the first e-journal was published and the distribution of e-journal turned out to be an instant success. Majority of the journals are now made available in digital form.

The publishers are now offering package subscription to electronic journals at highly reduced price as the publishing charges of e-journals have substantially come down, as compared to their print counterpart, which involved huge cost of printing and distribution. Subsequently, even bibliographic resources were brought in electronic form.

Soon, e-books also made their presence. These developments made the libraries to seriously rethink their collection development and information delivery policies.

While moving totally to electronic may be a distant possibility, a progressive shift from print to electronic, is being noticed.

MOVING FROM PRINT TO ELECTRONIC A CRITICAL ISSUE

While the print and online versions have their own advantages and disadvantages. However, to put the subject in perspective, some critical remarks are made here. Print resources subscribed/ bought are physically available in the libraries and form an asset. Online resources subscribed/ bought on one-time purchase can only be accessed by users, as the digital content is held remotely at the publishers' end.

This raises the issue of ownership *vs.* access and is a well debated point in the user and the librarians' communities. The fact, however, is that, in case of online resources, the libraries are currently dependent totally on publishers to access the subscribed/ bought content. This situation made the libraries to think in terms of ensuring perpetual access to the subscribed/ bought content. Of course, publishers too have their own concerns of protecting their content from misuse. It is, therefore, a mutual interest of both the publisher and the end-user to enter into an Agreement protecting each other's interests. This agreement is generally known as License Agreement.

LICENSE AGREEMENT AND ITS TYPES

A License agreement is a legal document and contract between the publisher and the institutional library. Both the parties agree to abide by the terms and conditions set in the agreement. There are basically three different kinds of site license agreements according to:

- The type of library,
- Product/ model, and
- Number of sites.

The agreements by the type of libraries include Academic/ Research, Government/ Corporate and Public and generally the variations are in terms of users, fees, etc.; The agreements by product/ model are based on the e-resources, such as E-journals, E-books and Bibliographic Databases. The agreements by site(s) are applicable according to the number of sites, such as single site, multi-sites and consortium. Although, the re-exist some Standard Licensing models, each publisher has his own Agreement and a close look at these indicate that there is a lack of consistency and standardisation. A few publishers have put up the copy of their site license agreement on their web site but others do not do so maintaining it as confidential document. However, signing of License Agreement has almost become mandatory. In fact, a well known publisher has a policy which stipulates that they will raise the invoice for an e-product only after the library signs the agreement. In a way, it is good that the library will know all the terms and conditions before buying the product. Other publishers send the agreement after the purchase order is raised and the payment is made. In such cases, it may be difficult to negotiate any changes in the clauses. The terms and conditions of the site license agreement are heavily tilted in favour of publishers. However, except a few, the clauses in the Agreement are generally subject to negotiations. The job of dealing with such issues would be much simpler for those Organisations which have a Legal Cell. It is advisable to refer the document to that Cell. But, as is generally observed, many Organisations do not have such Units which make it imperative for the Librarian to take up himself the responsibility of examining the legal aspects in the Agreement. In that case, the librarian needs to be very cautious in studying various clauses in the Agreement.

He/ she must ensure that the interests of his/ her Organisation are protected to the maximum possible extent. After going through the Agreements carefully, one has to first seek clarifications from the publishers on those points which do not seem to be very clear. Possible changes may be suggested to bring in more clarity. If certain terms are unacceptable, it is essential to request for changes/ amendments in the Agreement. Sometimes, it needs a hard bargaining and the librarians need to have strong negotiating skills.

KEY ISSUES IN THE AGREEMENT

Perpetual Access

Perpetual access is ensured by most of the publishers. But some publishers put a condition that the library should subscribe to at least one online journal or any online product of theirs. Otherwise, they will charge maintenance fee/ hosting fee. If the access is provided off-line, then they ask the libraries to bear the cost of production to provide the content on other electronic media, such as CDs/ DVDs, for local hosting. Some publishers prefer to use the term 'Continued Access' in place of 'Perpetual Access'. The terminological difference may have to be clearly understood. As one UK publisher puts it - the 'Perpetual Access' in their terminology refers to a limited period and the 'Continued Access' means indefinite period. Libraries need to ensure that their parent institution will not be put to disadvantage and take precautions to get inserted right terminology.

However, some publishers do not provide perpetual access at all to the subscribed content. If an online subscription is not renewed, the libraries will lose access even to the paid content. If that is the case, then the Licensing document must clearly state it. In such cases, the libraries need to think seriously about an alternative method of archiving either by continuing with print version or get archival year-end CDs/ DVDs, as offered by some publishers.

Withdrawal of Content

Publishers insert a clause that it reserves right to withdraw the content, which it no longer retains the right to publish or infringes copyright or defamatory, etc. While the last condition should be acceptable, the first two conditions may sometime put librarians in a fix. These situations may arise when a journal title is transferred to some other publisher. The new publisher may not permit the old subscribers to access this content, free. It is all the more critical if this content is substantial and/ or directly relevant to their users.

As a remedial measure, one can demand insertion of the following clauses - The publisher will make best efforts to convince the new publisher to provide access to the old subscribers or shall allow local hosting of such content. Also, if the withdrawal is substantial, then the publisher shall refund the amount proportionately.

Restrictions on Usage

Generally, publishers do not permit users to download entire journal issues and e-books. A standard condition to this effect may be found in License Agreement of all the publishers. There are publishers who even put a restriction on the number of pages and chapters printable from e-books. The decision of the libraries to buy ebooks from such publishers depends on how comfortable they are with the restrictions imposed by the publishers. A few publishers do permit the licensee to make an electronic copy and a hardcopy for backup purpose. However, the libraries need to create necessary infrastructure to preserve the content on their local computer server.

Access to Archives through Third Party

In the event of a publisher deciding to wind up his operations or merge with another publisher, it is an obligation on the part of the publisher to make alternative arrangements to provide access to archive of the licensed materials concerned. This is where the third party arrangement comes into picture. Many publishers have made arrangements with some external agencies for the long time preservation of their digital archive. Some examples are LOCKSS, CLOCKSS, PORTICO, and National Library of Netherlands. In a trigger event, it becomes the responsibility of these agencies to grant access to the content to the subscribers. The libraries should insist publishers to incorporate in the agreement a clause specifying the names of the agencies with whom the arrangements are made to provide access to the content in the event of publisher closing his business. Some of these agencies offer paid service, but since the subscribers have already paid for the content earlier, it becomes a debatable point whether the libraries can afford to pay again for the same content.

Inter-Library Loan (ILL)

Providing a copy of an article to another library (not-forprofit, Non--commercial) under ILL is generally permitted by most of the publishers, but with varying conditions. While the publishers expect subscribers to observe normal Copyright rules, some put specific restrictions on document delivery system. While one publisher permits only to send copies in print format, the other allows electronic transmission through secure network, but insists that the recipient library delete the file after printing a paper copy. Such clauses are Non--negotiable and the libraries need to accept them, so long some form of ILL is permitted.

Governing Laws

Business of digital content is only three decade old. Like any other business, there is a possibility that disputes might arise especially in terms of copyright rules, access problems etc. If such disputes remain unresolved mutually, the aggrieved parties have no option, but to approach Judiciary. This gives rise to the problem of jurisdiction as the two parties belong to different countries. The agreement is generally governed by the laws of the country of origin of the publisher.

However, some publishers are flexible on this issue. While some agree to sort out the issue in the court of subscriber's country, others agree to the condition that the aggrieved party can approach their respective countries. Alternatively, some publishers also allow for an independent arbitrator mutually acceptable to both parties.

Fees

Fees charged by the publishers for e-books, online journal packages, etc. varies from library to library, depending upon size of the user community. However, publishers also offer price cap in case a library agrees to go for a multi-year agreement. The base price and the price cap shall form part of the Agreement and as such need to be stated explicitly.

Counter-signed Copy

Original copy of the agreement is generally in duplicate and the two signed copies are exchanged between the library and the publisher. However, the Agreements of some publishers have only the acceptance column which needs to be signed by the Library. In such a case, libraries should keep with them one copy of the agreement.

General Conditions

Some publishers incorporate a clause in the agreement, stating that the content of the Licensed Material is 'subject to change without notice'. If accepted, this allows the publisher to alter the subscribed/ purchased content without notice. In this case, subscriber will be totally in dark about the changes effected, including withdrawal of any content.

To avoid this, the librarians need to insist for change in the clause appropriately by changing it to 'subject to change with prior notice to the licensee' (*i.e.* library). This will protect the end-user from any loss of content, as the user will have time to copy and store the content locally. Some publishers also incorporate a clause that the contents of the License Agreement should not be disclosed to a third party without their consent.

While the publishers urging to maintain secrecy is understandable, it may be difficult for libraries to accept such a clause, especially for those organisations funded by State/ Central Governments, which, according to the Right to Information Act, may have to be disclose the content to those, who seek it. Therefore, it is essential that appropriate changes are demanded in the clauses.

ELECTRONIC ACCESS RESOURCE AND THEIR TYPES

Direct Access Resources

These are the resources which can be used at any time, *e.g.* Databases available in CD form.

Advantages:

- Can be used at any time and only computer is required.
- Searching and downloading is easy and quick.

Disadvantages:

- Database CD can be protected from scratches or other things which may spoil it.
- Information contained by these is getting out dated with minute span of time.

Remote Access Resources

These are the server and client based information resources. These are the online resources in which location of the server is somewhere else, may be in another country and clients are located in different geographical location (countries), *e.g.* Science Online, Chemical Abstract Services (CAS), etc. This type of access can be given on specific range of IP (Internet Protocol) within the campus, access through username password in which information can be downloaded from anywhere with the help of Internet. Access through IP range, as well as username password is also there (in combined).

Advantages:

- Update is regular feature of these types of resources.
- Can be used by any number of users at a same time.

Disadvantages:

- Required Internet to use the resources.
- Processing of quarry depends on Internet speed and processing speed of the remote server. Some problems at the server can hinder information access.

Type of e- Resources

To keep bibliographical control over the published information, with the help of computer and communication technology various methods have been developed and adopted by the libraries from time to time. Broadly three types of e-resources are available to cater scholarly information needs of the users.

- *Bibliographical resources:* These are the resources provide bibliographical information only like- title, author, name of the journal, volume and issue number, publication date, publisher and most importantly an abstract of the entry. Bibliographic eresources are mainly containing information on single subject. These resources are not providing full-text but facilitating the user by providing linking facility to the fulltexts in some of the cases, *e.g*. Biological Abstracts (database covering biological sciences), MathSciNet (bibliographical database deals with mathematics), Chemical Abstract Services (biggest bibliographical resource for chemical sciences), etc.
- *Full-text E-resources:* These e-resources provide full-text of the document apart from its bibliographical information. The approach in these databases is journal-wise or publisher-wise only, *e.g*. American Chemical Society is the database and containing titles published by the American Chemical Society. The same way there are, Institute of Physics, Cambridge University Press, Springer Journals, Elsevier Journals and Taylor and Francis, etc. are various publishers who are providing access to full text journals/databases through Internet.
- *Portals/Aggregator products:* It is just like a super market, where one can get everything from a single shop. Portals provide a single interface to search various databases, *e.g*. Under UGC-Infonet: E-Journals Consortium Indian universities are accessing more than 20+ different databases or products. User has to search individually (has to open all the web sites one by one to search within them) for a single term if s/he wants to search in all the provided products then this exercise needs much time to cover all 20+ products. Here portals can help a user; portals will search the needed term in all the products from single interface. There is no need to go for individual database. Portal does not have its own contents but all the contents have been taken from the member publishers and provide the linking facility to the full-text. Ingenta and J-Gate are the examples of these portals. So as the aggregator products, aggregator purchased the contents (on mutual or legal understanding) from the actual publishers and providing the access to users, *e.g*. EBSCO, JSTOR and ProQuest are the aggregators who are providing access to 1000+ publisher's journals from single window. Aggregators cannot provide latest issues of journals but they keep some embargo period for access. But even smaller libraries can have important journals through aggregators due to various low price subscription models.

Some of the challenges that Electronic Resource Management systems and LIS Professionals claim:

- Acquisition processes for electronic resources typically are more complex than for printed materials. They may involve trials that require supporting technology, license terms that require negotiation, and systems configuration to ensure that users have access to the material for which a license has been agreed. A single information source, such as a journal, may be available individually or as part of different packages from several different sources using potentially several different interfaces. Access to an electronic version of a serial may depend on a print subscription so the two forms of material need to be linked for acquisitions purposes, and of course budgets for print and electronic materials must be consolidated for financial control.
- Libraries may participate in consortia for acquiring materials, further adding a layer of complication. Some titles or collections may be purchased for the entire consortium and others simply purchased for individual libraries through a consolidated order process. Costs must be allocated to different member libraries based on a variety of possible criteria.
- Different licensing restrictions for different publisher, suppliers or aggregators means that detailed information must be recorded and tracked in order to control access to electronic resources. Licensing information needs to be made available to users and to a wide variety of library staff. Ideally, licensing information should be actionable, that is to say, it should be driving the process of controlling access to the electronic resource itself.
- Users in many libraries rely more and more on electronic materials, yet resource discovery is not simple with electronic materials. Serial titles may have records in library catalogues, but catalogues may only include print titles, not all titles to which the library has electronic access. Libraries may supplement the catalogue with separate web pages of alphabetical or topic-based lists of serial titles. Holdings information may be difficult to keep up-to-date when new issues of electronic journals appear or when the titles or coverage periods available through different bundled services of aggregators change. In most libraries, electronic journal articles can only be directly searched through external electronic resources such as abstracting and indexing services, but they may also be located using local link resolver services. Keeping all these sources up-to-date and accurate and maintaining ease of use for the end user can be a considerable challenge.
- Getting access to electronic resources requires technology and technical support not required for print materials. Authentication and

authorisation services need to be set-up and maintained, in many cases both for on-site and off-site use by legitimate users. This may need to be done even before titles are licensed during trial or test periods. When users cannot access an electronic resource, local trouble-shooting will be required, whether the fault is with the information vendor's system, whether it involves a local system problem or whether it involves miscommunication such as failing to renew on time or to update IP address information.

- Libraries already have complex automated systems, including integrated library systems, library portals, digital asset management systems or link resolver services. Libraries may be producing alphabetic or topic-organised lists of electronic journals from other sources. These systems need to be integrated in some measure with electronic resource management systems in order to provide users with a coherent, easy-to-understand environment and staff throughout the library with a consistent service for consulting and maintaining information.

Responsibilities of LIS professionals to manage ERM systems:

- Manage the lifecycle of electronic resources from selection, subscription, licensing, renewal, access and to user support;
- Manage a small print serials collection including subscription, issues receiving and preservation;
- Negotiate license agreements to obtain the best possible terms and conditions, and assess vendor performance;
- Contribute to the development of policies and procedures to support efficient operations of technical services
- Administer use and development of Serials and Electronic Resources Management modules and linking management tools;
- Maintain systematic record keeping, update MARC records, collect and analyse data, and prepare reports related to electronic resources and associated issues;
- Work with Research Librarians on subscription and administration of licensed electronic resources, monitor contracts and maintain information accuracy in electronic resources management systems;
- Work with technical services staff in Acquisitions and Cataloguing and Metadata Services on procurement and bibliographic control of serials and electronic resources;
- Work with Systems Librarian to resolve technical problems and troubleshoot access issues for electronic resources and participate in the enhancement of ILMS related modules;
- Maintain awareness and engagement of trends and developments in e-resource acquisitions and management and transfers knowledge to staff across the library;

- Supervise a team of para-professionals;
- Participate in training sessions for library users

The serials/electronic resources librarian is responsible for all library continuation material in both print and electronic formats and for binding of print material. Reporting to the Associate Director for Technical Services, the librarian performs the following duties:

- Manages the serials unit of the library, establishing and documenting all necessary policies and procedures; hires, supervises, trains, and evaluates 3 support staff responsible for serials check-in, serials claiming, serials check-in record maintenance, data entry related to e-resources, binding, and sorting library mail;
- Manages all required work activities for the library's growing electronic resources including creating and maintaining electronic resource records in EBSCO's ERM Essentials and updating of any related check-in and order records; maintains licensing details, preferably electronically in EBSCO's ERM Essentials, or in paper format when necessary; monitors the lifecycle of library subscriptions to all electronic resources, including individual journals, databases, e-resources packages and other electronic content;
- Works with other librarians to coordinate the set up of trials for electronic resources; notifies Associate Director for Technical Services when orders resulting from trials should be placed;
- Monitors vendor performance; works with Systems/Emerging Technologies Librarian to set up and monitor usage statistics gathered through the proxy server, Serials Solutions, and/or collected directly from publishers and vendors;
- Coordinates with Systems/Emerging Technologies Librarian and Associate Director for Technical Services to troubleshoot access problems;
- Takes lead role in promoting electronic resources, working with both reference librarians and the Systems/Emerging Technologies Librarian to develop a wide array of activities that will increase the students' and faculty's awareness and use of the library's electronic resources;
- Works closely with Systems/Serials Library Specialist on claiming and replacement of print and other serials-related matters;
- Serves as a backup for placement of rush, faculty requests using a University of Pennsylvania purchasing card;
- Participates in a variety of library-wide planning activities and committees; participates in collection development activities; serves as serials liaison with other library and law school departments, library patrons, other libraries and organisations.

Bibliography

A.K. Gupta: *Digital Library and Education*, Pearl Books, Delhi, 2012.

Ajay K. Srivastav: *Digital Library Environment and Networking*, Sree Publication, Delhi, 2006.

Cheriyan Mathew: *Current Trends in Library Services*, Cyber Tech Publications, New Delhi, 2011.

Deepak Kumar: *Information Technology and Social Change : A Study of Digital Divide in India*, Rawat Publication, Delhi, 2006.

Efraim Turban, Dorothy Leidner, Ephraim Mclean and James Wetherbe: *Information Technology for Management*, Wiley Publication, London, 2003.

Hasnain Qureshi: *Principles and Practices of Library Science*, Anmol Publication, Delhi, 2006.

Indrajit Chatterjee: *Management Information Systems*, PHI Learning, Delhi, 2001.

J.B. Sharma: *Professional Leadership in Library Science*, Book Enclave, Jaipur, 1998.

K. Rajasekaran, R. Raman Nair and K.M. Nafala: *Digital Library Basics: A Practical Manual (With Software CD Inside)*, Ess Ess Publication, Delhi, 2010.

Ketan Sharma: *Management Information Systems*, Pacific Books, Delhi, 2011.

Khalid K. Faruqi and Mehtab Alam: *Library Information Systems and E-Journal Archiving*, Authorspress, Delhi, 2005.

Mange Ram and Ram Chander: *Recent Trends in Library Services*, Vayu Education of India, Delhi, 2011.

Omesh Aadhavan: *Development of Digital Library*, Oxford Book Company, Delhi, 2010.

Omesh Aadhavan: *Management of Digital Library*, Oxford Book Company, Delhi, 2010.

P. Balasubramaniyan: *Research Methodology in Library Science*, Deep and Deep Publication, Delhi, 2011.

P. Sashikala: *Management Information Systems with CD*, Dreamtech Press, Delhi, 2012.

P. Vidya Sagar: *Networking in Library Science*, Sonali Publication, Delhi, 2005.

R.C. Chakravarthy and P.R.S. Murthy: *Information Technology and Rural Development*, Pacific Books International, Delhi, 2012.

R.C. Mishra: *Information Technology and Poverty Reduction in South Asia*, Authors Press, Delhi, 2003.

R.K. Singh: *Basic Facts of Digital Library*, Shree Publication, Delhi, 2004.

Raghunath Pandey and M.N. Velayudhan Pillai: *World Famous Public Libraries*, Jnanada Prakashan, Delhi, 2011.

Ram Shobhit Singh: *Encyclopaedia of Library Information Systems and E-Journal Archiving, Vols. I-II*, Anmol Publication, Delhi, 2008.

S R Ranganathan: *The Five Laws of Library Science*, Ess Ess Publication, Delhi, 2006.

S.A. Kelkar: *Management Information Systems : A Concise Study*, PHI Learning, Delhi, 2003.

S.C. Dwivedi: *Digital Library (2 Vols-Set)*, Shree Publication, Delhi, 2005.

Sandhya Aggarwal and R.D. Mehla: *Library Services : Challenges and Solutions in Digital Era*, Ess Ess Publications, Delhi, 2012.

Savita Mittal: *Digital Library Resources*, Ess Ess Publication, Delhi, 2005.

Sreenidhi Iyengar: *Researches in Library Science*, Anmol Publication, Delhi, 1996.

Sudha Azhikodan: *Public Libraries in Malabar*, Serials Publication, Delhi, 2010.

T C Mohanti: *Research Methodology in Library Science*, Alfa Publication, Delhi, 2008.

V.V.V. Satyanarayana: *Modern Librarianship Ushering in Digital Library*, Authorspress, Delhi, 2006.

Vasu Deva: *Information Technology and Marketing Management*, Commonwealth Publication, Delhi, 2003.

Index

M

N

O

P

R

S

T

U

V

W

X

Index